P9-AFZ-113

DATE DUE

DEMCO 38-296

ENHANCING DEPARTMENTAL LEADERSHIP

ENHANCING DEPARTMENTAL LEADERSHIP

The Roles of the Chairperson

Edited by
John B. Bennett
and David J. Figuli

AMERICAN COUNCIL
ON EDUCATION
Series on Higher Education
ORYX PRESS
1993

Copyright © 1990 by American Council on Education/Macmillan Publishing Company

Copyright © 1993 by American Council on Education and The Oryx Press

Published by The Oryx Press
4041 North Central at Indian School Road
Phoenix, AZ 85012-3397

Printed in the United States of America

Library of Congress Cataloging-in-Publication Data

Enhancing departmental leadership : the roles of the chairperson /
    edited by John B. Bennett and David J. Figuli.
        p. cm. — (American Council on Education/Oryx series on higher
    education)
        Originally published: New York : American Council on Education :
    Macmillan, c1990.
        Includes bibliographical references and index.
        ISBN 0-89774-866-2
        1. Departmental chairmen (Universities) 2. Educational
    leadership. I. Bennett, John B. (John Beecher), 1940– .
    II. Figuli, David J. III. Series.
    LB2341.E645 1993   93-21575
    378.1'11—dc20   CIP

CONTENTS

PREFACE

Until quite recently, chairpersons at many institutions have toiled in relative obscurity and isolation. Without much institutional recognition or support, they have attended to the multiplicity of activities for which they typically have responsibility. Frequently they have labored alone, not realizing that other chairs have many of the same problems, vexations, and uncertainties. Often they have been sustained more by their own convictions about the importance of the position than by the attentions paid to it or to them by key campus administrators. Colleges and universities have been the beneficiaries, for no institution can succeed with poor chairpersons.

Fortunately, institutions have now begun to provide their chairpersons more help and recognition. Conferences, seminars, and workshops for chairs are now commonly available. Specific publications for chairs have emerged, including *The Department Advisor*—a national quarterly newsletter, for which most of the essays collected in this book were originally written and from which they are taken. The objective of *The Department Advisor* has been to provide department chairpersons assistance with the variety of tasks for which they have responsibility.

This collection of essays is the first in a series of volumes of the best current thinking about how to be a department or division chairperson. It is to be a resource for those new to the position as well as those with substantial experience. Topics and essays for the next collection of essays, and for the intervening issues of *The Department Advisor*, are invited.

Thanks must be given to all who have encouraged the development of this book and to its contributors. Special recognition is due Thomas A. Emmet for his leadership in developing *The Department Advisor*. Acknowledgement must also be given to Mary Christ for her work on the production of *The Department Advisor*, and to Mary Ann Hawley for her assistance in the myriad of editorial chores.

JOHN B. BENNETT
Adrian, Michigan

DAVID J. FIGULI
Greeley, Colorado

INTRODUCTION

The stature of an academic institution is in large part a function of the stature of its individual departments. It is at the departmental level that the real business of the institution—teaching, research, and service—is conducted. The ultimate success of the institution turns significantly on the degree to which objectives at the departmental level are both appropriately defined and realized.

CUSTODIANS OF ACADEMIC STANDARDS

Any organizational chart will testify to the critical role the chair plays, however unsung that role may be. Together, chairs set the academic tone of the institution. Mistakes they make can be difficult to undo elsewhere, and things left undone may be impossible to correct later on. Above all, it is the department chairperson to whom other institutional administrators must look for assurances of academic integrity.

Specifically, it is the chairperson who must monitor the departmental or divisional curriculum, ensuring that it meets the needs of a changing student body and the mission of the institution. It is the chairperson who is responsible for seeing that course assignments are made judiciously, and that individual faculty talents are aligned with instructional needs. It is the chairperson who is in the best position to promote racial and gender balance in the faculty and to encourage continued personal and professional growth. And it is the chairperson who must attest to the adequacy of instruction and research. No dean, provost, or president can easily speak to this issue. All are dependent upon chairs. Accordingly, it is the chair who must function as custodian of academic standards for his or her department or division.

Curriculum

This custodianship requires periodic program review to eliminate redundancies and excessively specialized courses. It requires monitoring patterns of present student demand and anticipating future student interests. It also involves adjusting departmental or divisional emphases as student capacities and societal needs shift, and as the institutional mission changes to reflect these shifts.

Chairs are at the level where services are actually delivered and so are eminently positioned to gauge the degree to which the appropriate programs are in place. The fit among student capabilities, faculty resources, and disciplinary developments is of fundamental importance. Even very traditional programs and courses of study and inquiry may need rethinking.

The actual delivery of instruction may also need to be reviewed. Curriculum and pedagogical presuppositions as well as such operational matters as the time of day classes are provided may need to change as the proportion of "nontraditional" students changes. The schedules of too many institutions are still arranged more for the convenience of faculty than they are to accommodate the needs of students. Some faculty are reluctant to change, but chairs are positioned to provide leadership on this issue.

Faculty

Consider some of the problems associated with faculty members that the chairperson must address. Almost all faculty today in the United States are struggling with a loss of relative purchasing power and a slippage in public esteem, together with the challenges to self-respect that inevitably flow from such developments. Higher education today can be described as what economists call a "mature industry," that is, one characterized by little hiring at the entry level, minimal mobility once within the institution, and restricted opportunity for advancement, resulting in a stable but aging workforce.

The disadvantages of working in such a situation are substantial, especially for those who entered the professoriate anticipating opportunities for advancement and mobility—and find instead that they are "stuck." Serious challenges to morale have sometimes resulted. Nonetheless, department chairpersons must promote continued faculty development and growth. Financial incentives in any quantity are rarely available. Instead, chairs must rely upon the traditional mechanisms of peer esteem and communal recognition, and they must enforce the requirements of a self-regulated profession.

Chairs report that within the faculty there are great variations in industriousness, with some individuals undaunted by almost any adversity, while others reflect the variety of afflictions and setbacks that come with age. Then, too, some faculty are simply cranky—with students, colleagues, and chairs alike—and are either oblivious to their disagreeableness or appear to take pleasure in the discomfort they inflict.

Additionally, a number of chairpersons must deal with strains between younger and older faculty members. Not infrequently the younger faculty come with better credentials than their older colleagues could sport at a comparable age and point in the development of their careers. As a result, the younger faculty may feel exploited, laboring under the impression that more is demanded of them. For their part, older faculty may feel that the rules under which they were hired have changed and that their contributions are no longer valued.

ROLE AMBIGUITY

These and other problems among the faculty then become problems for the chairperson. They are often compounded by the narrow and sometimes self-serving perceptions that the faculty may have of the chair. For instance, faculty can regard the chair as the chief clerk of the department or division. In these cases, faculty look to the chair to handle paperwork, to arrange for chalk and travel reimbursements, to allocate typewriters and computers, or to fix problems with the maintenance staff. Leadership in any more substantive or dignified sense is not what they have in mind.

At the other end of the spectrum are those faculty who have totally unrealistic expectations of the powers of the chair—viewing him or her in terms of a "white charger" fixation. When things go wrong or the department suffers setbacks, these faculty then blame the chair for events that may have been completely out of his or her control.

All these factors contribute to the frequent complaints of chairs regarding the role ambiguity they feel.[1] This role ambiguity or role conflict seems to trouble chairpersons in all sectors of higher education. The common factor is the discomfort felt in being expected to represent two sets of interests that are often competing and sometimes conflicting. Both faculty and administrators look to the department chair to advance their specific objectives. The chairperson is often forced to take the larger institutional viewpoint and to call for faculty loyalty even when such loyalty might conflict with personal and disciplinary interests and values. This situation is inherently awkward and stressful.

The difficulties reflected in these complaints of role ambiguity are also present in the inability of most chairs to draw upon the personal and interpersonal skills they developed for use in the classroom. Unlike professors, chairs are not experts in a specific area and have no special credentials to cloak them in authority. Both faculty and institutional collegiality require that issues be advanced more by the power of persuasion than by the power of the position. What worked to motivate student inquiry may not work to promote department vitality or to secure a common department direction. The cultivation of different interpersonal skills is usually in order.

Some institutions would do well to reconsider the expectations they have for their chairpersons and the degree to which they are actually prepared to reward individuals for their accomplishments as chairs. The biggest source of dissatisfaction among chairs is the lack of institutional appreciation they receive. Some chairs point to the toll that being chair exacts on their own teaching and scholarship. Others talk quite specifically about the incommensurability of the rewards with the duties. As one individual put it:

> The chair's job is the most difficult on campus in many respects. First, the continuous need for attention to details, second the need to make decisions which have an impact on the lives of those with whom you also deal on a personal basis, and third, when things go wrong the chair carries directly or indirectly a good share of the responsibility.[2]

Chairs at institutions suffering enrollment declines and other financial difficulties are most likely to experience these pressures. Institutions in such circumstances should consider ways to recognize and support the work of their chairpersons. Other institutions as well should consider thoughtful policies for rewarding chairs for accomplishments that may well have been purchased at the expense of teaching and research accomplishments. And all institutions should recognize the undesirability of selecting faculty members who have yet to secure tenure as chairpersons for fragmented, quarrelsome or otherwise difficult departments.

LOOKING AT THE FUTURE

The elements of successful leadership will vary according to the context. What works in one situation may not be possible in another situation or may backfire in a third. The specific requirements for successful leadership turn closely around recent developments at the institution or in the department, its history and tradition, the environing culture, and the personalities of key players. Still, some general trends are quite clear and the chances are good that many department chairs will wrestle with one or another of their manifestations.

Periodic evaluation of senior faculty
For the vast majority of chairpersons, increased attention to continued faculty growth and development will be necessary as the faculty continues to age. The continued aging of the faculty presents a troubling future, especially when combined with the recent federal uncapping of any mandatory retirement age. Obviously a number of questions will need to be answered with this new development, the meaning of tenure itself being perhaps the most critical. In any case, department and di-

vision chairs will likely find themselves giving increasing amounts of time and energy to development activities.

An important strategy in this context is the periodic evaluation of senior faculty. Most current evaluation practices emphasize the early stages of the faculty member's career. That is, most attention is paid to evaluating probationary faculty and to assembling sufficient data to warrant a thoughtful and judicious tenure decision. Once tenured, however, many faculty are left entirely to their own devices. Some faculty will do much better than others in these circumstances, as initiative and stamina are not evenly distributed. Policies reflecting an extreme individualism neglect the support which the community of peers can provide and which is at the heart of the concept of collegiality.

Properly constructed and introduced, a program of periodic evaluation of senior faculty performance by peers, can go far to prevent individual stagnation and loss of vitality.[3] Such programs harness the mechanism of the peer group and tap the individual's natural reluctance to appear as less than fully valuable in their eyes. And since each faculty member has the opportunity and necessity to identify the next step for his or her career, he or she retains a key element of control.

Entrepreneurship

In the future, a number of chairs will probably find themselves paying more and more attention to ways of generating funds outside the normal institutional structure. Current financial constraints upon institutions of higher education are unlikely to disappear in the next decade. Indeed, they may well increase as more public funds are diverted into medical, geriatric, and other social services required for an aging population.

In the context, enterprising chairpersons will be exploring ways to forge relationships with the commercial world. Such support can come in the form of funds to support salaries and laboratory expenditures, replacements for obsolete equipment, scholarships, internships and placements for both students and graduates, and exchanges of faculty and business or industry employees. Creative uses of faculty members as consultants may well emerge as a way to relieve the excessive dependency on their institutions that many faculty now feel.

Chairpersons themselves will have to continue paying attention to student recruitment, enrollment, and retention. Indeed, such attention will be critical to the survival of some departments and divisions, and will be necessary for the continued vitality and development of others. In many cases better as well as more students will be the object of aggressive campaigns.

Additionally, some chairpersons are already feeling the need to plan for the recruitment of large numbers of new faculty. Other chairpersons can see significant vacancies within a decade. The aging of the professoriate means the retirement of many faculty in the future and replacing them in some disciplinary areas will require creative and imaginative action by chairpersons.

Chairperson Reviews

For their own protection and job satisfaction, chairpersons are well advised to seek periodic reviews of their own performance, if the institution itself does not have such procedures in place. Periodic reviews can provide indispensable feedback and information on areas of strength as well as weakness, on department consensus as well as division, and on the degree to which faculty and chair perceptions about objectives and performance are in harmony or conflict.

Conclusion

The overall task of the chairperson is to create a unity and a common identity out of an assemblage of individuals. This is not unlike the job of herding a bunch of frogs. The academy is a bastion of rampant individualism. The chair must find ways of harmonizing this diversity and keeping it moving in the same direction. In some cases vastly different value systems must be accommodated. In other cases decisions must be made with radically limited information. In all cases, though, the chair has a unique opportunity to shape the department's self-perception and spirit.

NOTES

1. See John B. Bennett, "Ambiguity and Abrupt Transitions in the Department Chairperson's Role," *Educational Record* (Fall 1982): 54–57. Other illustrations of role ambiguity are provided in Elwood B. Ehrle and John B. Bennett, *Managing the Academic Enterprise*, New York: American Council on Education/Macmillan, 1988.
2. John B. Bennett, "Inside a Department Chairperson." *AGB Reports*, (May–June 1982): 52–53.
3. John B. Bennett and Shirley S. Chater, "Evaluating the Performance of Tenured Faculty Members." *Educational Record* (Spring 1984): 38–41. Another helpful resource is C. M. Licata, *Post-Tenure Faculty Evaluation: Threat or Opportunity?* Washington, DC: Association for the Study of Higher Education, 1986.

CONTRIBUTORS

Artin Arslanian
Vice President for Academic
    Affairs
Belmont Abbey College
Belmont, North Carolina

John B. Bennett
Executive Editor
The Department Advisor
Provost and Dean of the College
Siena Heights College
Adrian, Michigan

George E. Biles
Professor and Chair of
    Management
Kogod College of Business
    Administration
The American University
Washington, D.C.

Robert Boice
Director
Faculty Instructional Support
    Office
State University of New York,
    Stony Brook
Stony Brook, New York

Robert G. Cope
Associate Professor of Education
University of Washington at
    Seattle
Seattle, Washington

Donald V. DeRosa
Dean of the Graduate School
University of North Carolina at
    Greensboro
Greensboro, North Carolina

Kenneth E. Eble (*deceased*)
Professor of English
University of Utah
Salt Lake City, Utah

Elwood B. Ehrle
Professor of Biology
Western Michigan University
Kalamazoo, Michigan

Thomas A. Emmet
Chairman, Higher Education
    Executive Associates, Inc.
Special Assistant to the Presi-
    dent and Professor of
    Education

Regis College
Denver, Colorado

David J. Figuli
President, Higher Education Executive Publications, Inc.
General Counsel
Regis College
Denver, Colorado
Assistant to the President for Legal Affairs
University of Northern Colorado
Greeley, Colorado

Myrna Goldenberg
Professor of English, Modern Foreign Language and Philosophy
Montgomery College
Rockville, Maryland

Mark Hurtubise
Vice President and Dean of the College
Sierra Nevada College-Lake Tahoe
Incline Village, Nevada

William J. Hynes
Academic Dean for Campus Programs
Professor of Religious Studies
Regis College
Denver, Colorado

Antoinette Iadarola
Provost and Dean of Faculty
Colby-Sawyer College
New London, New Hampshire

Jerry R. May
Clinical Psychologist
Assistant Dean of Admissions
Professor of Psychiatry and Behavioral Sciences

School of Medicine
University of Nevada at Reno
Reno, Nevada

Robert B. McBeath
Medical Student
School of Medicine
University of Nevada at Reno
Reno, Nevada

Wilbert J. McKeachie
Research Specialist
Center for Research on Learning and Teaching
Professor of Psychology
University of Michigan
Ann Arbor, Michigan

John Minter
President
John Minter Associates
Boulder, Colorado

Sister Eileen Rice, O.P.
Program Director for Teacher Education
Siena Heights College
Adrian, Michigan

Howard P. Tuckman
Distinguished Professor of Economics
Director, Center for Economic Education
Memphis State University
Memphis, Tennessee

Lois Vander Waerdt
Attorney at Law
President
The Employment Partnership
Former Director of Affirmative Action
University of Missouri
St. Louis, Missouri

Charles O. Warren
President
State University of New York
College at Plattsburgh
Plattsburgh, New York

Quelda Wilson
Assistant Vice Chancellor–
    Personnel
University of California, San
    Diego

Robert E. Wolverton
Professor of Classics
Mississippi State University
Mississippi State, Mississippi

P. Anthony Zeiss
President
Pueblo Community College
Pueblo, Colorado

ENHANCING DEPARTMENTAL LEADERSHIP

PART ONE

Roles and Responsibilities of Chairs

The number of responsibilities department chairpersons face is large indeed. Functioning as the custodian of standards can easily require reducing conflict, redistributing departmental burdens and chores perhaps by interrupting comfortable and familiar routines, promoting affirmative action in a reluctant faculty, as well as attending to the major tasks of faculty and staff evaluation and development. Throughout, the chairperson must determine that students are being properly served, that the curriculum is updated, and scholarship is promoted. Running an airline on time may look easy by comparison.

The experience of Artin Arslanian as a department chairperson is typical of many. In "A Few Suggestions to New Department Chairs," Arslanian shares some pointers. Among them are the need to say "no" early, the importance of keeping the institutional context and tradition clearly in mind, and respect for confidentiality. Invariably, lofty goals are not easily or completely accomplished. The chair should be realistic about what is possible.

In "Chairing the Small Department," Wolverton provides a tidy review of several of the challenges facing all department chairpersons, as well as perceptive comments on those special circumstances the chairperson of the smaller department will recognize instantly. Wolverton also calls attention to the questions the current or prospective chairperson needs to ask him or herself regarding the satisfaction to be found in the job, and therefore how long, or whether, to be in the position.

In "Common and Uncommon Concerns: The Complex World of the Community College Department Chairs," Myrna Goldenberg reflects on the special characteristics and challenges for these department or division chairpersons or heads. Administrative appointment goes far, she thinks, in establishing the authority and the institutional accountability of the chair. In this sense, the chair's role ambiguity associated with collegial selection seems to recede. Likewise, both the nature of instruction and the omnipresence of the public within the community college define significantly the role of the chairperson. The lack of advanced courses in a two-year curriculum can accelerate burnout among faculty removed from the stimulation of deepened disciplinary connections. The chair must find ways to counter this faculty disengagement at the same time that he or she must contend with the omnipresent publics all claiming rightful ownership of the department's resources. Even so, this special relationship of the community to the college also presents special faculty development opportunities for the skillful chairperson.

Perhaps the most important talent for any department chairperson is the ability to communicate effectively. No campus has an excess of communication, and many are in a good deal of difficulty because of deficiencies in communication. Both faculty and upper-level administrators expect department chairpersons to convey information accurately and effectively.

In his essay "Communicating Effectively," Kenneth Eble observes how central effective communication is to everything the chairperson must do and be. Yet there are forces that work against efforts to communicate well. These forces must be resisted and communication enlarged beyond memos and mere transmission of information. Indeed, communication is intrinsically connected with the broader objective of enabling personal growth.

Every chairperson must relate to an academic dean, provost, or vice president. The relationship is special for both chair and dean. To the latter, his or her chairs are much like faculty members are to the chair—in both cases they function as the key constituency through which the leader must work and without whose cooperation little of lasting importance will get done. Wise deans recognize the indispensability of chairpersons and cultivate them accordingly. For their part, chairpersons also must see the dean as more than a necessary evil, for no lasting political advantage is secured thereby.

In "Chairperson and Dean: The Essential Partnership," Charles Warren analyzes the potential this central relationship offers to be a source of evolving or "transforming" leadership if mutual expectations are balanced and authority is shared. Warren provides several suggestions on how to get beyond the mechanical and transactional relationship—suggestions for both the dean and the chairperson. With proper cultivation from both sides, a transformational relationship can occur, with the potential of enriching the whole institution.

Good things rarely come easily, however, and many chairpersons find themselves confronting stress. Jerry May and Robert McBeath provide some help in "I Wanted to Be an Administrator; Now How Do I Cope with the Stress?" Ten common sources of stress for department chairpersons are identified; the effects of excessive stress upon performance and bodily efficiency are outlined; and concrete suggestions for managing the negative aspects of stress are provided.

1

A FEW SUGGESTIONS TO NEW DEPARTMENT CHAIRS

ARTIN ARSLANIAN

It was by a haphazard process of selection that I became chair of a medium-size department (10 FTEs). I came to the position unexpectedly and quite unprepared. This was true for many of the new chairs on campus. Most of us had not read about departmental leadership, and our requests to the administration of the college for an orientation seminar went unanswered. Although some of us solicited advice from experienced chairs on campus, it is safe to say that we embarked on our tasks with little experience but full of good intentions. We were resolved to nurture departmental collegiality, encourage excellence in teaching and scholarship, and improve the departmental image on and off campus. We soon learned that these lofty goals were not easily accomplished. We tried our best—with mixed results.

I jotted down a few pointers for the new chair when I recently moved to another college. These are distilled from my experience and the thoughts of other chairs. I share these knowing full well that differences in institutional size, mission, and philosophy may invalidate some of them.

- Always work within the philosophic and pedagogic tradition, and budgetary guidelines of your college or university. There should be a good fit between your plans and the institutional goals and realities. Ideas and methods considered brilliant in one institution might be damned in another with a different mission, tradition, structure, and clientele.
- Learn to say no early. Resources of all kinds are limited and are invariably outpaced by demand. Do not concentrate most of the resources on a few: all members should receive their fair share. However, make public the criteria informing the distribution of departmental funds and use them consistently: otherwise, you'll be (rightly) accused of favoritism or shiftiness.
- Fight the urge *to do something* as soon as a colleague complains against another or in case of a crisis. First, hear out all parties involved and try to ascertain the facts. Do not become an intermediary or messenger between the feuding parties—this will further complicate the problem. Call the grieving individuals to your office, discuss their con-

cerns and ask them to work out a solution, reminding them that we are condemned to live together as a family in these days of almost nonexistent career mobility.

• When chairing departmental meetings, state the issues and let all present have their say first. Do not begin by arguing your case or solutions as it will create the semblance of an adverserial relationship with those who disagree with you—they may not even bother to express their opinions. Try to maintain an atmosphere conducive to discussion by all members of the department at the price of not having sufficient opportunity to elaborate your position fully. If there is a minority view, give its proponents a second or third opportunity to make their case, but avoid taking formal votes that tend to create winners and losers. Summarize the majority view in such a way as to make some concessions to the concerns of the minority and announce it as the reflection of the department's thinking.

• Do not discuss the shortcomings and weaknesses of the department's members with others if you want to enhance your credibility and the image of the department. Always talk about their contribution, accomplishments and strength, especially in the case of those who are rumored to have criticized you in public.

• Avoid creating an inquisitional atmosphere when evaluating for tenure, promotion, salary raises or merit pay. Required, frequent, and systematic evaluations are the key to a potentially difficult and sometimes explosive situation. Frequent discussions with individual faculty members about teaching, publications, professional growth, and involvement in the life of the college community create a relaxed environment for open discussion. But make sure to give equal time to the faculty members for the evaluation of your performance as chair and discussion of departmental goals, problems, and priorities. If done frequently and systematically, this procedure will greatly ease the tense atmosphere that permeates yearly evaluations.

• Read the papers and publications of the members of your department, discuss their works with them, and honor their accomplishments in the department and in the wider college community.

• Make sure that candidates visiting the campus are treated professionally. Provide them with pertinent information about departmental needs, educational philosophy, salary and benefits, but refrain (and restrain others) from gossiping about the members of the department, the faculty at large, or the administration. Indiscretions of this sort have a way of haunting the department, and sometimes the college, whether that candidate is offered a job or not.

• If a colleague takes a problem to the dean's office before resorting to all the departmental procedures, do not invest additional time on the matter. Just inform the dean that the faculty member has failed to exhaust the departmental grievance procedures. A wise dean will refer the case back to the department, lest a precedent be set that will soon flood his office with requests from faculty.

• Do not check your mail after hours or on weekends. If there are problems, there is very little that you can do about them when everyone is away from the campus. Most probably the only thing you will accomplish is to ruin your evening or weekend!

I am sure that others can easily supplement this list from their experience. Let me close with a confession: I failed to follow some of these guidelines—and often paid the price!

2

CHAIRING THE SMALL DEPARTMENT

ROBERT E. WOLVERTON

In 1973 a marvelous book appeared bearing the intriguing title *Small is Beautiful: Economics as if People Mattered.*[1] Its author, E. F. Schumacher, posited observations, questions, and insights valuable not only to economics but also to higher education. If we agree with Schumacher that "people can be themselves only in small comprehensible groups,"[2] then we must ask the question, How small should academic departments be to allow people to be themselves? Or, to put it another way, How small is "small," in the welter of departments on most college and university campuses? For the purposes of this discussion, I will arbitrarily define a *small department* as one with no more than six full-time-equivalent faculty members. I feel quite comfortable with this definition, since my own academic discipline is the classics, and on many campuses, the department of classics (if it exists at all) is the smallest one, often vying with philosophy and religion for that distinction. I am certainly cognizant that small departments exist within professional schools, and I believe that much of what follows will apply to those departments as well as to small departments within schools of arts and sciences or the liberal arts.

FREESTANDING OR PROFESSIONAL: IT DOES MAKE A DIFFERENCE

Small departments can exist within any school or college on campus. Whether they are housed in a liberal arts college or in a professional school does matter, however. Within liberal arts colleges, small departments are, along with their larger counterparts, members of a "rugged-individualist" pattern: every department considers itself the most important, fights for its share of resources and students, and shares the spirit of organized anarchy that typically abounds in liberal arts colleges. Within professional colleges, however, small departments are parts of the whole, and the whole shares certain common goals and objectives to which all departments subscribe and contribute. All oars in the professional rowboat—engineering, business, pharmacy, or veterinary medicine—are pulled in the same direction, but in the liberal-arts rowboat, oars are splashing every which way, each trying to prove "we're number one." This difference of location can make small departments unequal in other significant ways; for example, faculty in small departments within a business college will demand much higher salaries than will faculty in small departments within a liberal arts college.

LEVEL OF CURRICULAR OFFERING: WHO TEACHES WHAT TO WHOM?

What business is our small department in? Is it offering programs and degrees at the baccalaureate level only? Does it offer a major? (If it does not, I would find it difficult to give the department the status of a department.) Certainly, the department hopes to attract nonmajor students for an occasional course and cannot expect to be overrun with majors. A balance must therefore be struck between those courses with appeal to nonmajors and those courses considered essential for majors in the discipline. It may be possible that faculty members capable of teaching majors and nonmajors with equal effectiveness populate the department's ranks; given a faculty position to fill or refill, however, the department chair must evaluate the current and projected needs of the department in both its major and service roles, its generalist and specialist commitments.

All disciplines splinter as the number of specialties increases. Given this fact of academic life, the small department must fix its sights on what it wishes to impart to its majors. In what specialities should faculty members be found and retained? On this question hang many others related to the mission and goals of the department. In classics, for example, should history, philology, or archaeology be preponderant? Greek or Latin? Thus, the old academic question comes to the fore again: Can we be all things to all people? For a small department, the obvious answer is no, but how does the department, or the college/university, decide what to offer?

When we move to graduate-level work, some of these questions become even more important. Granted that the department does not offer graduate courses to many nonmajors, there still must be concern for the specialties to be taught and the type of professors to be hired. In addition, the recruitment of quality graduate students becomes a must, and a certain level of support for those students will have to be found or provided. Further, the distinction between teacher and researcher will be sharpened, as the curricular offerings and types of students require differing faculty interests and competencies. Compensation and work loads of faculty must also be given more attention as curricular levels and offerings are maintained or changed.

Finally, the curriculum of our small department will largely shape the library requirements of the department. More research, done by graduate students and their specialist-professors, will demand greater access to national and international books and periodicals, either through campus acquisitions or through networks of computers, and neither of these is cheap!

PERSONNEL DECISIONS: THE HERT FACTOR

Foremost among any administrative tasks for the department chair of any size department is that involving personnel. The decisions to hire, evaluate, reward, and terminate make up the *HERT factor*. In a small department, these decisions are ipso facto more difficult; the department chair does know each person more intimately, the faculty know each other more intimately, and the distinction between objective and subjective evaluations becomes quite blurred. On the other hand, informal conversations, as well as formal evaluation sessions, can set a tone that encourages faculty in their individual and professional growth. Rewards may be few, but easier to apply within the small department. Termination is never easy, especially if the faculty member has tenure. On occasion, it must be done, either on ethical grounds, (e.g., a professor becomes addicted to drugs, alcohol, or because of plagiarism), or on financial grounds, (e.g., an emergency has been declared, and the faculty must be reduced in size). The HERT factor, more than any other single characteristic, may well determine the faculty member's decision to become a department chair, or the department chair's decision to remain in the position.

BUDGET DECISIONS: THE RAST FACTOR

Most departments, large or small, have needs: more faculty, more space, more students, and more money. It does fall to the chair to administer the departmental budget. The chair must request, allocate, spend, and tally up the monetary resources in each budgeting year or cycle. The *RAST factor* combines with the *HERT factor* to comprise the largest part of the chair's administrative duties. Knowing the institution's budgetary system is the first sine qua non; after that, knowing the department's possibilities, mission, and objectives is essential. In spite of the budgetary razzle-dazzle borrowed from business and industry, incremental budgeting seems to be the most widely used system within the academic world. This is not to suggest that incremental budgeting is easy! Decisions regarding the budget still must be made, and, more and more frequently, the decision called for is the reduction of the budget, even while the fiscal year is in progress. Maintenance, travel, supplies, contracts, and equipment may go to protect salaries of faculty and secretary.

The RAST and HERT factors come together at times, and they may constitute the proverbial "sticky wicket" when they do meet. Travel to professional meetings, library acquisition requests, computer time, equipment and supplies needs must fit within the typically inflexible annual budget. The department chair, knowing full well that money spent in one category or on one person cannot be spent elsewhere, will have to rely on more than dazzling footwork to spread scarce resources effectively, efficiently, and economically.

Another point at which the *HERT* and *RAST factors* meet is in the assignment of summer-school teaching. Typically, there are not enough classes for all the department's faculty members to teach full time in the summer term(s). Who will be given preference?—the older faculty whose summer salaries may boost their retirement income or the younger faculty whose summer salaries are needed to support families? It is possible, of course, to set up some sort of rotation, giving work in alternating summer terms to all faulty members.

A third point at which personnel and budget decisions cross is on the question of full-time or part-time employment. Fewer dollars may attract more part-time faculty to teach one or two classes, thereby lowering fringe benefit costs and perhaps bringing some "real-world" expertise into the classroom. On the other hand, can and should part-time people be used as student advisors or as members on standing committees of the department and college/university? This is rarely practical.

An alternative to a full-time position carrying tenure, or to the use of part-time personnel, is the establishment of short-term positions, (for example, three years), and the hiring of an incumbent every third year. Such a decision is not without its problems, however, since anyone hired into the position will be "on the make," receptive at any time to a better position elsewhere. Such turnover positions do not build a sense of stability within the department, but many institutions are employing them in this time of restrictive funds and declining enrollments.

MORALE: THE "WE ARE ALL IN THIS TOGETHER" SYNDROME

High among the skills required of the chair of the small department is that of maintaining good morale. This may be a rather intangible skill, but it is extremely important to the welfare of the department and to all the staff members individually.

No one in our generation has written more eloquently on the subject of morale than John L. Gardner. Following earlier volumes, such as *Self-Renewal*[3] and *Excellence*,[4] in which he offers much sound advice and wisdom, he completed a work called *Morale*.[5] All three of these books should be read and re-read by department chairs and all others who hold or aspire to hold leadership positions. From the most fundamental premise that, ". . . it's the task of the leader to keep hope alive,"[6] the department head must be able to inspire by example, to motivate by expectations and rewards, and to create synergism within the department. The most successful department heads and departments I have seen in my 35 years of experience in higher education are those in which high standards of performance have been set and met by every member of the department, including the department chair. The old saw "Do as I say and not as I do" is absolutely and totally a formula for failure, if practiced by a department chair. If synergism is to be attained within the small department—and it can be—the chair must be able to motivate people, establish high standards, reward performance, and set the example; as Gardner observed, "The only way to combat the worst in humans is to call for the best."[7]

Leadership style, the abilities to communicate and delegate, to listen well and act expeditiously, and to inspire by word and deed, must complement in a very positive way the establishment of goals, objectives, and standards of performance. With purpose, enthusiasm, patience, and tenacity, faculty members can make everything they do, and the department itself, models of high morale and solid reputation. No matter how small, the department filled with such enthusiasm and good results will be favorably noticed—by students, faculty peers, and administrators.

THE POSITION ITSELF: TO CHAIR OR NOT TO CHAIR?

The most basic decision hangs on these questions. Before agreeing to become a department chair, the faculty member must have satisfactory answers to such concerns as these: (1) Will I have the support of my colleagues, even when I am in the "no" position? (2) Is my leadership style compatible with that of my dean? (3) Do I have sufficient knowledge of the workings of the institution? (4) Do I tend to suffer stress when I am called upon to make a decision or present a position? (5) Do I have the thick skin to withstand the slings and arrows of outraged colleagues? (6) Do I tend to be more positive, more assertive, more aware of my department's role, and more optimistic? (7) If I find that being a chair is not for me, will I give up the position without regarding myself as a failure and return to my professorial role with equanimity and grace? (8) Do I want this job as chair for the right reasons? (9) Is it possible for me to chair this department and continue an active interest in my discipline by teaching and writing? (10) Do I want / expect this assignment to be a nine-month or twelve-month job? If twelve-month, what responsibilities will I have? (11) Is my family supportive of me as I move into this position? (12) Can I live with the ambiguities involved, recognizing that I will have to wear many hats as I represent the administrators to my departmental members, my departmental members to administrators, and my department to campus colleagues and off-campus friends and foes? (13) What price will I have to pay to get the position and to keep the position? (14) Do I see this position as the first rung on the ladder of an administrative career?

These and other concerns must be addressed fully and forcefully. No one has a gun at your head, saying, "You must be a department head, or else . . ." Some of the concerns cannot be finally addressed until one is in the position, but once in the position, one must be honest with oneself and with others on the question of remaining in the position.

Annual or regular periodic evaluations should be an expected feature of the position. While "top-down" performance reviews have been traditional, usually conducted by the next highest official, (e.g., dean or vice president), more and more there is the requirement of "bottom-up" evaluations, conducted by the faculty members who serve under the department chair. Certainly these latter reviews indicate the degree of satisfaction with and confidence in the department chair by professional colleagues. On the other hand, one faculty member with an axe to grind can undermine the effectiveness of the department chair in a number of obvious and subtle ways.

It is possible, therefore, for a department chair either to become so bland that no one is offended "above" or "below," or to become so aggressive that faculty and/or dean resolve to make a change. Caught in this dilemma, the department chair must consider his or her own best interests, the best interests of the greater number, and the welfare of the department itself. Without support from the top and from below, the department chair is in deep trouble and must assess his or her own professional future. Accountability has become a watchword, along with responsibility and authority, and accountability is best measured by some sort of regular performance review and evaluation. The day is past when the department chair can say, and mean, "I'm my own boss!" As the advocate for both the department and the college/university, the department chair does indeed serve two masters and does try to balance tradition and change, leading and being led. If the time should come when "driving" and "being driven" replace "leading" and "being led," then the time has come to consider making the move out of the chairmanship.

Tenuring a new department chair presents another special problem, since, as far as I know, no institution grants tenure to an administrator for being an administrator. It is incumbent, therefore, that, in the search for a new (outside) chair, special consideration be given to the candidates' academic, rather than administrative credentials. The department chair, hired only for demonstrated administrative skills, will hit a stone wall when faculty colleagues consider a recommendation for tenure. On the other hand, the search process that regards only academic capabilities can well produce a good example of the Peter Principle, in which a person reaches his/her level of incompetence. Again, a balance must be found in which academic stature makes the chairperson worthy of tenure while administrative stature—demonstrated or potential—makes the chairperson attractive enough to be hired by other, higher-level administrators.

Extinction is a real threat to a small department! With little administrative clout, with a small number of faculty and students, or with no positive reputation or vocal clientele, a small department is truly vulnerable. Calls for cost reductions, budget cuts or give-backs, and perceived savings through larger administrative units constantly bedevil any chair of a small department. The "big-fish" syndrome has caused the demise of many a department of classics, which suddenly found itself in the belly of a department of foreign language. The department chair in this sort of situation is much like the person given a slingshot to hunt an elephant! Moral suasion or the creation of guilt may be all that the department chair has in his or her arsenal, unless allies can be found among the larger and more powerful departments on campus. The hard task is to discover in advance the about-to-be-made decision that merger-extinction is "in the best interests of the institution." One fact is certainly true: once the small department loses its status and independence, the chances are extremely slim that it will ever have a rebirth (or resurrection) as a free-standing department. Thus, the chair of a small department must constantly be vigilant and stress all the positive goods that result from maintaining the department's independent status. In today's frame, however, it is no exaggeration to say that the small department is an endangered species!

PERSONAL AND PROFESSIONAL RELATIONSHIPS

Within a small department, where people can truly be themselves, relationships of a personal and professional nature can easily become blurred and work for the greater good or ill of all who comprise the department. It is much more likely that a collegial style of administering the department will be adopted, since departmental committees would otherwise be pointless, and an authoritative chairperson would not long be tolerated. The faculty in a small department may therefore display greater homogeneity of interests and outlooks, but this fact can work to an advantage. Anonymity certainly is not possible here, as it would be in a large department! The result is that a disruptive faculty member can have a much greater negative impact upon the small department, whereas in a large department a voice of disruption can be muted by other faculty members and working committees.

In like manner, a few disgruntled students within a small department can cause serious harm beyond their numbers. The familiar "80-20 rule" undoubtedly applies: the 20 percent of unhappy students can create 80 percent of the problems, and the chairperson and faculty members can find themselves spending an extraordinary amount of time and effort in trying to blunt or eliminate the criticisms and negativism of this vocal minority.

In the case of either disgruntled students or a disaffected faculty member, the chairperson will have to become involved. As the old spiritual put it, "There's no hiding place down here," and the chairperson must be able to restore dignity and trust within the department and to its various constituents.

SUMMARY

It is not accurate to state or believe that a small department and its chair are but a large department and its chair writ small. There are differences in the personal relationships of faculty with faculty, of faculty with students, of students with students, and of both faculty and students with the department chair. Frequently different audiences are served, and for different purposes. Small departments can make a difference to the campus and to all audiences, often far beyond the mere size of the department. If the quality of teaching is outstanding and known to be so, if the quality of scholarship and research is the envy of larger departments, and if the quality of public service exceeds the expectations of administrators and public alike, then the likelihood is great that the small department will be regarded as a jewel to be retained rather than a bauble to be discarded by the institution. Quality leadership of the department can create or improve the quality work done by faculty and students. While the department chair may not be the paragon who can, inter alia, walk on water, he or she can do much more than simply keep the department afloat in a sea of ambiguity. By dint of character, knowledge, example, and skills, the department chair can make the difference between excellence and extinction. How to identify such department chairs and support them in their positions may be the most significant— and most overlooked—undertaking facing higher education today. Such leaders will not only be effective, they will also administer their departments as if people mattered, proving again that "small is beautiful."

NOTES

1. E. F. Schumacher, *Small is Beautiful: Economics as if People Mattered.* New York: Harper & Row Publishers, Inc., 1973.
2. *Ibid.,* 75.
3. J. W. Gardner, *Self-Renewal.* New York: Harper & Row Publishers, Inc., 1963.
4. J. W. Gardner, *Excellence,* rev. ed. New York: H. H. Norton & Co., 1984.
5. J. W. Gardner, *Morale.* New York: H. H. Norton & Co., 1978.
6. *Ibid.,* 147.
7. *Ibid.,* 110.

3

COMMON AND UNCOMMON CONCERNS: THE COMPLEX ROLE OF THE COMMUNITY COLLEGE DEPARTMENT CHAIR

MYRNA GOLDENBERG

Recent articles charging community colleges with lack of definition and, therefore, with lack of purpose remind me of the ambiguity felt as the newly appointed chairperson of the largest department of a suburban community college. I was concerned about fulfilling my responsibility as chairperson of a department nearly as diverse in its programs and faculty as the community college was, and still is, in its purposes and personnel. In fact, a colleague inadvertently convinced me that the position of chairperson was ill-defined and, at best, ambiguous when he congratulated me and then quickly advised me that I was no more than a "first among equals." His words stimulated my agonizing process of role definition, a process that generates the type of questions that are valued more for the issues they raise than for the answers they yield. Those questions eventually led me to conclude that the major differences between community college chairs and chairs in other types of colleges are the result of the differences between the purposes of community colleges and the purposes of other institutions of higher education.

COMMON CONCERNS

I began the process of defining my role by posing questions about my responsibilities to my equals (my colleagues), to my dean, to the institution, to the profession, and to my discipline. I also wondered whether other chairs were as concerned as I was with these questions and whether the literature defined the role of the chair. Most other chairs were kind though unhelpful, or benignly tolerant of my questions—an attitude that I translated as verification of our reluctance to clarify the job beyond the position description printed in the Policies and Procedures Manual.

The literature was even less helpful, and could not provide the role models offered by a body of chairs. Uncomfortable with the non-strategy of "muddling through," I took comfort in my conclusion that all chairs—new or experienced, community college or four-year institution, arts and sciences or professional—begin with an absence of training and share a common set of duties. These center on preserving the academic integrity of the department through careful tending to department standards; periodic evaluation of the program of instruction as well as the instructors; sincere interest in the recruitment, well-being, and professional growth of the faculty; respect for the mission of the college or university; and a sense of professionalism built on genuine and healthy self-interest.

UNCOMMON CONCERNS

After months of experience and hours of thinking about and discussing the subject of commonly shared duties. I turned my attention to the differences among chairpersons, for, I believe, it is the differences more than the similarities among chairs that really provide insight into the role of the chairperson. Conversations with other chairpersons in my discipline led me to conclude that most differences, beyond the obvious ones of individual personalities and perceptions of leadership, result from factors beyond our control and are, in fact, attributable to institutional characteristics that define the institution in small and large ways. There are two institutional characteristics that influence the position significantly. The first is the chairperson's status in the organization as either administrator or faculty. The second is the type of institution, that is, a community college or other type of postsecondary institution. These externally determined circumstances are peculiar to the institution, and both characteristics will modify the role of the chair in predictable ways.

Status of the Chair

The first distinctive characteristic, administrative or faculty status, clarifies the authority that is vested in the position itself. Administrative status determines the extent and nature of the chair's supervision, evaluation, and salary adjustments regarding faculty and eliminates much of the ambiguity inherent in the "first among equals" concept simply because it is based on a hierarchical premise. Decision-making may or may not be collegial in departments chaired by administrators, but accountability is clearly fixed at the administrative level and cannot be shared collegially. Formal, rather than fluid, lines of authority define the administrator-chairperson's role.

"Community" Expectations

The second distinguishing characteristic of the chair that marks the significant division between chairs in a community college and chairs of any other type of postsecondary institution is derived from the word *community,* a word that imposes a set of expectations on the community college department chair that is different from the expectations faced by chairpersons in other types of colleges. Two distinct categories of expectations, the nature of the instruction and the omnipresence of the public, are so important that they deserve further discussion. These distinctions shape much of the chair's interactions with students, and, in large measure, influence the intensity of faculty burnout and the direction of professional development.

The Nature of Instruction

As a two-year college, the community college limits the number and type of courses that a department may offer and thus the extent of stimulation and scholarship that the curriculum itself provides the faculty. These limitations do little to maintain, let alone enhance, the deep connections of the faculty to their disciplines, connections which led them into teaching in the first place. The demands of a very diverse student population, the challenges of open enrollment, the continuing increase of remedial courses, and the problems of the multi-age classroom all combine to attenuate faculty commitment to the discipline. Furthermore, increasing specialization, which crowds out traditional academic studies, and decreasing student literacy present a paradox. The former requires faculty to strengthen their own disciplinary ties, and the latter, to improve pedagogy at a time when such efforts are scarcely appreciated and least valued.

The chairperson must, then, not only guard academic standards but also guard faculty from discouragement, burnout, and disengagement. It is the chairperson who must acknowledge the fact that the gratification derived from teaching remedial sections is not a substitute for the stimulation derived from teaching bright students and challenging subjects. It is the chairperson who must find ways to help faculty maintain, or re-kindle, the passion for teaching his or her subject in an academic situation characterized more by challenges derived from student diversity than by challenges borne out of scholarly pursuits. It is the chairperson who must find ways to protect the faculty from the vague but perceptible public disregard for the teaching profession.

The Omnipresent Public

The unique link to the public, the second distinguishing characteristic of the community college, provides a key to understanding the complex role of the community college chairperson. The community college, unlike other institutions, is integrated into the everyday life and formal and informal political structures of the community. It, alone among higher education institutions, lives with an omnipresent public.

Although they may compete for the same students, urban colleges and universities, whether public or private, generally draw from a larger, and, in most instances, denser geographical area than community colleges do. Even though these colleges and universities often develop programs that meet community needs, their primary mission, granting of the undergraduate or graduate degree, is not tied to community needs. Neither is the mission of the small liberal arts college closely related to community interests. To establish or improve relations with the community, these colleges may offer generous scholarships to local residents and support for community projects, but these activities are peripheral to the life of the college. Medical schools, too, may serve their communities in visible ways, but through their teaching hospitals, clinics, and model programs, they *use* the community as much as they *serve* it. The resolution of "town and gown" tensions, which pepper the history of many four-year institutions, affects the fortune of the "gown" less directly than a similar tension between a community college and its "town." In fact, the community college can neither thrive nor survive without the support of its community. Nor should it, considering its mission.

As a faculty member, I never doubt the fact that I have a public role. As a department chair, I learned that the role carries very broad public responsibilities. Because I live in the county in which I teach, I meet my former students everywhere I turn—at the supermarket, at shopping malls, waiting on my table in a restaurant, helping me select computer software, in line at movie theaters, at intersections waiting for a traffic light to turn green, as police officers who wave to me from their patrol cars, behind the bank teller's window, as repairpersons who make house calls, as the public school teachers of my children, and as members of the Kennedy Center audience, or as sightseers downtown. These encounters make me keenly aware of the unique public role of a community college faculty member. In a similar way, the cultural life of the small liberal arts college tends to keep the student on campus and to draw the instructor to the campus, facilitating their meeting. The difference, though, is that the faculty member of the small liberal arts college expects to meet students *on* campus while the community college faculty member can barely escape such meetings *off* campus. Thus, for community college faculty members and for department chairpersons who live in the community, the college intrudes upon and essentially permeates their lives.

THE COMPLEX ROLE

The close and, in fact, critical relationship between the community college and its community dictates a large portion of the department chairperson's daily responsibilities. For example, a substantial part of any chairperson's job is dealing with the students and with the public. There are the usual complaints about grades, complaints about faculty, charges of unfair treatment, and comments about course content and standards. A chairperson in a community college responds to students of traditional age in much the same way as do the chairs elsewhere. Community college students, however, are older than their counterparts in four-year colleges and are likely to treat the complaint process more seriously than the 18- to 22-year-old student.

The average community college student (in his or her late twenties) normally does not make an appointment to see the chairperson to ventilate about an instructor. Instead he or she brings a substantiated case, a complaint based on evidence, to the chairperson. I found that the issues in these student complaints were seldom "off the wall" or foolish allegations. They were, instead, problems of expectations manifested as lack of confidence (prevalent in re-entry women who present issues too complex for discussion here) or, in the cases of senior citizen *cum* undergraduate, differences borne out of "remembrance of things past." In any case, these students were unhappy about their own performance, the performance of the other students, or the instructor, none of whom may have measured up to "how it should be" or "how it was." Their problems touch on the more profound issues of declining literacy and the diminution of the traditional formal academic life.

For the chair, these complaints have the immediacy of a time bomb because the students who complain are also citizens with ties to the local newspapers, the various civic groups, and often the funding agencies of the college. It is not easy for some of the older students, many of whom already hold undergraduate or graduate degrees, to understand the open enrollment policy, indigenous to the community college, and to accept the additional tax burden of extended schooling. Community college department chairs may find themselves explaining the differences between community colleges and four-year baccalaureate-granting colleges to dissuade student visitors or telephone callers from recommending to the county council or state legislature the transformation of the college into a four-year institution. I developed a 10-minute talk on the history, mission, and value of the community college in order to diminish, or deter, these adult students' evangelical zeal. Normally, however, these students raise the complex issue of meeting the need of the adults in the community for more challenging (read "junior/senior" but not university/graduate level) courses.

Faculty Development and "the Community"
The chairperson has the responsibility of making faculty sensitive to the political reality of an omnipresent public and to the power of this type of public. There are few community college chairpersons who have not, in "off-duty" hours, heard community residents comment on faculty in their departments. Negative comments, especially in small communities, may become the fuel that a disgruntled council member or hostile legislator can use to block funding. Favorable impressions multiply geometrically and stimulate deserved or undeserved support. In either case, the public dimension of community college teaching is weighty.

The chairperson, who has the responsibility to encourage, recognize, and reward effective teaching also has the responsibility of making each instructor understand the connection between the classroom and the county council or state legislature. For the astute chairperson, the omnipresent public can also provide the stimulation for faculty development and commitment to the community. The chair can turn that connection into specific suggestions for faculty development. As the person who is most familiar with the individual strengths and interests of the faculty and also knowledgeable about community expectations and projects, the chair has the opportunity to make connections and create teams composed of faculty and community members. These teams put faculty, and thus the department and the college, in highly visible and often highly rewarding places. At the same time, they fill legitimate community needs.

The chair can suggest co-sponsorship of department lectures and other activities with appropriate community organizations and can help establish a variety of links between the college and community that call upon the faculty's scholarly interests or specific expertise. By matching faculty talent with community projects, the chair can support faculty nominations to local museum boards, research groups, and similar programs. For example, department chairs can form a cadre of speakers to present, in informal settings, recent research to high school teachers. In some disciplines, such as English, department chairs can establish a telephone consulting service, limited to grammar and usage questions, that is open to selected county or city government agencies during specified faculty office hours. In other disciplines, chairs can arrange for exchange programs, or two-way internships, between industry and the college. Few community agencies and organizations refuse technical support from area faculty, and most colleges can accommodate these types of professional development activities that connect the classroom with the community and ultimately with the political structure governing the college.

Professional development through community service has enormous potential because it avoids many of the obstacles frequently associated with staff development, such as faculty "defensiveness . . . or detachment"[1] or remote centralized efforts that pre-package faculty development programs. This community-related approach complements the approach to faculty growth that is based on stages of career development. It provides a response to the need for "validation of self-worth . . . [and the] wish to become a 'senior' member of one's world, to speak with greater authority."[2] It can be a positive intervention strategy for the mid-career faculty members who require sources of satisfaction and gratification different from those needed at earlier career stages.[3] It also encourages the increased productivity that one author finds is the result of a "rather free wheeling/dealing, entrepreneurial, non-supervised [department] environment."[4] Needless to say, community-related faculty projects may lure faculty away from academe. However, when the chair exercises the leadership necessary to the position and initiates faculty-community connections, he or she begins the process of engaging faculty in meeting department and college goals and establishes a model for others to consider.

Repeatedly, we hear and read that the community college "is what it is today because of its ability to adapt to changes in its environment, which in turn is due to the quality of its staff and their ability to change.[5] Because that adaptability resides most prominently in the department, the chair is instrumental in facilitating the changes demanded of the college by the community. Thus, the nature of the community college itself, which is formed by the community's interests and needs as well as by interests and abilities of the faculty, does indeed shape the definition of the chairperson's position. The omnipresent public should influence recruitment and development of faculty. While the traditions of academe and those of a particular discipline certainly influence the role of the chairperson, there also exist the resources, needs, abilities, and expectations of the community, all of which define—in at least an equal measure to academic tradition—the responsibilities of the community college department chairperson.

I am grateful to my valued colleague and very dear friend Barbara Stout for her responses to this paper and for our lengthy dialogues on the role of the community college department chairperson.

NOTES

1. Claxton, Charles S. *Community College Staff Development: Basic Issues in Planning.* Atlanta: Southern Region Education Board. 1976, 9.
2. Baldwin, Roger. "Adult and Career Development: What are the implications for Faculty?" *Current Issues in Education.* Washington, DC: AAHE. 1979, 14–15.
3. Mathis, B. Claude. "Academic Careers and Adult Development: A Nexus for Research." *Current Issues in Education.* Washington, DC: AAHE. 1979, 22.
4. Blackburn, Robert T. "Academic Careers: Patterns and Possibilities." *Current Issues in Education.* Washington, DC: AAHE. 1979, 26.
5. Hammons, Jim and others. *Staff Development in the Community College: A Handbook.* Los Angeles: UCLA. 1978, 59.

4

COMMUNICATING EFFECTIVELY

KENNETH E. EBLE

If I were to name the single most important skill necessary to being an outstanding department chairperson, I would pick out the ability to communicate. But having said this, I check myself, not because communicating is not important, but because it is not really a single, separate skill. It is intermingled with everything an administrator does, defines the important parts of a chairperson's job, and is, moreover, largely inseparable from what a chairperson is. In many ways (the thinking that one does and the important tasks performed in private) and in small ways, almost everything a chair does or might do eventuates in communicating something to someone else. Thus, the idea that communicating is a separable skill, and often a secondary one, should be modified to regard communicating as the defining characteristic of being a chairperson at all.

Perhaps the notion that communicating is merely an acquirable skill or something a person is or is not good at has gotten support from President Reagan's success as "the Great Communicator." But as suspicions toward his public utterances grew and the number of press conferences dwindled, the possibility arose that the President as a communicator had been neither very great nor very communicative.

As regards chairpersons (and much of what I will say here applies to all administrators), the conditions of their employment unfortunately often emphasize communications as a useful but secondary skill. They must be scholars and teachers first, perhaps academic leaders, and be able to administer things. If they have some grace and wit and clarity and profundity of expression that is possibly to the good, but not demanded. Faced with the conflicting demands placed upon them and the dangers in declaring themselves, many move to communicating less, to hunkering down as the safest posture of all.

Some chairpersons probably do come into office with some idea of being a "Great Communicator," and may suffer the same fate as Presidents pursuing that line. The forces that create a glut of scholarly periodicals and a flood of articles are hardly perceptible in generating a high level of discourse on the many vital matters affecting education within and outside departments.

SOME CHALLENGES

Although there are chairpersons who are picked because they are leaders and spokespersons, conditions do not favor such appointments. In the first place, the choice of chairpersons is limited to the members of a department. It is further limited by a reluctance to move excellent scholars and teachers from what they are doing best into positions they may do well or poorly. And whatever the choice, the person most often comes into it trailing relationships already established and with a necessity of maintaining relationships, not with employees, but with colleagues and friends. The practice of rotating chairs with relatively short terms does not greatly alter these limiting conditions; rather, it adds another, that over a cycle of twenty years and a turnover of five or more chairpersons, the pool of likely chairpersons is further depleted.

It is no wonder then that chairpersons find communicating a problem. To make matters worse, among the first lessons learned is that every written message is likely to be misunderstood, unheeded, or resented by someone. Spoken utterances have a chance of immediate qualification and explanation, but that takes the kind of time and patience that chairpersons quickly find in short supply. There is, then, a natural drift to safe communicating, which, pushed to its maximum point of safety, is not communicating at all.

Within the snarly anarchy that defines faculty self-governance, such a posture can be quite acceptable for a time. No academic body has much of a tolerance for memos, nor does it have as much stomach for being instructed as for instructing someone else. A near-lifetime of trying to convey relatively simple information about teaching makes me think there is little receptivity to any information that falls outside of specialized scholarly interests. And few chairpersons hurt their chances for survival by holding too few department or committee meetings.

And yet there is work to be done, and as regards college and university teaching, work that not only profits from but is dependent on a good deal of communicating and gathering. Perhaps that is another reason why research, pursued in private, funded at a distance, and responsible to no one but the researcher, has such a high place among academic values. And that may also explain why a chairperson can seem to be functioning adequately by limiting communication to the functional or inclining toward no communication at all.

But despite the conditions I have described and a general faculty fondness for being let alone, a chairperson cannot avoid the necessity of communicating and the desirability of communicating well. The presence of students and the bureaucratic necessities of processing, if not educating, them, require a good deal of communicating. And the oddity of people being together but not talking or gathering sooner or later affects a department. Some member or members of a faculty will want to break the silence. Like General Halftrack wanting to hear from the Pentagon, they may want to hear from the Chair. If all that is forthcoming is functional communication, the notion can be established that the chair is or has become a mere functionary.

SOME SUGGESTIONS

So a chairperson should be wary of becoming, like Dickens' Tulkinghorn: "a tight unopenable oyster of the old school." Necessities for communicating will not disappear, and the human qualities that make communicating integral with a person's being should not be suppressed in some mistaken notions about safe administrative functioning. If chairing a department is often looked upon as a sacrificial act and the performing of it drudgery, it is because too little is made of its opportunities and joys. Writing and talking and communing with students and faculty are recognized pleasures of academic life. For a chairperson they are twice blessed. They are not pleasures stolen from preparing classes and reading papers, but central requirements of the chairperson's job. And for chairpersons, as for the faculty and students they serve, joys are greater for being shared joys, individual achievements greater for their part in the shared achievements of others.

It is an attitude, one of taking the risks that go with communicating and of counting on satisfactions greater than those risks, that promotes effective administrative communicating. Raising the level of communicating by department chairs resides in selecting chairpersons who are capable of translating that attitude into a variety of ways of communicating; of keeping before themselves and others the importance of communicating; and of overcoming the various excuses, cautions, and frustrations that go with trying to communicate.

As to selecting chairpersons, whatever course is followed should include a request for a written statement from the candidate outlining his or her conception of the position, of the department's functions and aims, of the department's place in the broader education of students, and whatever else might reveal both the person's professional beliefs and ways of expressing them. Serious candidates—for some would be eliminated as having little to express or expressing it poorly—would be expected to have further open discussions with faculty and students as part of the selection process.

Recognizing the importance of communication should be a central aim of inducting new chairpersons into their jobs, though getting an institution to provide an induction program is a prior necessity in most institutions. The importance of communicating manifests itself in so many ways. I will list a number of expectations to be carried out by a chairperson.

1. A chairperson should find a variety of ways to improve the effectiveness and quality of routing communication. Memos do not have to be uniform and uniformly dull. Letters do not have to be stuffy. Repeated written reminders are only one way of gaining a faculty's attention.

2. A chairperson should enlarge communication beyond that necessary to department functioning. If memos and summons are in bad repute, it may be because that is all an administrator seems capable of sending out. It should not be the exceptional chairperson, but every chairperson, who frequently addresses in writing and speaking the issues that animate faculty and student conversations, that shape the education of students and activities of faculty, that articulate both ideals and objectives and ways of achieving them.

3. A chairperson should be a conduit through which a wide range of ideas, opinions, and activities going on elsewhere are brought to the attention of the faculty. Good writing and speaking grow out of wide reading, experience, and observation. As the chair necessarily must operate within a wider range than individual faculty, so it is the chair's responsibility to make that wider range available to faculty in effective ways. For the time that one occupies a department chair, much of one's reading and experiencing should get done with a view to bringing relevant and important items to the attention of faculty and students and other administrators.

4. A chairperson should recognize that communicating is at the heart of the most important responsibility of any administrator: getting the best out of the individuals he or she serves. In this respect, communicating has other forms than writing and speaking. It can be the act of walking to someone's office rather than always having them come to yours, of removing barriers to access—the secretary to be approached, the anteroom to wait in, the telephone voice asking, "Who is calling, please?" It can be showing up for some faculty or student activity out of both honest interest and a sensed need to lend support. It can be pats on the back and kicks in the ass and the picking up of people who have stumbled.

5. A chairperson should not give up the vital and skillful communicating that goes with being a good teacher. The department faculty are now the students, fully as much in need of instructing in some ways as students—and probably more resistant to it. That fact, if it be a fact, merely increases the chance to hone one's teaching skills.

6. A chairperson should aim some speaking, writing, and appearing at the wider public upon which support of a department ultimately depends. One responsibility is to place the department before the university administration, and not merely in responding but in initiating, and proposing, and informing.

Beyond that, there is the wider public. No university department except the athletic department has any body of reporters greatly interested in its business. If the work of a department is to be made known at all, the news will have to come from the department. The chairperson must take on the job of public relations. For every department has a public, and a more important one than most realize. Departments are vaguely aware that their undergraduate majors go somewhere; often only majors who become graduate students may be more closely followed. At the least, department chairs should maintain communication with identifiable groups of alumni, such as the large numbers in many departments who become public school teachers. In addition, every good chairperson should make some effort to see that the department has some visibility in the community at large. Education is not as dull a subject as the ordinary newspaper's scanty treatment of it would lead one to believe. If it seems so, the fault is in part that few chairpersons try to communicate the excitement of learning that takes place, now and again, within their purview.

7. A chairperson should try to leaven the deadliness of much academic prose. There is much that is pleasurable, comic, and thought-provoking in any place where large numbers of students and faculty are brought together daily. Some of this could be communicated by a skillful department chair who is willing to challenge the distinctions between poetry and prose, song and speech, dance and marching to an academic two-step. In any department of size, there should be an internal publication or publications, a newsletter that has some literary as well as news-gathering merit.

Not all of the above expectations need be carried out by the chairperson. Here as elsewhere in an administrator's work, delegating is important. At the same time, the chair must remain at the center of communication, to establish a center for knowing what is going on and to act upon what is being argued here: that communication is one task that is too important to be delegated entirely to others.

EXCUSES AND CAUTIONS

The final point I wish to make is that even given a chairperson with a disposition to communicate effectively and an ability to marshal department resources, excuses and cautions and frustrations often stand in the way.

The majority of excuses are those of having too much to do and of planning to do it tomorrow. These are human weaknesses, present in everyone. That is why I think in the soul of every good chairperson, dwelling side by side with magnificent qualities of leading and serving, are the habits of a good bookkeeper. Chief among these habits is that of keeping a running account of assets and expenditures—a balance sheet for apportioning one's time and skills to all the necessary tasks for which there seems never to be enough time. Few administrative preoccupations—budgets, supplies, schedules, reports and complaints—can be separated from communication. Failing to communicate because of the pressure of other tasks is not an excuse: it is funking the whole job.

As to procrastinating, maybe there is nothing that can be done about it except what we do with students: keep haranguing against it. In the past decade, much of my own zeal to confront procrastinators has been tempered by the fact that a giant industry—Federal Express, Purolater, and Express Mail—has been built on the habits of people to put things off. What could be sent for 25 cents on one day gets sent for $12.95 the night before it is due. I do not mind attacking a human weakness, but I have no wish to undermine the economy.

I have already indicated my impatience with caution in communicating—in mentioning the risks of saying something and the safety of remaining silent. And yes, there are arguments in favor of the memo not sent, the letter not mailed, the meeting not called. Poor administrators are tolerable chiefly because of the things they might do that their ineptness keeps them from doing. But learning, I think, does not thrive on caution. I have been struggling to learn French for thirty years. My failure may be blamed on lack of intelligence, defective hearing, or a lack of genuine motivation. But much must be blamed on my being cautious, on being unwilling to get out of the safe position I occupy with respect to the language I know and face being misunderstood, humiliated, and reviled in a language I cannot even understand. But my caution with French is a private matter. A chairperson who would affect positively the learning of others cannot let caution lead to silence.

Finally, frustration is not the same as caution, nor is it an excuse, though it may lead to excuses. Most of the common frustrations are what a commitment to teaching should have already conditioned a chairperson to face. A chairperson's silent rage at a perfectly clear statement being misunderstood or ignored by some part of the faculty is little different from a teacher's suppressed desire to kill those students who never quite get the assignment right. As we continue to be teachers, we cultivate patience, keep extra copies of all instructions, and live with a certain amount of slippage between what we say and write and what students comprehend. Chairpersons must be at least as patient, persevering, and ingenious, and still expect some slippage.

A larger frustration besets anyone charged with some obligation to assist others for their own and the common good. The frustration is that those most in need of assistance do not show up and are the hardest to reach. Chairpersons may have less difficulty in this respect than freelance improvers who issue calls for voluntary participation in improving things, addressing issues, or wrestling with problems. But departments vary greatly in what any chairperson can expect as to the degree of voluntary commitment leading to committee service, and reading unenveloped mail, or even attending department meetings. Similarly the amount of coercion that can be employed is a delicate, or perhaps explosive, matter.

SUMMARY

Once again, I am drawn to say that what one is left with is the power of persuasion: Establishing a level of commitment, articulating expectations, and holding these expectations before the community of faculty are ways to proceed. However frustrating the results may be, there is justification in making the effort. However few are reached by an effort to extend one's range of communicating, they are more than those reached if no effort had been made. And reinforcing the inclinations and efforts of the easily reachable is worth doing in itself.

In concluding, I realize I have spent no space on some of the unseemlier aspects of communicating. For example, the chairperson's role in facing frictions, antagonisms, disturbed factions, and individuals. It is a truism that such violences often arise from people either not speaking to each other or having spoken too much. Chairpersons must deal with them as they can. But in chiefly discussing positive ways of communicating effectively, I have not quite passed over this other side. A department in which communication is frequent, varied, and open, and which has the force, lightness, and direction that a good chairperson can provide, is less likely to foster wrangling, misunderstandings, and sulking. As that affects a chairperson, there will be fewer reasons for hunkering down and more reasons for gaining satisfactions from the job and for communicating those satisfactions to others.

5

CHAIRPERSON AND DEAN: THE ESSENTIAL PARTNERSHIP

CHARLES O. WARREN

In recent years the role of department chairperson has received increased attention. Numerous articles and books have been published, regional and national workshops are held frequently, and at least two periodicals related to this topic have national circulation. In-depth analysis of the chairperson's critical, central position in academic leadership and organization is greatly needed and long overdue.

Many of the recent writings have elucidated the complexities, ambiguities, and vagaries of the role of chairperson. This chapter will concentrate on a particular aspect of the position—a professional relationship that seems, or that should be, central—in the hope that a more general understanding of mutual expectations and goals might emerge.

LEADERSHIP: A SHARED RESPONSIBILITY

Whenever we begin to think and write about a particular role or position within the academic community—chairperson, president, dean, professor—the danger arises that focused attention may lead to a feeling of overwhelming responsibility, often accompanied by a sense of isolation, on the part of those in the position. What should be emphasized more, and what this essay attempts to advance in model form, are notions of mutual responsibility, shared authority, and balanced expectations.

A fundamental premise for the "essential partnership" is that the dean's role carries with it considerably less ambiguity than that of the chairperson. The dean's view of institutional mission and the nature of academic leadership should be well formed, placing him or her in a position to communicate readily the values and necessity of the partnership.

The need for overt communication between the dean and chairpersons, especially new appointees, seems obvious, and most would argue that of course it happens. More frequently than not, I fear, such interaction deals only with the mechanical, routine features of the professional association. The philosophical moorings of the chairperson's position, the challenge of shared, dynamic leadership, often go unexplained—perhaps due to the press of time or to the embarrassment some seem to experience when exploring values of philosophy or, worse still, to a devaluing of such matters.

The general literature on leadership is too voluminous and, in some cases, too taxonomic to explore at this time: helpful reviews of leadership styles for new chairpersons are suggested within relatively recent works by Tucker,[1] Bennett,[2] and Booth.[3] More appropriate here, I think, is the highly perceptive and insightful conceptualization offered by James MacGregor Burns in his brilliant book *Leadership.*[4] Incisively, Burns differentiates two categories of leadership: transactional and transformational.

Transactional leadership is quite familiar to all of us: it involves, as Burns states, "the exchange of valued things"; the purposes of the individuals involved are related, but not blended. Transactional leadership then involves a "swapping" of one service for another between leader and followers, often with independent objectives. The teaching role of the leader is absent. By contrast, leadership of a *transformational* nature calls for an evolving interaction so that "leaders and followers raise one another to higher levels of motivation and morality." Transforming leaders have a supportive, caring attitude, their questions have a positive ring, they encourage other people to excel, and they reflect a grasp of mission, of common cause. They embrace the teaching role of leaders and they "seek significant change that represents the collective or pooled interests of leaders and followers." The application of Burn's concepts to the essential partnership is direct and useful.

THE DEAN'S ROLE: SUPPORT AND EXPECTATIONS

The initial onus in this partnership is on the dean. Early on in the chairperson's tenure, the dean should lead in the exploration of process and the desired characteristics of the professional interaction.[5] Transactional events are inevitable, and they are needed. That should be understood. But the dean must move directly in pointing out the mutual benefit for all concerned—students, faculty, administrators—in jointly exhibiting transforming leadership.

Whether the supervisor is president or provost and whether the charge is institutional or divisional, the dean must receive strong support of the partnership idea from those higher in the administrative line. The commitment to dynamic, transforming leadership must begin with the president and extend throughout the administration. If that commitment is not present in the dean, any current ambiguities in organizational structure, function, and leadership will continue and increase.

With this background, let us consider some reasonable expectations the chair might have for the dean who is attendant to the essential partnership.[6]

• The willingness of the dean to share knowledge and detailed information with chairpersons, individually and collectively, is critical. Not only do chairpersons need such information to generate organizational trust and effective leadership at the departmental level, but greater understanding and wisdom can result directly from knowing collective circumstances. Recently at our institution, a dean, for the first time at a chairpersons' retreat, shared extensive, detailed budgeting and resources information for each of the divisional departments, followed by chairpersons' explanations of critical departmental needs and objectives. The result was a strong feeling of mutual concern and support. In fact, one chairperson commented, "I didn't realize that relatively we (our department) were in such good shape—I'm amazed at how well several departments manage with such limited resources."

• The replacement of myth and suspicion with openness and realistic information contributes greatly to a sense of common purpose, even when the facts are not nearly as positive as *all* concerned would hope. Such information also is essential if chairpersons are expected to participate effectively in budgetary and academic planning. Most of us are and will be, for some time, in a fiscal environment where growth in one area demands resource relocation from another. By sharing information forthrightly, by offering rational justification for tentative decisions, and by listening openly to cogent counterargument, deans and chairpersons can practice transforming leadership that is demonstrably beneficial at all organizational levels.

• The dean must take the lead in reducing the amount of unproductive record keeping and paperwork expected of the chairperson. Word processing and other forms of departmental office automation should be a continuing goal of the dean, as should the insistence that fellow administrators resist the natural management impulse to inundate chairpersons with low-priority, often overlapping requests for data and reports.

• Departmental review and planning retreats, led by the chairperson and dean, should occur periodically; the sharing of common views *and* honest differences with departmental faculty is often salutary. At least annual retreats and frequent meetings between the dean and the divisional or institutional chairpersons are functional. Likewise, all chairpersons and deans—at institutions with multiple schools or divisions—should meet with the president and provost once or twice during the academic year. As discussed earlier, the open sharing of data, ideas, and plans at all such occasions will help establish and preserve a pervasive sense of mutual trust and respect. Our experience in practicing this approach for these and even broader forums over the past few years, while falling short of a panacea, has contributed very positively to a more idea- and issue-oriented environment, one where answers are directly available from all administrative leaders, especially the chairperson. The dean, through persistent reference to plans and objectives and through sincere praise for meaningful accomplishment, must help create an atmosphere that nurtures the sense of partnership and negates the notion of professional isolation and futility.

THE CHAIRPERSON'S ROLE: CONTRIBUTING TO THE PARTNERSHIP

While preserving the integrity of the crucial relationship to departmental faculty, the chairperson also must be clearly committed to the validity of the essential partnership.

Some reasonable expectations of the chairperson include the following:

• The chairperson should clearly convey to departmental colleagues the sense of partnership, the feeling that there is no isolation, that the dean is readily accessible and a dependable source of accurate, clear information. The absence of a mythical, extradepartmental enemy will not diminish the influence of the chairperson, nor will the mere pretense of its presence permit the expression of transforming leadership.

• Chairpersons *must* relay information to their colleagues in a timely and accurate fashion. Many deans express the perception that critical information or even casual statements have been subsequently misrepresented or not passed on at all. Such action represents either detached, sloppy leadership or a posture from which perceived political advantage is derived; neither practice fits the model of the essential partnership.

• Completion of an effective communications circuit depends also on the chairperson's willingness to pass along needed information from the departmental level to the dean and other appropriate administrative offices. Timely, clear communications of data, plans, and serious concerns of faculty colleagues enhance and ensure an open environment and a sense of shared purpose.

• While a strong advocacy for departmental needs and objectives is the chairperson's fundamental sine qua non, a clear grasp of institutional mission and a willingness to discuss, interpret, and explain divisional and/or institutional priorities are critical.

• Careful planning and periodic assessment of departmental and individual faculty objectives give the chairperson a clear vision in presenting to the dean the case for particular resources at particular times. In turn, the dean's timely response allows the chairperson to balance departmental expectations, collectively and individually; consequently, the partnership is strengthened.

• Certain sensitive situations or problems with negative overtones are, arguably, placed legitimately at the feet of the dean, provost, or president; the exclusion of the chairperson from culpability might be essential to preserve the integrity and effectiveness of the position. Conversely, other situations exist—questions of promotion and tenure, substantive student grievances, poor academic advisement, etc., where, for the lack of a better cliche, the chairperson must simply "bite the bullet." Transforming leadership or even effective transactional leadership is not possible if certain inviolable principles are abridged. The willingness of the chairperson to make or concur with thoughtful, difficult decisions is a basic characteristic of transforming leadership *and* the essential partnership.

SOME SUMMARY THOUGHTS

Dealing with ambiguity and competing principles is a realistic component of almost all campus administrative leadership positions. That is especially true for the department chairperson. While some degree of ambiguity and complexity will always persist, a model is available that should result in a more positive, supportive professional environment. This is the model built on the unique professional relationship of chairperson and dean—a relationship that calls for an essential partnership.

Through a mutual willingness to clarify goals, share essential information, explore the nature of effective leadership, and communicate widely and openly, the chairperson and dean have an opportunity both to enrich their own professional experiences and to enhance those of students and faculty and administrative colleagues. The proposal is not unrealistic, but neither is it a total solution. The essential partnership is pragmatically idealistic and can be a source of transforming leadership practiced subsequently throughout the institution.

NOTES

1. Allan Tucker, *Chairing the Academic Department*. 2nd ed. New York: ACE/Macmillan, 1984.
2. John Bennett, *Managing the Academic Department*. New York: ACE/Macmillan, 1983.
3. David B. Booth, *The Department Chair: Professional Development and Role Conflict*. Washington, DC: AAHE:ERIC/Higher Education Research Report No. 10, 1982.
4. James MacGregor Burns, *Leadership*. New York: Harper & Row, 1978.
5. David Booth reports a personal communication, considered representative of a new chairperson, that states: "We have no orientation program for chairs, formal or informal. I am an incoming chair of a department and my only preparation is that of observing informally the activities of the outgoing chair." Booth goes on to discuss a study by A. K. Bragg in which she reports that, from a sample of 39 chairs, one-third had no consultation with their predecessors and another

one-third collaborated infrequently; only one-fourth reported frequent interaction with the outgoing chair. In *The Department Chair: Professional Development and Role Conflict*.

6. For a number of practical hints to the dean, see John B. Bennett, "A Chairperson's Notes to the Dean." *AAHE Bulletin* (June 1982).

6

I WANTED TO BE AN ADMINISTRATOR; NOW HOW DO I COPE WITH THE STRESS?

JERRY R. MAY
ROBERT B. McBEATH

Becoming a department chair is a natural step for many competent faculty. To be a leader of our colleagues is an honor and a means of representing our discipline's orientation to the school or university as a whole. It allows us to become involved in the university's larger mission. Yet how many times have you asked yourself, How did I get into this job? or stated, The stress of this job is getting me down. Is being a department chair stressful? Actually life is stressful, and it is not clear that being a department chair is more stressful than anything else in life. Basically we must recognize that the job is stressful at times and we must learn how to cope and function effectively during these times.

As we have talked to administrators at midmanagement levels, like department chairs, ten common sources of stress have been identified:

1. *It is common to feel caught in the middle.* Being caught between the faculty and the administration can be trying.
2. *Upward mobility.* The movement from being one of the flock to the leader can, at times, lead to isolation and role confusion.
3. *Bureaucracy.* The bureaucracy becomes more real. Edicts from a higher authority must be filtered through you to your faculty.
4. *Personality conflicts.* Dealing with personality conflicts between faculty and/or staff now rests on your shoulders.
5. *Time demands.* Demands upon time and constant interruptions are commonplace. All faculty and staff believe that their concerns are important and that their problems are yours. You may feel guilty if you take time for yourself or angry that no one values your need for private time. As the myth has it, administrators always have spare time.
6. *Student/teacher alienation.* There is a sense of underlying responsibility for student/teacher alienation. The message is that the ultimate responsibility lies with the department chair.
7. *Discipline-specific issues.* Each department has its own potentially volatile issues. For example, the anatomy department's han-

36

dling of cadavers, or the education department's dealing with complaints about a graduate who has become a child molester.

8. *Meetings*. There is a steady stream of meetings, reports, and political appearances.

9. *Unexpected issues*. Having to deal with unexpected issues from the faculty or administrators is a frequent occurrence.

10. *Evaluations*. One of the most stressful reasonsibilities is the periodic evaluation of faculty and staff. One must be objective and candid on evaluations and yet work with these individuals on a daily basis. One wants to be supportive of each faculty member's development, yet part of the job description is the evaluation of job performance.

This list is by no means exhaustive. However, most of these stressful situations are common in the lives of college administrators. We either falter or cope with the incessant pressure of these stresses depending upon our perception of the problems, their frequency, intensity, and duration. Arnold Bennett said "your own mind is a sacred enclosure into which nothing harmful can enter except by your permission." This is easily said but difficult to control. This chapter will show you how to identify your stressors, outline their effects on your body and performance, and, finally, present a few concrete suggestions for preventing or managing the negative aspects of stress in your work day.

IDENTIFICATION OF STRESS

Almost everyone is aware of the association between stress and illness. We have all heard the comments, "I'm going to get an ulcer over this" or "I'm going to have a nervous breakdown." Such comments reinforce the idea that somehow too much stress is unhealthy.

The concept of stress means different things to different people. Stress, as defined by Selye, is a "nonspecific response of the body to any demand made upon it."[1] It is how the body reacts on a physiological level to any type of demand. These demands are called stressors. Many different stressors such as heat, cold, sorrow, or joy may elicit an identical biochemical response in the body. Although individual stressors may initiate a specific response (e.g., cold causes shivering), they also produce a nonspecific demand on the body to reestablish homeostasis (e.g., normality). The mechanisms used to reestablish homeostasis involve a complex association between the brain and the body in which a variety of hormones and nervous system responses combine to restore the body to its original state. We have the ability to perceive an event as pleasant or unpleasant, and this perception plays an integral role in how our bodies react to that event. It should be noted that there is no such thing as a life free of stress. In fact, stress is a necessary ingredient for life and without it the organism fails to thrive and eventually dies. The problem arises when the intensity and duration of the stress response eventually overtaxes an individual's ability to function.

The human body has a finite ability to restrict and adapt to internal and external stimuli. The presence of a stressor over an extended period of time can eventually deplete the person's resistance capacity and lead to illness. Table 1 outlines several of the warning signs of negative stress. You may wish to put a check next to the specific physical, emotional, or behavioral signs that you experience. If you check many of these items, the remainder of this article may be of interest and help to you.

TABLE 1 Warning Signs of Negative Stress

Physical Signs

( ) Fatigue
( ) Pounding of the heart
( ) Dryness of the throat or mouth
( ) Insomnia, an inability to fall asleep or stay asleep or early awakenings
( ) Frequent or lingering colds
( ) Trembling and nervous tics
( ) Grinding of the teeth
( ) Increase or decrease in appetite
( ) Increased sweating
( ) Diarrhea
( ) Indigestion, queasiness in the stomach
( ) Vomiting
( ) Pain in neck or lower back
( ) Increased premenstrual tension
( ) Missed menstrual cycle
( ) Headache
( ) Weakness
( ) Dizziness
( ) Weight gain or loss
( ) Shortness of breath
( ) Stuttering or other speech difficulties
( ) Increased pitch in voice
( ) Nervous laughter

Emotional Signs

( ) General irritability
( ) Hyperexcitability
( ) Depression
( ) Boredom
( ) Restlessness

( ) Stagnation
( ) Overpowering urge to cry, run, or hide
( ) Difficulty relaxing
( ) Need to generate excitement over and over
( ) Feeling people do not appreciate you—feeling used
( ) Inability to laugh at yourself
( ) Increased feeling and expression of anger, or being cynical
( ) Inability to concentrate, the flight of thoughts
( ) Disenchantment
( ) Feeling of unreality
( ) Feeling life is not much fun
( ) Not enjoying your job
( ) Desire to quit job
( ) Mind going blank
( ) Feeling afraid
( ) "Free Floating Anxiety"—that is to say, we are afraid of something but we do not know exactly what it is
( ) Always feeling under pressure to succeed
( ) Hyperalertness, a feeling of being "keyed up"
( ) Automatic expression of negative feelings
( ) Disappointment in yourself or others
( ) Increased rationalization
( ) Feeling indispensable
( ) Obsessions
( ) Unable to enjoy or compliment colleagues' successes
( ) Fault-finding
( ) Nightmares

Behavioral Signs

( ) Tendency to overwork
( ) Difficulty with routine daily work
( ) Decrease in job performance
( ) Increased use of alcohol
( ) Increased use of nonprescription drugs
( ) Increased use of various medications, such as tranquilizers or amphetamines
( ) Increased use of tobacco
( ) Less time for recreation
( ) Less time for intimacy with people around you
( ) Less vacation time
( ) Overworked, but cannot say no to more work without feeling guilty
( ) Hypermotility, which is the increased tendency to move about without any reason
( ) Inability to take a physically relaxed attitude, sitting quietly in a chair or lying on a sofa

( ) Feeling that sex is more trouble than it is worth
( ) Speaking up less and less at gatherings, and then only speaking negatively
( ) Difficulty setting goals
( ) A tendency to be easily startled by small sounds
( ) Finding yourself further behind at the end of each day
( ) Forgetting deadlines, appointments, etc.
( ) Accident proneness—under great stress, whether it is positive or negative, one is more likely to have accidents while at work, driving a car, or during athletic events
( ) Making a foolish mistake
( ) Blaming others for poor performance

"The feeling that you've done a job well is rewarding. The feeling that you've done it perfectly is fatal." (Anonymous) Most achievement-oriented individuals are perfectionists. Yet trying too hard to be perfect will usually increase our stress beyond an optimal performance level. There is a myth that would lead us to believe that if we are not doing something well, we must simply try harder. Unfortunately, many of us, even department chairs, use this logic not only with ourselves but with faculty and staff. It is important to remember that both you and your

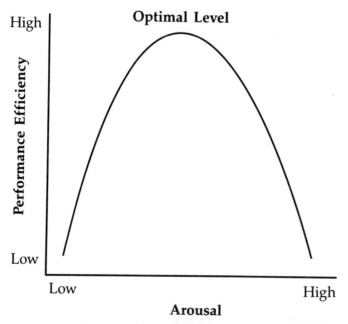

FIGURE 1 (anxiety, emotion, attention, concentration, stress, motivation)

faculty tend to be over-achievers. In most circumstances where performance is deteriorating, we must learn to moderate our arousal level, an effort which will lead to a reestablishment of maximum performance. Figure 1 demonstrates the well-documented relationship between stress and performance. Highly motivated people who are not doing well, if pushed, will only do worse.

Guidelines for Coping with Stress
It is sometimes very helpful to remember six basic guidelines for counteracting the negative effects of stress:

1. Forgive yourself (with no strings attached).
2. Forgive others.
3. Do not compare yourself with others.
4. See your good side.
5. See the good in others.
6. Be positive about today. Do not dwell in the past or the future.

DEALING WITH DIFFICULT PEOPLE

We all know difficult people. Notice that most of the ten stressors identified by department chairs center around interacting with people. They can have such a negative impact on us. We silently wish, If only everyone could be more understanding and agreeable. One of the first steps in knowing how to deal with difficult people is understanding some of the different categories of personality styles. Bramson[2] divides difficult people into seven categories:

1. Hostile aggressives
2. Complainers
3. Silent and unresponsive persons
4. Super agreeables
5. Negativists
6. Know-it-all experts
7. Indecisive stallers

It helps to know which types we are dealing with. Remember that we ourselves may fit into one of these categories. Understanding the response to stress in ourselves and others can help us cope. Bramson believes that there are six fundamental steps in dealing with difficult people:[3]

1. Assess the situation.
2. Stop wishing the difficult person were different.
3. Put some distance between you and the difficult person.
4. Formulate a coping plan.
5. Implement your plan.

6. Monitor the effectiveness of your coping strategies, modifying them where appropriate.

Relationship Tension

All people, whether difficult or not, can be affected by how we communicate. The quality of the relationship can depend upon our style of interaction with others and some of our traits and attitudes. It is important to remember that positive communication increases self-esteem in ourselves and those around us. Frequently, as administrators, we are dealing with problems and therefore tend to communicate in a negative fashion. We have found that there are seven basic factors that increase relationship tension:

1. *Negative communication.* Negative communication tends to reduce self-esteem in the other person and produce defensive behavior.
2. *Being judgmental.* This can be communicated by tone of voice or through an authoritarian opinion that usually ends up in our defending ourselves and saying that the other person is wrong.
3. *Acting superior.* Presuming a higher rank, quality, or importance than the person with whom we are interacting.
4. *Too much strategy.* The definition of strategy is "the science and art of military command exercised to meet the enemy in combat under advantageous conditions." If we are overly strategic, the other person will feel like a pawn in a contest that we are trying to win.
5. *Self-centeredness.* When we act like we are not concerned with the desires, needs, interests, or problems of others, relationship tension will be increased.
6. *Being opinionated.* This is undue adherence to our own opinion or preconceived notions. We act as if we have all the answers, we are the teachers, and the others only need to be taught.
7. *Controlling.* This occurs when we exercise restraint or direct influence over another and provide the total structure and format of the interaction.

Encouraging Nondefensive Behavior

All of us have the tendency to use one or more of these negative factors. It is important to monitor your own interactions with others and see which ones you tend to use. Fortunately, there are corollaries to these tension-producing factors which help us cope, reduce relationship tension, and encourage nondefensive behavior. These can be important tools in a person's coping strategies when dealing with difficult people.

1. *Positive communication.* Remember that positive communication increases self-esteem and cooperation. Catch somebody doing something right each day. It can be the smallest bit of behavior,

but pointing out a positive thought, feeling, or behavior can help override many of the negative problems of the day.

2. *Try to understand.* Ask questions, for example. "Tell me more about it," "I would like to understand this more." We suggest you avoid asking the question, "Why?" Linguists have taught us that "Why" questions in adulthood tend to produce defensive behavior in those with whom we are interacting.

3. *Equality.* Attempt to be on an equal plane with the other person and avoid acting superior. We have found that truly superior people rarely have this need to *act* superior.

4. *Flexibility.* In listening to the other person, attempt to remain flexible and not have too rigid a plan or strategy. The other person may be giving you valuable information which could lead you to change any plan you may have.

5. *Sharing others' feelings.* Simply identifying the other person's feelings enables that individual to feel heard. An example would be, "I hear that you are angry, and I would be too." Identifying the feelings in others rather than ourselves can help reduce our own self-centered feelings at the time.

6. *Open-mindedness.* Demonstrate that you want to hear, versus remaining opinionated.

7. *Problem-solving.* We suggest that you first get the other persons involved in problem-solving. Many times they will have a very good answer. This means you will not have to work as hard and you can reinforce them for a good idea. Problem-solving is step seven and should not be attempted until the thoughts and feelings have been expressed. Do not try to control the problem-solving situation.

We have found that the sequencing of these factors is significant in reducing relationship tension. Managers tend to be viewed as problem-solvers, and may solve problems too early, before trying to understand how the aspects of equality, flexibility, the sharing of others' feelings, and being open-minded can help reduce stress and more effectively cope with and solve the problem. We suggest that you practice these factors that are known to defuse relationship tension. Certainly spontaneity, laughter, and the ability not to take everything so seriously are some of the most important stress-relieving strategies. A little appropriate humor in the day can make our busy schedule more tolerable. In addition, the use of aerobic exercise and recreational activities tailored to individual interests and age is a very important part of any plan for reducing tensions and stress.

RELAXATION TRAINING PROGRAM

A very straightforward method of dealing with physical manifestations of stress is learning how to relax. The relaxation training program can be one of the most beneficial psychological techniques to keep us at an optimal level of performance. Those exercises should be conducted on a daily basis for ten to fifteen minutes, and then, if you feel situationally tense, just prior to a stressful situation, the sensation of relaxation can be recalled mentally within just a few seconds.

In practicing the relaxation technique, it is important to pay attention to the environment. The relaxation training should take place in a quiet surrounding that is comfortable and that will facilitate maximal concentration. The technique outlined is based upon a method described by Bernstein and Borkovec.[4] The procedure allows us to relax deeply various muscle groups of the body. There is a specific sequence to follow.

1. Attention should focus on the specific muscle group.
2. A specific muscle group is to be tensed.
3. Tension is maintained for a period of five to seven seconds (this duration is shorter in the case of the feet).
4. The muscle group tension is then released.
5. Attention should be maintained on the muscle group as it relaxes for an additional twenty to thirty seconds.

Remember that the goal of progressive relaxation training is to help learn to reduce the muscle tension in the body far below levels normally achieved. The procedure produces relaxation in sixteen different muscle groups.

While you are relaxing, it is important to concentrate on breathing. Breathe normally while relaxing, but during each exhalation or breath out, think of pushing the tension out of the body. The muscles of the body normally contract or become tense with breathing in and release and relax with breathing out. Synchronizing this breathing out as you are also concentrating on relaxing the muscles can enhance the effect.

We believe that if you understand and practice these stress management philosophies and techniques, being a department chair can be rewarding and fun.

NOTES

1. H. Selye, *Stress Without Distress*. New York: The New American Library, Inc., 1984.
2. R. M. Bramson, *Coping with Difficult People*. New York: Anchor Press/ Doubleday. 1981, 4.
3. *Ibid.*, 130.
4. D. A. Bernstein and T. D. Borkovec, *Progressive Relaxation Training: A Manual for the Helping Professions*. Champagne, Ill: Research Press, 1973, p. 25.

SUGGESTED READINGS

Asken, M. J. and May, J. R. *Sports Psychology: The Psychological Health of the Athlete.* New York: S. P. Medical and Scientific Books. In Press.

Burns, D. D. *Feeling Good.* New York: William Morrow and Company, Inc., 1980.

May, J. R. Relaxation Training Videotape. Reno: Office of Communications and Broadcasting, University of Nevada, 1985.

Zimmerman, I. M. "Stress: What it does to Judges and How it Can be Lessened." *The Judges' Journal* 20 (No. 3 1981). 4–9.

PART TWO

Faculty and Staff Hiring and Evaluation

It takes little reflection to realize that the best solution for problems is their prevention. One implication for chairpersons is that attention paid to hiring the right people pays off enormously in the reduction of problems the wrong people could later create. The careful, reasoned, and deliberate selection of faculty colleagues is as important as nurturing them. Investing time and energy in both hiring and nurturing will strengthen the ability of the chairperson to create a vital and vigorous department, recognized as such by those within as well as without.

In "Quest for the Best: Successful Proactive Recruiting Strategies," William Hynes provides a number of suggestions about taking the initiative in faculty recruiting. The authorization to proceed with a search presents an unparalleled opportunity to improve and/or redirect the department. It should not be wasted by any of several kinds of passivity: insufficient review of department needs and future possibilities, poor networking and advertising of the needs to be filled, inadequate reflection upon the benefits the department and institution have to offer the right candidate, or unenthusiastic interviewing and review of credentials.

Affirmative action is an important consideration in the hiring process. However, attending to matters of equity and gender/racial/ethnic balance is equally important in considering retention, promotion, salary increase, and so on. The chairperson has important roles to play in both contexts. In "Women in Academic Departments: Uneasy Roles, Complex Relationships," Lois Vander Waerdt provides helpful suggestions. Throughout her essay she emphasizes the role the chair can play in assessing the climate for women and minority students.

Second only to hiring in its long-term impact upon the department is the evaluation of those already on board. Decisions made today can have an impact for good or ill for years to come. Uniformly a matter of discomfort for department chairpersons, evaluation of faculty colleagues is usually approached with ambivalence. While conceding the importance of evaluation for the health of the department, chairpersons often experience stress over the potential their involvement in these activities may have on long-standing relationships with colleagues.

In his essay "Faculty Evaluation: The Roles of the Department Chair," John Bennett addresses this element of negativity and some ways of placing it in constructive context. Properly done, faculty evaluations are developmental in that they prevent problems from developing, identify and focus on problems not prevented earlier, and so reduce the potential for conflict and anomie within the department. They have a role in promoting planning within the department as well. Traditional distinctions between activities appropriate for probationary and for tenured faculty remain important, especially since most institutions emphasize the evaluation of non-tenured faculty, often leaving any systematic evaluation of tenured faculty to a matter of chance. Yet it is precisely tenured faculty today who may be in most need of the developmental help that periodic evaluations can provide.

Part-time or adjunct faculty members are also an important constituency for department chairpersons. Indeed, at some institutions, especially community colleges and some urban four-year institutions, adjunct faculty can greatly outnumber full-time faculty. Those adjuncts with full-time positions elsewhere can bring to the classrooms invaluable perspectives from their hands-on experience. And adjuncts also provide staffing flexibility and budgetary relief. On the other hand, they are often especially difficult to integrate into departmental affairs and traditions and they can present challenges for the chairperson on the monitoring of quality instruction.

In "Managing Part-Time Faculty," George Biles and Howard Tuckman provide a variety of suggestions on auditing human resource management practices. Properly done, such an audit helps to determine whether part-time faculty are being used efficiently and effectively. Biles and Tuckman also provide a sample outline for a policy and procedures manual for part-time faculty.

Chairs are frequently supervisors of staff, as well as leaders of faculty. Different procedures and values may apply in supervising staff, and chairs should be alert to the differences. Secretaries are a key resource, as are administrative assistants, and laboratory and research technicians. In "The Department Chair's Leadership Role in Supervising NonFaculty Personnel," Donald DeRosa and Quelda Wilson provide help by reviewing key relationships with nonfaculty staff and providing a number of suggestions for maintaining good staff morale.

7

SUCCESSFUL PROACTIVE RECRUITING STRATEGIES: QUEST FOR THE BEST

WILLIAM J. HYNES

Professor Sam Procrustes, long-standing chairman of the theater department, was asked by one of his theater colleagues about the status of the search for a new technical director, with particular interest in one candidate. "Oh, Pamela Lukas-Scheider? No, she isn't a finalist. She's too high-powered for our small university and besides I think she has already signed a contract with a more prestigious institution. I didn't even think it worthwhile to keep her in the running. Our best bet is probably Charlie Fowler who has taught parttime for us for the last several years. He's a known quantity, the students like him, it won't cost anything to bring him to campus and our salary is more than he's able to make through part-time employment."

The search for a new person in humanities was taking an extraordinary length of time. Interviews had occurred over a month ago, but no announcement of a selection had been forthcoming. When queried, Professor Diane Hunter responded: "Yes, it has taken a long time but we are still negotiating with our top choice. He really wants to join us and it's only a question of whether we can put together the right package of things to suit his professional and personal needs. The salary that we're offering is near what he's making now. We are trying to tailor an offer which will meet his specific needs so that we can have a positive decision in the next few weeks."

These two examples take us to the heart of proactive recruiting and hiring. They remind us that perhaps no other decision has as much to do with the growth and well-being of a department as the careful and deliberate selection of new colleagues. A chair who practices proactive hiring does far more than simply place an ad in *The Chronicle of Higher Education,* sit back and let the applications roll in. A proactive approach provides active ways of identifying the type of faculty member you need, raising your chances that such people will join your applicant pool and increasing the likelihood that, once you have made your own choice, the person you choose will in turn choose to join you. Given the lack of mobility in most areas of our academic profession, one should select a colleague with only slightly less care than choosing a spouse. In fact, comparing tenure rates with divorce rates reveals that a choice of an academic colleague may well be more permanent.

Proactive recruiting is a combination of active strategies and techniques employed by the chairperson to increase the probability of identifying and hiring the best available person for the department, someone who will not only do the job, but improve the overall quality of the department and move it discernibly ahead. The search for a new colleague is a critical opportunity to improve the position of the department both in relation to your institution and in relation to comparable departments elsewhere. A proactive approach can also turn an impending act of drudgery into a stimulating venture that receives the energy assigned to any high priority.

There are five essential elements to this proactive approach: (1) clearly defining what you want and what you have to offer, (2) casting your net as widely and effectively as possible so you are likely to get the best pool of candidates—particularly through good networking, (3) implementing adequate screening and interviewing procedures, (4) fostering positive attitudes and synergy within the interviewing community, and (5) following through with your top choice after the interview, with strong emphasis upon listening and responding to his or her particular needs before, during, and after you have crafted your offer and the candidate has reached his or her decision.[1] Although these procedures and techniques are not primarily designed for recruiting minorities, they can easily be used to increase minority presence.

DEFINING WHAT YOU WANT AND WHAT YOU HAVE TO OFFER

The clearer you are about what you want in the new person, the more efficient your search will be. Unfortunately, far too many search committees follow the old Latin dictum "Solvitur Ambulando—Solve it as you go." A search should always occur in the wake of significant discussions by the members of the department, in conjunction with the dean, regarding the needs shared by the department and the college or university. All too often, there is only the vaguest sense of the future within the department and only an inchoate awareness of the need for new blood and the type of person needed. Ideally, a chair and the dean will have been engaged in some meaningful long-range or strategic planning.[2]

Lack of clarity on the part of the search committee will not only result in a lack of cohesion within the search but, in the worst case, this vagueness may communicate itself to the applicant. It is important to remember that the candidate's own anxiety is probably already at a peak and does not need to be exacerbated. Unless you subscribe to Professor

Kingsfield model from *The Paper Chase,* the role of the chair should be to do everything possible to diminish a candidate's anxiety.

Furthermore, if you are serious about looking for really excellent candidates, remember that these people are likely to be in particularly high demand. This is especially true of candidates who are minorities and/or from such fields as business and computer science. When faced with a choice between two institutions of relatively similar merit, such a candidate will more than likely choose the institution that seems to have the clearest sense of itself, what it seeks in a candidate, and what difference this new person can make. If you wish to heighten further the perception of institutional coherence, make clear who will be responsible for judging the success of the candidate as a faculty member, and identify the standards by which such a judgment will be made.

More often than not, a search is precipitated by an unexpected vacancy, an unanticipated gift from the budget process, or an administrative fiat. In such cases, the push to start a search may occur before the necessary discussions described above have taken place. The best advice at such times is to delay the search until you know where the department is headed. Make do with part-time faculty. If you are in a system where you will lose the position unless it is filled, try to fill it with a one-year temporary appointment. If you must fill the position with a full-time tenure-track person, place your formal advertisements, but word them in a way that, while providing a reasonable level of specificity consistent with what you now know, will leave you some room to evolve further. Set a closing date far enough ahead go you can have sufficient time for this refinement. Such an interim period could allow you time to bring in a consultant who might help everyone achieve a much better idea of the type of person needed.[3] Thus, if you have not had such discussions, or if these have yet to produce a clear idea of what you want, buy some time. It can make all the difference.

In your strategic discussions, you should have focused upon the distinctive qualities of your department, institution, and locale. These will be significant factors for the perceptive candidate in assessing whether or not to join you. Bear in mind that candidates are themselves concerned about the lack of faculty mobility: they want to make sure that their choice will prove itself to have been a good one over time. A candid assessment by you of the current and future benefits of choosing your institution, when coupled with an equally candid assessment of your top candidate's abilities and interests, will give you an optimum chance of negotiating a successful conclusion to your search. The quality of life in your faculty, the cultural advantages of your community, your proximity to the sea or mountains, or your ability to shape the person's departmental responsibilities, may ultimately have more to do with your ability to secure your top candidate than the attractiveness of your salary scale.

GETTING TOP CANDIDATES IN YOUR APPLICANT POOL

Placing appropriately worded advertisements is only the beginning of the proactive hiring process. The chair needs to "work" his or her contacts. This means making contact with anyone who may know of a good candidate, particularly someone who may not be actively looking for a new position, or someone who is looking but may be unaware of the opening at your school. At the very least these networks should include chairs or deans at other comparable schools. They may know of someone who is looking or should be, for example, a person who is locked into a frustrating situation that is unlikely to change. It also happens that more than one excellent candidate may have surfaced in an earlier search elsewhere. Every specific network has its own limitations, however. Contacts at major graduate schools may be useful, but be sensitive to the reality that some tend to oversell their own graduates. The "old-boy" network of the past functioned with great efficiency but with equally clear sexist and racial biases. The more diverse your networks, the more likely it is that the myopia of one network will be offset by another.

Another technique is to search out the leaders in the appropriate field and seek their advice. One department head took the time to read a major book of essays in the subfield for which the department was about to begin a search for a junior person. He then called the authors of the best essays, complimented them on their ideas, and asked them whom they might recommend as up-and-coming individuals.

ADEQUATE SCREENING AND INTERVIEW PROCEDURES

Some schools are riddled with complex procedures, while others are casual in the extreme. In good stoic fashion, virtue lies somewhere in the middle. Some chairs of large departments immerse themselves continuously in the business of hiring; others in smaller departments plunge far less often into the process and may have a problem getting geared up for it. The existence of clear procedures helps assure that any hiring proceeds in an organized and systematic manner. Whether adopted at the institutional or department level, these procedures should provide: formulation of a job description; authorization to initiate a search for the position; budgetary commitment for a specific salary range; guidelines for the search or interviewing process; designation of an authorized person to speak with the candidates and their references; guidelines for the type of information needed from the candidates at various levels of consideration (initial pool, semi-finalists, finalists); clear definition of the relationship between the committee and the dean; and an outline of the activities that will occur (i.e., whether the finalists will be asked to address a class or present an overview of their research to the faculty).

It is imperative that the chair or the person delegated to handle the search have a list of these procedures from the start. Some procedures wisely include sample letters for communicating with candidates at each stage of the search. These letters can offer model language to assure that the appropriate information and materials are solicited in a consistent manner and at the right junctures.

It is a simple truth, but one worth repeating, that an interview process should provide a breadth of different opportunities in which to assess the important qualities of the candidates. In my judgment, the best searches are those which incorporate a specific written response from the candidates after the first cut. At that point you will have identified the best candidates. A written statement can be solicited in any number of ways: for example, you can request a short statement of the candidate's own educational philosophy, a personal response to the mission statement of the institution, or a more extended reply to a series of particular questions from the search committee.

The first cut is also a good time to familiarize the remaining candidates more fully with your institution. When you ask them for a personal statement, you can also provide them with a packet of selected materials. Pick those items that will give them an accurate picture of the best in your college or university. Consider sending a viewbook or catalog, departmental brochure, recent faculty lecture, long-range plan, faculty handbook, et cetera. If the salary range was not explicitly mentioned in the advertisements or if you have a salary scale, include this as well. At this juncture, nothing can take the place of a first class set of materials. These materials can form the first part of the interview process. Through them the candidate will begin to know the institution and have the opportunity to become more interested in you. In turn, the candidate's written response will provide you with an opportunity for judging his or her familiarity with these materials; the thoughtfulness of the response, and the degree of reciprocal fit which seems to exist between the candidate, and the values, traditions, and sensibilities of your institution.

Calling references is one of the most maddening and time-consuming aspects of a search. It is always difficult to find the time to do the calling, play telephone tag and, then, on the bad days, receive less than forthright responses. Nonetheless, calling references is an essential part of the process. It serves to help offset the human tendency to stereotype: to project everything we need on to one candidate with the degree from the "right" school or to undervalue the expertise of another from the "wrong" area of the country. To borrow and slightly revamp a line from Will Rogers, people who do not call a candidate's references get precisely the candidates they deserve.

You do well to strike a "loose-tight" balance between structure and casualness in interviewing referees. On the one hand, for consistency's sake you may wish to have a series of prearranged questions at hand. On the other hand, give the referee time to be expansive about the candidate's strengths or to wander beyond a given question. Be sure to ask about the person's weaknesses and be particularly attentive to subtle verbal hedges or tonalities. If necessary, ask follow-up questions. Many chairs find it useful to go beyond the references listed by the candidate. If you have your own personal contacts within the candidate's home institution, call them for a more confidential reading of the prospective faculty member. Investigation may reveal that the candidate, cast in a saintly light by his or her resume, may be roundly hated within the home institution and perhaps for good cause.

An important opportunity presents itself between the time of calling references and the firm selection of finalists. You may wish to consider conducting a short telephone interview with each of the probable finalists. This can serve a variety of functions. First and foremost, it can provide you with direct experience of the candidates' ability to articulate a position verbally, a sense of their curiosity and logic, and, in the case of nonnative speakers, whether they have sufficient mastery of English. Do not tell the candidate that he or she is a finalist at the start of the telephone discussion. In this way, if a significant defect is discovered, you have not obligated yourself to bring this candidate in for the personal interview. If everything goes well, extend the invitation to the candidate to visit as a finalist at the end of the telephone interview. At this point, you may even be able to use the call to discuss dates and the logistics of the visit.

Once finalists have been selected, most institutions utilize a standard set of formal and informal circumstances in which to assess the finalists' abilities. Even if this is not required, you would do well to consider having faculty and staff members from outside your immediate department participate in the interviewing process. The candidate you choose will probably have to have specific expertise in your area and be an able spokesperson for the area to other sectors of academe. This can also serve to build a wider understanding of the department within the faculty at large and build a sense of anticipation at the arrival of a new faculty member. In institutions which put particular stress upon the cogent and reasoned argument, a public lecture or classroom presentation by the candidate may be in order. Research institutions may wish to provide an opportunity for the candidate to present some current research to a group of fellow specialists. Institutions priding themselves on excellence in teaching can request copies of the person's teaching evaluations. Informal situations, such as lunches, dinners or cocktail parties, are crucial opportunities for assessing a candidate's social skills. As Dr. Johnson remarked: "Speak that I may know you." A few institutions now include a site visit to the finalist's home institution. However, this is a double-edged sword: what it provides in terms of empirical information or confirmation, it can take away in terms of confidentiality, particularly if the person does not ultimately change institutions.

Many institutions have protocols designed to put candidates at ease so they can interview under the best circumstances. For example, if the interview schedule is particularly intense, you may wish to suggest that out-of-town candidates arrive the night before the interviewing begins. Provide each candidate with a detailed program of the interview schedule. Because serious candidates may plan to stay an extra day to survey the area, the type and cost of available housing, and cultural amenities, you may wish to have maps, cultural directories, and even the cards of several good realtors at hand.

When done properly, proactive recruiting and hiring is one of the best long-term investments you can make for your department and institution. In the short run, however, the process is time consuming and not inexpensive. Short term expense is readily visible in terms of travel, housing, and entertainment for each finalist. Less obvious, but equally important, is the valuable time of all parties concerned with the search. Making an excellent choice, one which matches carefully the abilities of the candidate with the needs of the institution, will increase the likelihood of the person staying at the institution for a long period of time. However, even when someone chooses to leave after a short time, the pattern of proactive searching and hiring will have a cumulative benefit for the institution.

POSITIVE ATTITUDES AND SYNERGY WITHIN THE INTERVIEWING COMMUNITY

By the time you are finished with the interview process, you want the candidate to have an accurate picture of your college or university as it is today and what you hope it will become tomorrow. By the same token, you want to have an equally accurate picture of the candidate at present, and what he or she is likely to become after joining your institution.

The quality of the people in the interview group makes a significant statement about the quality of the institution as a whole. A major factor influencing the finalist's decision to join you will be his or her assessment of the quality of the potential colleagues at your institution. Select the best faculty and staff from within the department and institution for the interview committee; they are a crucial means whereby you can attract the best faculty from outside the institution. However, because these same people are most likely to be over-committed already, you will have to build a convincing case that their assistance is pivotal. Nonetheless, it is this group which is probably best suited to communicate "the challenges, the excitement, the satisfactions, and even the joys to be found in a particular position."[4]

The goal of a proactive interview should be to excite the candidate about the synergy of an institution and his or her potential role within it so that negotiations become almost secondary. Of course, you must be honest about contrary forces and personalities. If these are significant within the department or institution, you may wish to schedule a selective interview with representatives of these forces. In a small department, this is unavoidable. In all cases, the candidate should be briefed by you at the start of the interview process regarding the entire cast of players, particularly those who may represent negative forces. At the end of the interview process, it is an excellent idea to debrief the candidate: assess his or her level of perspicacity, counter any misinformation which may have come to the fore, and get a sense of the candidate's inclination toward the position.

Several years ago, a small science department in a liberal arts college was having difficulty hiring a tenure-track faculty member. Several different searches had each produced excellent candidates, but none of these candidates accepted an offer. Everyone was puzzled. It turned out that the chair had a very low image of the college and every time he was alone with a candidate he rattled through his list of reasons why a bright young scientist would not be interested in coming to this college. Each candidate assumed that the chair was imparting a less than subtle message not to become serious about the institution. When a new chair assumed leadership in the department, the next search was successful.

A proactive search is helped considerably if the department involved makes up its "corporate mind" as early as possible not to accept anything less than its top candidate. This will go a long way to assuring that the top candidate is in fact hired. If you do not secure your top candidate, give very serious consideration to reopening the search process.

CLOSING IN ON YOUR TOP CHOICE

Once you have identified your top choice, a continuing proactive attitude can increase the likelihood that your finalist will accept your offer. Central to this process is careful listening to your top choice's personal and professional needs. What motivates this person? What are the top candidate's five-year professional goals? What sort of personal environment does her or she desire? What mix of research, teaching, and publication seems likely to result? What are the weaknesses he or she perceives about coming to your school? Can these be offset in any way? Does a decision to accept your offer hinge upon a spouse being able to find a position in the area? Can you put the spouse in contact with influential members of the appropriate professional communities? Does the candidate want to make a difference within the institution? Can you hold out this prospect?

Listening carefully in this way will allow you to put together a special mixture of items that will appeal to your top choice and increase your odds of successfully bringing this person to your department. In addition to this crucial focus upon the person and his or her needs, you must have the support and trust of your administration in order to craft a sufficiently attractive offer.

Every question the person raises during the interview process should be answered immediately or shortly thereafter by phone or mail.

If a certain topic of discussion seems to connect the candidate with a particular faculty member, encourage that faculty member to follow up with a note or bibliographical reference. Have key members of the interview group drop personal notes to the candidate.

In the case of a reluctant candidate, it may help to enlist someone outside your institution to plead your case or court your candidate. For example, what if your top candidate is in great demand and is having doubts that your institution is the right step on his or her career path? Why not solicit support from several senior people in the field, particularly if they know both the candidate and your institution well? Such people can serve as ideal bridge figures.

Time can be both an enemy and a friend in getting your first choice. When you are seeking a highly sought-after candidate, your search will need to move along at a faster than normal pace. The pace is always faster when you are seeking a minority faculty member and/or when you are seeking someone from those fields where there is great demand for professionals.

Once you have offered your first choice the position, however, time can work to your benefit. If your first choice is clearly a quantum distance above your next candidate, you may wish to indicate to your first choice that he or she is your clear preference and that if he or she does not accept, you plan to reopen the search. This is not intended to induce feelings of guilt, but rather to communicate candidly to your top choice how outstanding you believe he or she is, what a difference the individual could make at your institution, and just how serious you are in trying to get this person to join you. By the same token, if this person asks for more time, give it if you can, but be sure to stay in continual contact.

Concluding the search by gaining the consent of your first choice is the most critical moment in a proactive search. As already indicated, the most important thing you can do as chair is to listen to the needs of the person you wish to have join your department. Let me give you one comprehensive example of how this final crucial stage proceeded in one instance by returning to the second case with which this article began.

Careful listening by Professor Diane Hunter revealed that the top candidate, Arthur Booker, although very interested in joining her institution and heading the humanities department, was still somewhat reluctant. This stemmed from his deep disappointment when his current institution failed to keep promises made when he had originally been recruited. He was also scheduled for a sabbatical which he would lose if he left his home institution. Furthermore, if he had to change institutions, he was inclined to return to another area of the country where he had attended graduate school. In fact, Booker had applied for two positions in that geographical area.

Unfortunately, Booker was already making a salary perilously near the top of Hunter's authorized range. Thus, she began to talk with Booker about a complex offer that included some research time, picking up a small financial obligation currently held by his home institution, and the possibility of new major financial resources becoming available for his department. More importantly, sensitive to his concern about being burned a second time by promises unfulfilled, Hunter managed to have Booker meet many of the principal players at her institution, including a prominent member of the board of trustees, the president, the vice president for academic affairs, and the academic dean. This helped reassure Booker that the variety of formal and informal promises being made would be honored by the institution in the years ahead.

Although Booker was now clearly interested in the offer, he still wondered whether there might be a closer approximation of the Holy Grail at one of the other two institutions that were courting him. Because Diane Hunter was so sure he was absolutely the right candidate, she suggested that he go for his interview at the better of the other two schools. Booker did this and returned to say that it was not nearly as satisfying as he had hoped. Now Hunter formally extended the carefully tailored offer to Booker. He accepted with enthusiasm.

In the two years since this incident, Booker has transformed the humanities department. He has gotten rave reviews from his colleagues. Although he continues to be sought after by other institutions, his experience with his new institution continues to be so good that he has not bothered to respond to recent "feelers."

Proactive hiring is nothing more and nothing less than taking the time and effort to make sure the person whom you recruit and hire stands to improve your department and the quality of life in your college or university substantially.

NOTES

1. Lois Vander Waerdt, "Women in Academic Department: Uneasy Roles, Complex Relationships." *The Department Advisor*, Vol. 1. No. 2 (Summer 1985), 1–5.
2. John Minter, "Positioning the Department for Survival and Growth: An Exercise." *The Department Advisor*, Vol. 1. No. 2 (Summer 1985), 6–7.
3. Daniel H. Pilon, "Using Consultants Wisely."in *Advancing the Small College. New Directions for Institutional Advancement*. No. 13. San Francisco: Jossey-Bass, 1981, 93–108.
4. Louis F. Brakeman, "Hiring and Keeping the Best Faculty." in *Issues in Faculty Personnel Policies. New Directions for Higher Education*, No. 41. San Francisco: Jossey-Bass, 1983.

8

WOMEN IN ACADEMIC DEPARTMENTS: UNEASY ROLES, COMPLEX RELATIONSHIPS

LOIS VANDER WAERDT

A graduate student, filing a sexual harassment charge against a professor after three years of severe harassment, stated that she had not come forward earlier because her department chairperson had discouraged her from making waves and had told her that to do so would seriously damage her career.

A department recently has become known nationally for its productivity, and campus-wide for an ambience conducive to scholarship and learning. The department has a number of tenured women. All of the women were recruited by a chairperson who, when he arrived from another institution, noted the homogeneity of his colleagues and deliberately set about to change that picture.

THE CRUCIAL ROLE OF CHAIRPERSONS

Both of these stories illustrate the impact a chairperson can have on a department. The treatment of women students and faculty members is becoming progressively more important because of the increasing numbers of women in all parts of the academic population.

Between 1972 and 1982, women's enrollment increased more rapidly than that of men, accounting for nearly four-fifths of the student population growth during that period. Today, women comprise the majority of undergraduate students. At the graduate level, the proportion of men and women earning doctorates within each field has changed substantially in the past decade. In 1982–83, 34 percent of doctorates in all fields were earned by women.

Ten years ago, the major problem for women on campus was initial access: admission to an undergraduate or graduate program or being hired at an entry-level teaching position. The problem today is advancement through academe and the professions. Women students and faculty are less likely to advance as far or as fast as their male peers. After exposure to the masculine educational environment, women are often less confident about their chances for success and are less likely to apply to graduate school than men of equal ability and achievement.[1]

As women students become the undergraduate "new majority," their education will become more central to the postsecondary enterprise. The attrition rate of female students, particularly from nontraditional fields of study, is a matter of departmental and institutional interest. The field of economics is illustrative of the impact of the educational process on women. In 1983, women comprised 52 percent of students enrolled in economics courses, 30 percent of undergraduate majors, 21 percent of doctoral students, 14 percent of doctoral degrees awarded, 16 percent of assistant professors, 11 percent of associate professors, and 4 percent of full professors.

As the number of white middle class males attending colleges and universities shrinks, departments must increasingly turn to students who have not traditionally been of interest to them: women, members of racial minorities, part-time students, and older students. Institutions and departments that fail to educate women for the same professions as white males will see their traditional social and financial support eroding in the future. Institutions also have a legal and moral responsibility to ensure the full participation of women in academe and in the workplace. The social costs of underutilizing women are considerable: scientific discoveries not made; art, music, and literature not created; talent wasted and potential not developed.

Academic chairpersons, as administrators and as leaders in their departments, can affect the departmental climate, making it more hospitable for women. They can review departmental policies and practices to ensure that such do not discriminate; utilize an evaluation process that is both nonsexist and fair; influence department choices to include women and women's issues; formalize the mentoring of women students and junior faculty; and defuse the sexual issues that too often intrude between students and faculty.

REVIEW DEPARTMENTAL POLICIES AND PRACTICES

In one geology department, the highlight of undergraduate training for majors was a senior field trip—open only to men because of perceived chaperoning problems. At another institution, the chairperson of the biochemistry department routinely tossed women's applications aside and announced that anyone who wanted a woman could take his pick. Many veterinary schools traditionally admitted only token numbers of women, ostensibly because women lacked the physical strength to deal with large farm animals. The women who were admitted, however, were selected not on the basis of strength or speed, but because they had high grade point averages—3.5 as opposed to the 2.5 required of men. Men are far more likely to be hired for tenure-track positions, to be tenured, and to gain full professorships.[2] The appearance of women in assistant professorships and lectureships—"revolving door" or "folding chair" appointments—"produce[s] a superficial look of equality quite without substance."[3] All of these practices relate to the numbers of women and to the decidedly masculine environment in the departments.

Faculty women, who represent less than 15 percent of department numbers, and women students, in departments in which women are a minority, experience all the problems of discrimination and isolation characteristic of tokens. Such women report feeling less confident of their abilities, less willing to take risks, and less able to negotiate for their needs. They experience performance pressures, marginality, and role encapsulation.[4] Chairpersons play a crucial role in ensuring that women are admitted into graduate programs and hired for tenure-track positions.

A chairperson at a midwestern university began to change the demographics of his department by carefully monitoring candidates' vitae. When he observed that women were being discounted because of their "deficiencies," he ensured that discussions of men's vitae included similar critical thinking. After all, everyone has deficiencies if one is determined to find them. He allowed the inclusion of men, whom he believed privately were unlikely to accept an offer, as well as women on final lists in all the searches, and when the "star" male candidates declined, he moved immediately to negotiations with female candidates.

Because the department had two openings that first year, he used the choice of women for both positions as a recruiting tool in his negotiations with each. Both women accepted, each eager for a colleague of the same sex in the traditionally male discipline. The next year, another woman was hired. All presently are tenured members of the department. They support one another, mentor women students, and have improved both the level of scholarship and the ambience of the department.

Chairpersons can affect the quality of teaching in the department by encouraging a textbook and an audio-visual selection process that includes fair treatment of women's contributions and of women's issues. Traditionally, these issues have been omitted from textbooks. One history text, for example, devoted six pages to the six-shooter and one paragraph to women's suffrage. Many textbooks and films show women primarily in subordinate roles and men primarily in authoritative roles.

Seminars and colloquia can include women as presenters and can focus on women's issues. At one college, a seminar coordinator developed a study procedure to stimulate interest and involvement in women's studies on a campus-wide basis. The public acknowledgement of women's studies as a legitimate area of scholarly endeavor improved the atmosphere for both faculty and students.

NONSEXIST AND EQUITABLE BEHAVIOR AND PROCEDURES

Part of the masculine ambience of many departments is activity that is demeaning to women. Some professors mix slides of naked women with photographs depicting various diseases, tell off-color stories in class, engage in sexist humor, or include sexist art—centerfolds and pin-up posters—in the decor of their offices. One professor had a small sofa in his office, above which hung two prints of female nudes, to the discomfort of his female colleagues and students. Another professor's exam included the following characters: Chasity Prudebody, Cissy Sleazey, and a pet snake named Virginity. Women in computer science have complained about obscene messages sent to them through the system, such as one involving a naked woman used to demonstrate the computer's graphics capability.

Other behaviors affecting women students are more subtle. Faculty members may discourage women by not taking them as seriously as men, by patronizing them, by getting to know male students informally but confining conversations with women to required meetings. Professors may pay less serious and active attention to women who are graduate students or junior faculty than to men by interrupting them, giving them minimal responses, ignoring them entirely, seeking opinions from men more than from women, crediting comments and ideas to men but not to women, and adopting a posture of inattentiveness when talking with women but the opposite when talking with men. Male colleagues and mentors may respond with surprise and doubt when women express demanding career goals, or they may treat women in an overprotective or patronizing manner. These disparaging behaviors lead women to believe they are unwelcome or viewed as incapable. Women lose valuable time and energy dealing with these unnecessary doubts and conflicts.

Leaders in faculty development are aiding those who want to become more aware of their own subtle behaviors that discourage students. Others are exploring the complex connections between sex-of-student and sex-of-teacher in order to isolate those verbal and nonverbal classroom behaviors that facilitate the participation of women students. The impact of sex on interactions in school and in society has become a major focus of research on many fronts, both in and outside academe.

Chairpersons can determine how a concern with classroom climate can best be integrated into the mission, priorities, and style of their departments. Some may use in-class questionnaires, class interviews, or questions addressing the issue of an equitable learning environment on course evaluations.[5] Others may videotape class sessions. More research-oriented departments may encourage research projects incorporating women's issues. Chairpersons can include information on the issue of classroom climate in workshops for faculty and teaching assistants, and can ensure that all new faculty are informed of an institutional commitment to an equitable classroom climate through seminars and informal meetings.

The Classroom Climate: A Chilly One for Women?, a publication of the Project on the Status and Education of Women, suggests that chairpersons utilize the active support of respected faculty who share the objective of improving the learning climate for women; ask heads of units, either formally or informally, what they are doing or have done to ensure an equitable classroom climate; mention it in speeches to reinforce its importance as an institutional priority; circulate pertinent materials to the academic community; discuss classroom climate informally at parties, luncheons, and meetings; and sponsor workshops, seminars, or other sessions on this topic.[6]

FORMALIZE THE MENTORING OF WOMEN STUDENTS AND JUNIOR FACULTY

We are learning that women's experience in the mentoring process is often vastly different from men's. Because senior male faculty members are likely to be more comfortable with those like themselves, more informal associations occur between male students and their professors and between junior male faculty and their senior mentors than between women and these potential mentors. For women students, supportive out-of-class relationships bear greatly on their self-esteem and self-confidence.[7] A female faculty member observed that she had been a member of her department for three years before any of her male colleagues invited her to their homes for dinner with their families—and then only after she was married! Another woman in the same department recounted a similar experience and added that new male colleagues, whether married or single, were routinely invited to dinner at senior colleagues' homes during this same period. Junior men are more likely to accompany their departmental mentors to the cafeteria for lunch and thus are introduced to others on campus. They are more likely to jog or play tennis with senior colleagues than are junior women in the department. Women's relationships are centered in a different context than those of their male peers. In fact, the formalized context of the annual evaluation may be the only real contact a junior woman has with the chairperson of her department.

The problem is enormous, but strong leadership from chairpersons can greatly improve the departmental atmosphere for both students and faculty. Chairpersons can foster formal and informal gatherings to encourage interaction among graduate students, junior and senior faculty. Chairpersons can encourage the development of written materials to provide newcomers with information on the steps to advancement within the department, institution, or discipline.[8] This "map" is particularly important for older women whose recollection of the system may be quite different, especially if they previously attended a different type of institution, or were enrolled in a different major.[9]

The Project on the Status of Women suggests that "multiple mentorships" may resolve many of the traditional mentoring problems. A chairperson may encourage a "set" of academic mentors for each entering junior faculty person that includes people in and outside the department and institution who are familiar with some aspect of the junior person's field. A chairperson can assist new faculty members in identifying senior faculty in other departments for a wider institutional perspective as well as for access to senior colleagues who need not make tenure and promotion decisions and who do not compete with them for department awards. The Project suggests the establishment of a two-stage mentoring process in which newcomers are initially paired with a senior person of the same sex and race and then helped by that person to find additional mentors with different strengths throughout the organization.[10]

Because chairpersons often control course and committee assignments, they steer a junior faculty member toward success or failure by the extent to which they assign convenient course meeting times, a manageable number of course preparations, and helpful committee assignments. One chairperson flattered a junior woman by assigning her to the prestigious curriculum committee, which met frequently and which the woman found engrossing. Her contributions significantly changed the focus of departmental research and teaching in her own sub-discipline. This came, however, at the price of her own scholarship. When she was reviewed for tenure, the same chairperson led the opposition to her becoming a tenured member of the department. Interestingly, a junior man had arrived the same year. The chairperson assigned him to the library committee, which met once a year and briefly. The chairperson encouraged him to devote his primary energies to his scholarship, and supported him for tenure. He is now an associate professor, while the female peer, denied tenure, has left academe.

RELATIONSHIPS BETWEEN THE SEXES

Campus life is not always as college recruiters portray it. A major problem for approximately 20 percent of undergraduate female students and 30 percent of graduate students and junior faculty is sexual harassment.[11] Sexual harassment has a detrimental effect on the individual faculty and students who are victims as well as on the climate of the department in which offenders operate freely. The harassment ranges from the atmospheric—jokes about the female anatomy—to sexual favors demanded in exchange for academic and professional advancement.

Sexual harassment alters women's attitudes toward their institutions and may have long-lasting negative effects on their perceptions of the rest of the male teaching staff, as well as decreased confidence and effort in their own academic work. Student victims avoid certain professors, change their majors, transfer to other institutions, or drop out of school. Faculty victims restrict their contacts with their colleagues or may leave the institution. Sexual harassment is not a minor inconvenience. It changes the lives of and extracts high costs from its victims.[12]

Sexual harassers are tolerated in academic departments because "society doubts that men are capable of sexual restraint." Sexual harassers are often defended with the shrugged observation, "After all, they're only human." A middle-aged professor, notorious for pursuing sexual relations with female students, offered a variation: "If you put me at a table with food [coeds], I eat."[13] Harassers rely on their colleagues' reluctance to intervene in student-faculty relationships, on academe's tolerance of other idiosyncrasies, and on vitae that list publications but do not mention improper relationships with students or colleagues.

Students and faculty are reluctant to report such experiences. "Even though I wanted to tell the dean, I was afraid it would just mean more trouble." "I guess I should have reported him to somebody, but I didn't know who. No one would have believed it anyway." A survey by the Iowa State University Committee on Women found that no woman who had experienced one of the three most serious forms of sexual harassment included in the survey reported it to a university official. Women recognize the failure of academe to cope with harassment institutionally. One student summarized this viewpoint: "They can't even figure out how to find places for all of us to park, so what can they do about the things these jerks say to us in class?"[14]

The reluctance of women to report these experiences indicates a breakdown in the ability of higher education to deal with a problem of great magnitude. Higher education's diffuse power structure, indirect accountability, and cumbersome grievance procedures often result in resolving sexual harassment problems through attrition: students graduate or transfer; faculty are reluctant to risk damage to their own careers by coming forward; the complaint process wears the victim down; the issues become confused, and time erodes anger.

Chairpersons can have a major effect on the departmental climate by making clear that sexual relationships are inappropriate to a collegial atmosphere, by encouraging victims to come forward, by taking complaints of sexual harassment seriously, by listening carefully to these complaints and perhaps discussing them with the campus director of Affirmative Action, coordinator of the Women's Center, or another appropriate institutional official. Chairpersons *must* act promptly and reasonably when informed of a sexual harassment problem. To ignore the complaint, to urge the complainant not to make waves, or to counsel the victim against pursuing the matter may subject the institution to litigation and the chairperson to *personal* liability.

Chairpersons can help to defuse the sexual issues that are part of the tensions of mentoring by encouraging faculty to meet with students in places that discourage sexual intimacy, such as departmental offices, labs and other work-related settings; by leaving doors open; by suggesting that discussions proceed professionally, whether they include personal or professional concerns; by avoiding sexual joking or innuendo, comments about personal appearance, and intimate confidences; by calling one another by name rather than by terms of endearment; and by stressing to women in the department that any suggestion of a sexual or romantic relationship should be confronted firmly—"I'm very flattered by your affection for me, but I don't want to ruin the working relationship we've developed."[15]

CONCLUSION

Chairpersons often feel powerless because of the ambiguous nature of their position in the department: they are truly neither administrators nor peers. Whereas a dean can often require that something be done, a chairperson usually must use more subtle means of accomplishing change. These changes are substantially easier if the institutional environment is hospitable to such changes. Nonetheless, chairpersons, deans, provosts, and presidents can play a critical role in developing an institutional climate more amenable to women.

Those of us who work with many different departments on our own campuses see the real impact that chairpersons can have. We hear from faculty members about the effect of a new chairperson's priorities on their professional lives. We see how the demographics of a department can change when a chairperson asserts leadership in this area, and how the ambience of a department is affected by his or her leadership style. Chairpersons who turn their attention to improving the departmental climate for women students and faculty will be viewed as promoting their departments' best interests.[16]

NOTES

1. *Academic Mentoring for Women Students and Faculty: A New Look at an Old Way to Get Ahead.* Project on the Status and Education of Women, Association of American Colleges, 1983. See also Laraine T. Zappert and Kendyll Stansbury, *In the Pipeline: A comparative Analysis of Men and Women in Graduate Programs in Science, Engineering and Medicine at Stanford University,* Stanford, California, n.d.

2. The hiring record of 25 leading universities shows that women faculty in science and engineering are twice as likely as their male counterparts to be hired for positions without a future. At the present rates of hiring and promoting women, there will be no significant change in the gender demographics of these science de-

partments for the next 25 years. Lilli S. Hornig, "Women in Science and Engineering: Why So Few?" *Technology Review* (November/December 1984): 40–41.

3. Hornig, 49–41.
4. Rosabeth Moss Kantor, *Men and Women of the Corporation.* New York: Basic, 1977.
5. Such questions include: Does this teacher call on women students as often as on men? Recognize women as readily as men when women raise their hands? Treat men's and women's comments with the same degree of seriousness? Make disparaging comments or use sexist humor? Make a special effort to treat women and men equally such as by avoiding sexist language, using sex-balanced class examples, etc.? See *The Classroom Climate: A Chilly One for Women?* Project on the Status and Education of Women, Association of American Colleges, 1982, 13.
6. *The Classroom Climate: A Chilly One for Women?* 14.
7. *Out of the Classroom: A Chilly Campus Climate for Women?* Project on the Status and Education of Women, Association of American Colleges, 1984, 2.
8. *Academic Mentoring for Women Students and Faculty.* 11.
9. See also Suzanna Rose, ed., "Building a Professional Network," in *Career Advice to Women Scholars*, Springer, 1986. Rose suggests that advice informally communicated through a socialization process includes how to approach certain individuals in the department, how formal criteria *really* are weighed, and the unwritten criteria for tenure.
10. *Academic Mentoring for Women Students and Faculty.*
11. Billie Wright Dziech and Linda Weiner, *The Lecherous Professor: Sexual Harassment on Campus.* Boston: Beacon Press, 1984, 116.
12. *Ibid.,* 13.
13. *Ibid.,* 87.
14. *Ibid.,* 36.
15. *Academic Mentoring for Women Students and Faculty.* 13.
16. In the spring of 1989, the Supreme Court decided *Hopkins* v. *Price Waterhouse,* a case that will have a significant impact on personnel decisions made in academic departments. Hopkins was denied promotion because of her abrasive and unfeminine personality at a time when 47 less productive males were promoted. Chairpersons who lead their departments toward evaluations based on performance and on clearly articulated criteria will save costly challenges to tenure and promotion decisions.

SUGGESTED READINGS

Billie Wright Dziech and Linda Weiner, *The Lecherous Professor: Sexual Harassment on Campus.* Boston: Beacon Press, 1984. A highly readable, sensitive and sophisticated book about sexual harassment on campus. *Highly recommended.*

Publications by the Project on the Status and Education of Women offer comprehensive and original examination of a number of problems affecting academic women. Publications are available from the Association of American Colleges, 1818 R Street, NW, Washington, DC, 20009, (202) 387–1300.

• *The Classroom Climate: A Chilly One for Women?* Offers specific questions for faculty awareness and attitudes, details behavior that can create a cold climate for women, offers a Student-Faculty Communication Checklist, suggests a Student Perception questionnaire, and offers a Curriculum Analysis Project for a Social Sciences Student Perception questionnaire.

• *Out of the Classroom: A Chilly Campus Climate for Women?* Recommends policy for administration, personnel, and curriculum in areas such as communications, admissions and financial aid, and provides an institutional self-evaluation check-list.

• *Academic Mentoring for Women Students and Faculty: A New Look at an Old Way to Get Ahead.* Describes mentoring and its problems for women, outlines model programs, and suggests improvements in mentoring that would benefit women.

Casey Miller and Kate Swift. *The Handbook of Nonsexist Writing.* New York: Harper & Row, 1980. A thorough and readable account of sexism in the English language. The authors include many examples contrasting sexist and nonsexist writing.

Suzanna Rose, ed. *Career Advice to Women Scholars: Getting Jobs in Psychology and Related Fields.* New York: Springer, 1986. A product of the American Psychological Association's Task Force on Strategies for Getting and Keeping a Job, this book gives advice on women's survival in academe for graduate students, older women students, and junior faculty that is practical, well-balanced, and well written. Chairpersons may wish to read it themselves and to recommend it to the women in their departments.

Marilyn Schuster and Susan Van Dyne, eds., *The Selected Bibliography for Integrating Research on Women's Experience in the Liberal Arts Curriculum,* second edition, Northampton, MA, 1984. Identified materials for classroom assignments and teacher preparation in seventeen fields, including art and architecture, biology, classics, economics, government, history, literature, music, philosophy, psychology and education, religion, science, sociology, theatre, and the Third World. The bibliography is designed to enable college teachers to understand the significance of research on women and to incorporate these insights in every class they teach, whether a woman-focused or an integrated course. Each entry has been recommended by teachers who have used it successfully to present a balanced view of human experience, with attention to sex, race, class, and culture, in courses in the liberal arts. Available for $5.00 from Susan Van Dyne, Associate Professor of English, Smith College, Northampton, MA, 01063.

Bonnie Spanier, Alexander Blom, and Darlene Boroviak, eds., *Toward a Balanced Curriculum, A Sourcebook for Initiating Gender Integrating Projects*. Cambridge, MA: Schenkman Books, 1984. Promotes the revision of the introductory curriculum to include knowledge about women. The book is a product of a three-year Curriculum Development project at Wheaton College (MA) culminating in a conference held in June, 1983. It combines the theoretical aspects of integrating women's studies with more practical tools such as bibliographies, course descriptions and guidelines. It serves as a resource handbook for faculty and administrators and others interested in implementing curricular changes to include women's experiences. Available for $18.95, cloth; $11.95, paper from Schenkman Publishing Co., 190 Concord Ave., Cambridge, MA, 02138.

The Sourcebook for Integrating the Study of Women into the Curriculum. A looseleaf-style notebook containing sample materials from the ten projects participating in the Northern Rockies Program on Women in the Curriculum as well as other projects in curriculum change. Includes program descriptions, resources, assessment materials, and bibliographies. Available for $22.00 plus $1.50 postage and handling from Betty Schmitz, Letters and Science, Montana State University, Bozeman, MT, 59717.

9

FACULTY EVALUATION: THE ROLES OF THE DEPARTMENT CHAIR

JOHN B. BENNETT

DEALING WITH THE NEGATIVITY

By common report, one of the most difficult chores for department chairs is the evaluation of faculty colleagues. Dealing with unsatisfactory faculty performance and evaluating faculty colleagues are ranked by department chairs as two of their most challenging responsibilities. The reasons given by both new and old chairs are often the same. Only the very self-confident seem untroubled by faculty evaluation, and their time in office is usually short.

Demands on time are certainly one complicating factor. Chairpersons are themselves already busy enough without the extra burdens that annual or periodic evaluations—and the accompanying paperwork—can impose. Even when things are running smoothly demands on the calendar can be extensive. When faculty members feel their involvement in evaluation activities is a distraction from teaching and research, chairs need to spend additional time arousing or redirecting their enthusiasm and dealing with their complaints.

Besides large commitments of time, faculty evaluation activities can presuppose decisions on some difficult conceptual and procedural issues—including such matters as the relationship between measurement and evaluation, the role and degree of confidentiality (particularly as it applies to peer judgments), and methods for providing constructive feedback. The chair must play a leadership role in securing a departmental consensus on these issues, and developing this consensus can be politically demanding.

Probably the most significant difficulty in making faculty evaluations is the personal element. According to many chairs, most faculty see the process of evaluation as threatening in one way or another. One observer notes, "resistance to being evaluated appears to grow out of three basic concerns: resentment of the implied assumption that faculty may be incompetent in their subject area, suspicion that they will be evaluated by unqualified people, and an anxiety that they will be held accountable for performance in an area in which they may have little or no training or interest."[1]

Given this resentment, suspicion, and anxiety, many chairs wonder how to maximize the possibility of benefit and to minimize the risk of damage to morale. And the morale in question includes their own, for as with few other activities, faculty evaluation can intrude directly into personal relationships and carries great potential for disruption. Most chairs report that even well-established friendships are subtly tested during evaluation activities. Other, shorter-term relationships can all the more easily become affected by elements of suspicion or even hostility.

Adding to these difficulties in evaluation are our long-standing traditions of professional courtesy and academic freedom as well as the substantial problems created by increased academic specialization and generalized societal distrust. "There is no one here who can really appreciate what I am trying to do, much less anyone who is able to measure my success or lack of it objectively," is a not uncommon faculty attitude. As a result, few chairpersons enjoy the stress of conducting faculty evaluations. Indeed, one may wish to be a little suspicious of those who appear to derive pleasure from evaluation activities.

On the other hand, faculty evaluation is also judged to be one of the most important of the chairperson's tasks. As Allan Tucker notes, "Probably no other activity has more potential for strengthening or weakening the department over a period of years."[2] Recommendations and decisions made today can have an impact for years to come. Faculty evaluation can strengthen the department as people come to feel appreciated for their contributions and supported in their efforts to grow and improve. It can weaken the department when institutional flexibility in dealing with inadequate performance is reduced through procrastination and when good faculty leave because the reward system fails to recognize their contributions.

The impact of faculty evaluation is pervasive. Students, faculty, and staff are all affected by evaluation—be it good or bad. And the multiplier effect is at work when evaluation results are used to determine the assignment of courses and funds. As a result, it becomes almost impossible to isolate from the many other responsibilities of the department chair, those for assisting the professional growth of the individual faculty member, for using institutional resources wisely, for avoiding litigation, and for meeting appropriate public concerns about accountability.

Faculty evaluation is primarily the responsibility of the chair. He or she is ultimately the custodian of department standards. Faculty peers have a general professional responsibility, but no one else has the specific administrative duty to oversee curriculum direction and faculty accomplishments in areas proper to the department or division. Of course, deans and personnel committees have their appropriate roles to play in faculty evaluation but at almost all institutions it is the chair to whom they look for guidance.

As a result of this responsibility, chairs often report feeling real personal conflict between supporting peer colleagues and assessing or evaluating their performance and accomplishments. The one presupposes collegiality while the other risks disruption of collegiality. Of course, support of colleagues can not mean acquiescing in weaknesses or overlooking deficiencies. But it is one thing in an atmosphere of informality and collegiality to pursue honestly with colleagues one's judgment of their strengths and weaknesses, and quite another thing to reflect these honest judgments in reports to the institutional authorities.

Experts in faculty evaluation distinguish between formative and summative evaluation activities—those designed to assist individual growth or development, and those whose outcomes are to be used in institutional resource decisions such as promotion, tenure, or salary determinations. On almost all campuses time, money, and other pragmatic considerations work against having totally separate procedures and instruments for these two objectives. The chair must devise ways of pursuing both objectives, and care must be taken that information secured specifically for formative purposes not be utilized in summative decisions.

The success of the chair will be highly dependent upon the atmosphere in the department. One of the most important elements is the trust level, given the history and traditions as well as the individual personalities involved. Some chairs are in remarkably favorable position, through no work of their own. Others, again through no fault of their own, are chairs with contentious, immature, or volatile colleagues.

Perhaps I am simply describing the most conspicuous aspect of what is commonly called the role ambiguity of the department chair.[3] He or she has the uncommon and often uncomfortable role of mediating between the administration and the faculty, of dealing with the expectation that he/she be an advocate from both sides, and of clarifying policies or correcting the mistaken thinking of the other side. Such expectations are impossible to meet, of course, but what the chair must somehow do is reflect the broader perspectives of the institution as well as those of the department and the profession.

In reflecting these broader institutional perspectives in faculty evaluation, chairs can anticipate resistance from colleagues and reluctant participants. At evaluation time, the investment one has in one's work can translate into territoriality or into forms of political posturing. For instance, occasionally one will hear references to academic freedom as justification for avoiding assessment activities. The chair should then insist that the principle of academic freedom supports the notion of relative autonomy in the choice of teaching approach and methods, but does not sanction complete privacy in this process or total exclusion from peer judgments on either the appropriateness or the success of these choices.

When evaluation of tenured faculty is under consideration, some individuals may charge that any rigorous form of evaluation will create hostility or permanent insecurity, thereby defeating the very purpose for which tenure was awarded. But dampening cooperative and collegial relationships, increasing unhealthy competition, or developing permanent insecurity are outcomes of evaluation only if people insist that they be. Obviously, any form of evaluation risks generating apprehension or insecurity. But such is ultimately the price to be paid for having an academy, in the same way as the very process of searching for and finding truth requires assessments by others—what we call peer-review. And clearly the need for personal and professional growth does not end with the award of tenure.

Perhaps the best way to avoid these and other forms of resistance is through regular discussions on the need for professional self-regulation and the best way to promote it. Ultimately, the purpose of faculty evaluation is to increase the effectiveness of self-regulation within the profession. As Chester Finn recently observed in a searching criticism of the quality of higher education: "the primordial issue of quality control is the rigor of the standards (and, of course, fairness of the procedures) by which faculties evaluate their own present and potential colleagues. For if the professoriat is the heart of the system of collegiate governance, at least with respect to academic affairs, its most solemn task is to see to its own membership."[4]

The difficulties of evaluating faculty colleagues and of being evaluated are certainly real, but so too are the benefits. At a minimum, the benefits for individual faculty members include increased self-esteem and the sense of control that can follow with increased self-knowledge. Regular occasions for assessing where one is in the development of one's career are a means to secure enhanced self-direction and self-esteem. Periodic negotiations with chairpersons can provide objectivity and assistance as well as the possibility of receiving institutional resources for the pursuit of jointly agreed-upon plans.

At the very least, we all need positive reinforcement as well as jolts out of complacency. We need the institution and important individuals within it to tell us that we are appreciated, and instruction on areas where we have become unimaginative or intellectually unbalanced or out of date. Without regular evaluation, the conditions of continued professional growth are left too much to chance, and to the uneven distribution of individual stamina.

Nor is there any reason that broader departmental and institutional planning should be neglected in the evaluation process. The chair must be both innovator and conservator. He or she has to promote, and often initiate, curricular reform and revision, while at the same time resisting fads and unwise enthusiasms. We know that some faculty members pursue intellectual and professional interests tangential, or even opposed, to those of the institution. Other faculty cease being as productive as their abilities would permit. The key point here is that the department must be more than the sum of its parts. Individual interests must be reformulated to meet institutional needs and the chair must orchestrate this process. Evaluation activities and processes can be an invaluable tool in accomplishing this redirection.

The outcomes of successful faculty evaluation programs can only be to promote academic excellence, institutional integrity, and public confidence. This is an enormous challenge for everyone involved from institutional administrators to department chairs to individual faculty members. Creativity, self-confidence, mutual respect, and a sense of humor are but a few of the resources needed. But how can we speak of excellence in the academy if we do not place priority on periodic evaluation of our endeavors?

LOOKING AT PERFORMANCE—AREAS AND EVIDENCE

What specifically might one look at in such assessment efforts? The customary distinctions between teaching, research, and service can be misleading if held too rigidly, but are so rooted in our tradition that they seem unavoidable.

Instruction should be reviewed in terms of both content competency and delivery/design skills.[5] Multiple sources of evidence should be used and should accommodate the different instructional settings (for instance, the classroom, the laboratory, and the clinic). Content competency is best judged by appropriate peers, not students. Colleagues know whether an individual is up-to-date in the area. However, students are probably best positioned to comment on elements of the individual's delivery skills. Such skills include the ability to present the inquiry in a fashion which elicits student respect and interest—an essential element of instructional effectiveness.

Design skills include the ability to construct appropriate learning experiences and instruments, and to utilize adequate measurement devices. Success in applying design skills includes the degree to which the instructor is both prompt and helpful in his or her evaluation of student exercises. Sources of student comment about these faculty abilities include the familiar formal student surveys and ratings as well as less customary exit interviews of graduating, transferring, or "stopping-out" students.[6]

Content competency and delivery and design skills are different matters, and individuals may excel in one and not the others. However, they do come together in the ability of the individual to teach a mode of scholarship and not only its outcome. Enlisting students to conduct the inquiry at hand is ultimately what teaching should be. It involves an appreciation of the logic of the inquiry and its payoffs as well as its limitations. It certainly should not result in the replication or cloning of the teacher.

Some faculty will resist the notion that students are qualified to assess their teaching effectiveness. The literature on evaluation is reassuring, though, as long as one distinguishes among content competency and delivery/design skills as the three areas that make for effective teaching.[7] The studies establish that, on the whole, students are reliable judges of delivery skills and it is not difficult to secure their opinions. Such opinions are usually generous, and the more so in smaller classes and in elective rather than required courses.[8]

Along with the chair, colleagues must come forward with comments on matters of content competency. It can be difficult on occasion to elicit these judgments from others, as some faculty are reluctant to comment on areas far outside their own specialization. A variety of creative devices may need to be explored. One which should not be overlooked is the rather penetrating question, Would you recommend that your own child take this person's class or work with him or her on a research project?

Access to the data on the basis of which chair and colleague evaluations are to be made is an issue that must also be faced squarely, especially the question of classroom visitation. Experts in the field of faculty evaluation are divided on this issue. John Centra is rather negative about the reliability of data based upon classroom visitation. Peter Seldin feels that visitations can contribute to the process of instructional improvement.[9] An additional consideration that is rarely discussed is the enhanced intellectual sharing and excitement that can result from classroom visitations. Whether or not classroom observation occurs, the materials supporting the instruction can and should be periodically examined to determine their appropriateness and adequacy to course objectives and learning assignments.[10]

Can one judge teaching effectiveness by measuring the amount of student learning that has occurred? This is a difficult and vexing issue. On the one hand, there must be some positive correlation. Other things being equal, the more effective teacher can claim a greater amount of student learning. But can we say with sufficient confidence that he or she is responsible for causing (creating, effecting) that learning? An effective teacher will present the inquiry with enthusiasm, pitching it at a relevant level and demonstrating its importance, thereby inviting the student to participate. To accept the invitation is in the hands of the student.

Associating teaching effectiveness too closely with learning achieved also has problems beyond that of properly assigning responsibilities and initiatives. The very act of measuring learning is complicated and, in some cases, quite expensive. Course outcomes vary and can include sophisticated intellectual competencies and aesthetic values as well as the acquisition of information. Influences outside of class, such as roommates and study colleagues, are factors that need to be considered. There is also the large problem of comparing judgments about one class (for instance, honors English) with those about another with very different objectives and levels of student ability (for instance, remedial English).

The conditions for effective teaching should also be recognized and support should be given to faculty for their contributions. I have in mind the varied ways in which individuals can enhance the teaching effectiveness of other faculty, can contribute to learning outside the classroom, and thereby create a more productive atmosphere within the department. In this context, academic advising is a task of no small departmental significance, considering its impact upon student success and attrition. The department chairperson should be interested in student perceptions on such matters as the accessibility, availability, knowledgeability, openness, and interest of the faculty adviser. Surveys or questionnaires can provide helpful information. Institutions credit such advising differently, some placing it under teaching and others considering it to be a form of service.

Many feel that a second area of performance—research or creative or scholarly activity—is easier to assess than teaching effectiveness or excellence. However, one should avoid relying too heavily upon some of the traditional criteria and sources of evidence. Some customary practices amount to avoiding first-hand judgments about the accomplishments themselves. I have in mind especially reliance upon such matters as citation indices and the criteria of refereed journals in judging the quality of publications. Citation indices are often incomplete, fail to reflect the impact of more recent publications, and are inherently neutral in their judgment of the quality of the work being cited. The study may well be cited because of flaws in design or data, rather than because of its excellence.

Likewise, editors of refereed journals make acceptance or rejection decisions on bases beyond those which reflect directly on the quality of the piece—editorial bases such as balance among topics and backlog of commitments. In any case, good essays can appear in nonrefereed publications, and presence in a juried publication is no guarantee of excellence. Incidentally, chairs in research institutions may wish to use outside evaluators to assess the quality of instructional materials as well. If outside evaluators are used, their judgments should be sought at the departmental level (rather than the college level) in order to be incorporated within the department's own planning processes.

For most chairpersons, though, scholarship is judged by a variety of activities of which publication is only one. A baseline definition of scholarship is staying abreast of the field. Evidence of such achievement is varied and includes contributions to symposia, development of new courses, special exhibitions, and research projects with students. Chairs also need to consider ways in which faculty progress on long-term research projects can be noted and credited in the evaluation process. Otherwise faculty will feel that only short-term activities are recognized and rewarded.

Third, activities and accomplishments in the area of service can be difficult to gauge and assess. Clarity needs to be established at the outset regarding the populations to be served: the institution (and whether it be at the department, division, college, or institutional level; or, alternatively, with student organizations and activities), the profession or discipline (perhaps through work in regional or national associations), or the broader public (perhaps through contributions to government bodies). Likewise, it is important to be clear about what counts as service and what does not, both inside and outside the institution.

Some of this clarification must occur at the college or institutional level. Some decisions will flow out of the institutional mission or type of governance, as in the case of the institution with strong and close religious affiliation. But other matters rest with the department and distinctions will need to be made. Ought one, for instance, to count as a service contribution consulting activities for which one is extensively remunerated by agencies outside the institution? Is not one thereby rewarding an individual twice for the same activity—an activity that may very likely be secured at the expense of service contributions to be department or institution?

Likewise, clarity should be secured regarding the connection between one's disciplinary or professional competence and various types of civic responsibilities and activities. Is membership on the local school board an activity for which service credit should be given someone in chemistry? How about work with the area scout council for someone in physical education? Incidentally, the degree of an individual's involvement and accomplishments on institutional committees can be determined by discreet inquiries with the committee chair, or with other committee members if the individual is the chair.

Some of these same considerations will apply to the evaluation of adjunct or part-time faculty, especially those comments relating to teaching effectiveness. Chairs can anticipate special problems with part-time faculty, but most of these problems stem from their limited participation (rather than their limited motivation) in departmental or institutional affairs. Special orientation activities should be conducted and other ways explored to provide the part-timer with as much information and sense of departmental identity as possible.

The best way to emphasize individual responsibility and to incorporate individual initiative within the evaluation process is through a growth plan or contract.[11] Such an approach permits the individual to suggest the areas in which he or she proposes to concentrate for the next year or so. These suggestions flow out of a prior process of self-evaluation. The department chair can then indicate areas of special departmental need or interest and the process of negotiation can occur. In what is actually a version of the growth contract, individuals at a number of institutions are permitted to choose from within a preset range the precise weights to be attached to their various areas of responsibility and performance.

Evaluation activities can certainly be overdone, and chairs need to be alert to the signs of overuse and overkill. A mechanical approach and attitude is one warning sign. For example, student evaluations could be sought each term only for new and revised courses and for faculty who are up for retention, tenure, or promotion decisions. A more relaxed schedule could apply to others, especially tenured faculty, for whom a comprehensive evaluation every third or fifth year may well prove much more helpful than the typical rushed, fragmentary, and often pro-forma annual evaluation.[12]

In any case, the chair needs to create a climate in which appropriate attention is paid to individual contributions to the departmental mission and objectives. The evaluation procedures should be clear to all. Credit should be given for innovative efforts, even if unsuccessful, and the workhorses of the department, however unimaginative, should be recognized. How contributions to the department are recognized may vary considerably according to institutional size, governance, and tradition.

Collegiality, for instance, may play a very large role in smaller institutions. Willing participation in departmental activities, cordial and constructive relationships with colleagues, and ready accessibility to students, could easily have the same importance as a regional or national reputation in one's field has at research-oriented institutions. The overriding issue for all departments is the institutional mission, and the role of the department within it. This establishes the charter of departmental citizenship.

Several years ago, Peter Seldin outlined some national trends in evaluation. Among his findings are: more sources of information are being used in faculty evaluation (as compared with periods of five and ten years earlier); there is more involvement in the design of procedures by those affected; and there is more attention being paid now to issues of reliability and validity. With regard to instructional effectiveness, there is increased use of systematic student ratings, syllabus review, self-evaluation, and classroom visits. Overall, there also seems to be more importance attached to research and publication, to public service, and to activity in professional societies.[13]

CONNECTIONS WITH DEVELOPMENT

The connection of any faculty evaluation activities with development or growth and improvement should be clear and strong. Evaluation activities provide the basis from which relevant and effective faculty development can occur. Indeed, evaluation itself is developmental at its core. It prevents problems and provides quick identification of those not prevented. Always important, faculty evaluation and development are even more so today as traditional means for facilitating personal growth have been eroded or have disappeared altogether.

We are all too familiar with the radical reduction of mobility and the loss of stimulation and revitalization earlier provided by new colleagues and surroundings. This is compounded by the less challenging and rewarding teaching situation many face at institutions that are now admitting students whom they would earlier have regarded as inadequately prepared for college. And as if these factors were not enough, the need for systematic attention to faculty development becomes overriding when one considers that many, if not most, of the tenured faculty of today were tenured during the great expansionary period of the 1960's. Hungry for faculty at that time, a large number of institutions tenured individuals who today might not receive reappointment if indeed they could have secured an initial contract.

In addition, faculty expectations for development are now changing. Common agreement on a fairly clear and narrowly defined range of activities is being reconsidered. Formerly, one pursued a restricted range of inquiry—and one did so over the whole range of his or her career, all of it spent in higher education. The one-dimensional model of a successful academic career is in some disarray as the traditional conditions of mobility, specialization, and public approval supporting it have eroded. Growth through advancement in one's specialized professional or disciplinary field is changing to growth through diversification. This can require new thinking about work load, leaves, and retirement attitudes, policies, and procedures. And of course new roles in faculty development will then cause or require new forms of faculty evaluation.[14] Department chairs need to be sensitive to these changes.

NOTES

1. Raoul A. Arreola, "Establishing Successful Faculty Evaluation and Development Programs," in *Evaluating Faculty and Staff*, ed., Al Smith, New Directions in Community Colleges, 41. San Francisco: Jossey-Bass, 1983, 86.

2. Allan Tucker, *Chairing the Academic Department*, 2nd ed. New York: ACE/Macmillan, 1984, 143.

3. John B. Bennett, "Ambiguity and Abrupt Transitions in the Department Chairperson's Role," *Educational Record* (Fall 1982): 53–56.

4. Chester Finn, "Trying Higher Education: An Eight Count Indictment," *Change* (May/June 1984): 47f.

5. Raoul A. Arreola presents this helpful distinction in "Evaluation of Faculty Performance: Key Issues," in Peter Seldin, *Changing Practices in Faculty Evaluation*. San Francisco: Jossey-Bass, 1984, 82.

6. There are several standardized student rating forms available nationally. The best known are probably the IDEA instrument from

Kansas State University and the SIR from the Educational Testing Service. John A. Centra presents a variety of forms in his *Determining Faculty Effectiveness*. San Francisco: Jossey-Bass, 1979. Other forms and a helpful bibliography are presented in Richard I. Miller, *Evaluating Faculty for Promotion and Tenure*. San Francisco: Jossey-Bass, 1987. One may want to separate the evaluation of the course from that of the instructor, thereby alleviating some of the concern the faculty member may feel about being tarred by the unpopularity of the course itself.

7. A helpful review of the evidence is presented by Jesse U. Overall IV and Herbert W. Marsh in "Research Currents: Students' Evaluations of Teaching, An Update," *AAHE Bulletin* (December 1985): 9–13.

8. Centra, *Determining Faculty Effectiveness*, 30f.

9. Centra, *Determining Faculty Effectiveness*, 154f., and Seldin, *Changing Practices in Faculty Evaluation*, 143.

10. A helpful instrument that relies upon dossier materials for the peer review of undergraduate teaching is included in Neal Whitman and Elaine Weiss, *Faculty Evaluation: The Use of Explicit Criteria for Promotion, Retention, and Tenure*. Washington, DC: AAHE-ERIC/Higher Education Research Report No. 2, 1982.

11. Lawrence H. Poole and Donald A. Dellow, "Evaluation of Full-Time Faculty," in Smith, *Evaluating Faculty and Staff*, 19–31.

12. Some suggestions in this connection are provided in John B. Bennett and Shirley S. Chater, "Evaluating the Performance of Tenured Faculty Members." *Educational Record* (Spring 1984): 38–41. Also helpful is C. M. Licata, *Post-Tenure Faculty Evaluation: Threat or Opportunity?* Washington, DC: Association for the Study of Higher Education, 1986.

13. Seldin, *Changing Practices in Faculty Evaluation*, 73f.

14. W. Todd Furniss has raised a number of these issues in his provocative book, *The Self-Reliant Academic*. Washington, DC: American Council on Education, 1984. In addition, the American Association for Higher Education has provided a helpful instrument for assessing faculty vitality in its "Vitality Without Mobility: The Faculty Opportunities Audit." *Current Issues in Higher Education* 4 (1983–84).

10

MANAGING PART-TIME FACULTY

GEORGE E. BILES
HOWARD P. TUCKMAN

Chairpersons of academic departments must, among many other duties, manage the part-time faculty staffing function. To insure that students have adequately trained and well-prepared part-time faculty members assigned to teach courses is one of a chairperson's key responsibilities. Part-time faculty members have both short- and long-term impact on student academic careers. No doubt many readers of this essay have vivid recollections of both successful and disastrous learning experiences under the tutelage of one or more part-time faculty members.

It is important that the recruitment, maintenance, development, and utilization of part-time faculty be effective. Considerable research supports the notion that organizations that manage people effectively possess certain characteristics. Among the more obvious of these are:[1]

- A genuine concern for people
- A positive view of staff members
- Good training, development, and advancement opportunities
- Good compensation programs
- Low turnover
- Good internal communication
- A commitment to human resource management

Conversely, organizations that do not manage people effectively also possess identifiable characteristics including:

- A lack of awareness of people as assets
- An absence of concern for people
- Management in an autocratic or bureaucratic manner
- Rigid and/or inflexible management style
- Limited staff development opportunities
- Ineffective internal advancement processes
- Poor internal communications
- Unclear or outdated policies
- Policies that are inconsistently administered or altered in difficult times

To promote effective outcomes and diminish poor organizational performance, managers need to evaluate their policies and procedures.

Department chairpeople should be no less effective in managing their staff than managers in other organizations. This means that they should seriously consider a human resource management audit to determine whether part-time faculty are being used efficiently and effectively.

AUDITING HUMAN RESOURCE MANAGEMENT PRACTICES

Auditing, according to the Institute of Internal Auditors, is "An independent appraisal activity within an organization for review of operations as a service to management."[2]

A part-time faculty human resource management audit:

1. Assesses the current state of a department's part-time faculty management policies and practices.
2. Defines what a department's part-time faculty human resource management practices should be, based on careful assessment of predetermined performance standards.
3. Develops action plans for moving from state (1) to state (2), specifying how to modify and improve the department's part-time faculty human resource management policies and practices.

A part-time faculty human resource management audit should provide answers to the following questions:

1. Do part-time faculty members perceive departmental policies and practices as justifiable and equitable?
2. Is the departmental chairperson implementing policies and practices in a consistent and objective manner?

A departmental part-time faculty management effectiveness audit should satisfy the broadly defined, long-term, and general interests of the institution. It should also satisfy the narrower, shorter-term and specific interests of the departmental chairperson, members of the full-time and part-time faculty, and students of part-timers.

A MODEL FOR AUDITING PART-TIME FACULTY HUMAN RESOURCE MANAGEMENT

What should an audit model for part-time faculty human resource management policies and practices look like? Each step is explained in brief below.

Step 1. Analyze whether or not part-time faculty human resources functions are being managed in an effective manner. This analytical process involves looking for *"triggers for action."* The departmental chairperson may choose to audit his or her part-time faculty human resource management practices periodically. More often, chairs will wait until a "red flag" indicates that something should be changed. We consider a "trigger for action" a signal indicating a need for an audit.

Step 2. Determine how badly changes are needed. This is done by comparing the current state of part-time faculty human resource management practices and policies with predetermined and desired standards of performance. Part-time faculty performance standards must be developed and promulgated in clear and unambiguous terms.[3] By comparing part-time faculty performance standards to current practices, information can be obtained on both whether a human resource management practice must be changed and how important such a change would be.

Step 3. Develop an action plan designed to improve part-time faculty effectiveness by taking a department from Step 1 to Step 2.

Presumably, a department chairperson reading this essay is thinking about steps 1 and 2 already, otherwise the essay would never have caught his or her attention. We, therefore, assume that Step 1 has been completed. We further assume the reader has thought about or at least is now cogitating over Step 2. This leads to Step 3—developing specific action plans that will improve part-time human resource management policies, practices, and procedures. Until action plans are articulated and undertaken, an audit is incomplete.

ACTION PLAN FOR IMPROVING PART-TIME FACULTY HUMAN RESOURCES MANAGEMENT POLICIES AND PRACTICES

One of the most important management actions leading to the improvement of part-time faculty performance is to write and disseminate a part-time faculty policy and practices manual.[4] Such a manual can be organized into three sections:

Section I provides an overview, description of, and introduction to the larger academic institution.

Section II consists of specific contractual matters and performance expectations for the part-timer.

Section III explains the administrative procedures and policies that need to be followed for the part-timer to function effectively as a teacher or researcher.

The specifics of any outline will be shaped by an institution's setting, mores, and needs as well as by the unique demands of the discipline(s) represented in the department. They will also be shaped by the needs of the full- and part-time faculty employed in the department. Hence, the outline for two departments at different institutions may not be exactly the same. Set forth below is a sample part-time faculty human resources management policies and procedures manual. The material presented below assumes that there are several useful generic categories of information that all department chairpersons should consider in developing an action plan. Substantial economies of scale can be obtained if sections of the manual are developed at the institutional, rather than departmental, level.

A Sample Part-Time Faculty Human Resource Management Policy and Procedures Manual

Section I

Introduction to The Institution

☐ Provide a brief *History of the Institution*.

☐ Discuss the institution's *Accreditation Standards*.

☐ *Board of Trustees (Regents)*—Provide information about institutional governance policies.

☐ *Institution Administrative Organization*—Provide a thumbnail sketch of the institution's administrative organization.

☐ *Concept of the Institution*—Provide information on the philosophy, mission, role, and tasks of the institution. Include comments about the institution's commitment to superior education: whether it is public, private, residential, nonresidential, inexpensive, and/or expensive. Describe and define the institution's role in the community.

☐ Provide data on the *Student Population*.

Section II

Part-Time Faculty Contractual Matters

☐ Provide a statement on the *Institution's philosophy on the use of part-time faculty members*—Institutions may employ part-time faculty members whose skills and teaching abilities qualify them as effective teachers. This is a desirable practice because, often:

- Part-time faculty members have an ability to introduce ideas from the world of work into a classroom.

- Part-time faculty members offer special courses, technology, or programs that may not attract enough students to warrant employing a full-time instructor.

- Part-time faculty members offer special courses which are scheduled at a location and time when full-time faculty are unavailable.

- Part-time faculty members allow a department to test new courses and programs in order to build a curriculum.

- Part-time faculty members enable the institution to adapt to fluctuating enrollments.

☐ *Equal Employment Opportunity*—Provide a clear statement of the institution's equal employment opportunity policy

☐ *Type of Contract*—The length and nature of the part-timer's attachment to the institution should be clearly specified. The document should state the terms under which termination can take place.

☐ *Part-Time Faculty Teaching Responsibilities* should be clearly spelled out. At a minimum, the following duties and responsibilities of the part-time faculty member should be addressed:

- To conduct assigned classes in accordance with the catalog description.

- To develop behavioral learning objectives for each course.

- To hold every class for the scheduled number of minutes in the assigned class room.

- To ensure that standards of teaching are maintained worthy of accreditation standards.

- To submit mid-term grade reports and final grade reports *on time.*

- To submit to the appropriate academic supervisor a copy of the final examination and a copy of the syllabus, reading lists, and other instructional materials.

☐ Each part-time faculty member's file should contain specific *documents:*

- A current resume or curriculum vita including information on which to base an appointment decision, such as degrees received, teaching experience, and professional affiliations.

- An endorsement from the teaching unit administrator recommending the appointment.

- Student teaching evaluations when available.

- Publications, if any, in a field pertinent to the course subject matter.

- Valid academic transcripts.

☐ *Appointment Documentation*—These policies should specify that a member of the adjunct faculty is appointed for a finite period of, for example, two years. The appointment should be formally considered for renewal at the completion of the appointment period. Renewal should occur only after an analysis of course load requirements has been made, verification of satisfactory teaching evaluations has been completed, and a review of the part-time faculty member's academic and professional progress over the previous appointment period has been undertaken.

- *Evaluation Criteria*—An institution should have a variety of evaluative techniques, including student ratings, peer evaluations, and supervisory ratings.

- *Criteria for Promotion*—Promotion criteria need to be articulated for persons eligible to become long-term part-time faculty members.

- *Grievance Procedures*—Part-time faculty should be provided formal procedures to air grievances.

- *Separation, Layoff, Discharge for Cause, and so on*—A statement should be included specifying that an academic institution has the right to terminate a part-time faculty member because of insufficient class enrollments, economic exigencies, or cause.

- *Academic Freedom*—It should be noted that part-timers have the right to explore controversial issues and topics.

- *Part-Time Faculty Professional Development*—Policies should be outlined.

- *Fringe Benefits*—Benefit packages, or the lack thereof, should be carefully spelled out.

- *Salary Rationale*—The institution should offer its rationale for part-time faculty compensation. If part-time faculty salary is based on a prorated amount of full-time faculty salary, the procedure should be explained.

Section III

Administrative Matters

Poor administrative procedures can have a negative impact on part-time faculty effectiveness. A Part-Time Faculty Policies and Procedures Manual should include information on the following topics:

Audio-Visual Aids—How to check out and use audio-visual aids.

Audit Procedures for students to audit a class.

The basis for *Awarding Course Credit.*

The institution's policy on *Campus Visitors.*

The institution's policy on *Cheating and Plagiarism.*

Class Admission—Policies on admitting students not on an official roster should be spelled out.

Class Attendance requirements.

Class Length and the policies regarding adherence to these lengths.

Class Scheduling. Who is responsible for scheduling.

Class Assignment—How rooms are assigned and who to see about getting rooms changed.

Clerical Services—How to arrange for typing, reproduction, makeup examination proctoring, and so on.

Closed Class—Part-time faculty should be advised how to exclude students wishing to enroll late, or when a class has attained maximum enrollment.

Conference Areas—Where a part-time faculty member can hold office hours.

Copyright Law—Clear statements of this law need to be made.

Course Outlines, Course Goals, and Course Objectives—A statement on how to prepare these should be provided.

Course Records—Requirements for maintaining these.

Curriculum Planning—The role of part-time faculty member, if any.

Custodial Services—How to obtain these.

Emergency Procedures, Examination Policies, Fire Drill Policies and *Grade Appeal Procedures* should be included.

Grade Change Procedures, Grade System, Withdrawal From Classes, and *Reporting of Grades* should be delineated.

Identification Cards—Procedures for obtaining and updating should be provided.

Procedures for *Canceling Classes, Monitoring Independent Studies, Key Acquisition, Library Use, Turning in Lost Materials, Delivering First Class and Campus Mail,* and *Parking on Campus* should be spelled out.

Part-Time Faculty Absence From Class—Policies need to be carefully explained.

Policies regarding *Smoking, Eating and Drinking in classroom,* acceptable and unacceptable *Student Conduct, Student Financial Aid,* how to obtain *Student Records* and *Textbook Desk or Examination Copies* should be included.

Policies and procedures concerning who selects *Textbooks* need to be clarified.

SUMMARY

Auditing part-time faculty human resource management practices is, at first blush, an exercise in common sense. Although the elements of an action plan are familiar to the department chairperson, periodic audits are still necessary. Although a department's part-time faculty may appear to be both performing well and happy with their situation, there are often trouble spots that can only be ferreted out through scrutiny and investigation. Proactive chairpersons should therefore periodically audit their part-time faculty human resource management practices. If such an audit reveals that human resource management policies and procedures should be established or changed, we recommend an action plan including the categories provided in this essay. Effective human resource management involves forward thinking. The establishment of part-time faculty human resource management policies in advance can provide students and the department with more effective and committed part-time instructors.

NOTES

1. S. W. Alper and R. E. Mandel, "What Policies and Practices Characterize the Most Effective HR Departments." *Personnel Administrator* (November 1984): 120–24.
2. V. P. Kuraitis, "The Personnel Audit." *Personnel Administrator* (November 1981): 30. See also R. L. Mathis and G. Cameron. "Auditing Personnel Practices in Smaller-Sized Organizations: A Realistic Approach." *Personnel Administrator*. (April 1981): 45–49.

3. G. E. Biles and R. S. Schuler, *Auditing Human Resource Management Practices*, Alexandria, VA: American Society for Personnel Administration, 1986. This book compiles survey results from various corporate human resource departments—inputs from the American Society for Personnel Administration functional area committees, and surveys of recent human resource management literature—into audit statements that can serve as human resource management performance standards.

4. G. E. Biles and H. P. Tuckman, *Part-Time Faculty Personnel Management Policies*. New York: American Council on Education/Macmillan, 1986. This book covers the full range of personnel issues—from pay, compensation, and benefits to appointment, promotion, and tenure decisions, due process, grievances, affirmative action, and the responsibilities of part-time faculty members.

11

THE DEPARTMENT CHAIR'S LEADERSHIP ROLE IN SUPERVISING NONFACULTY PERSONNEL

DONALD V. DeROSA
QUELDA M. WILSON

The role of department chair as leader of the faculty, while challenging, is rooted in shared experience and common values. The role of the department chair as manager of the staff (i.e., nonacademic personnel) is a less familiar one and, therefore, can be more vexing.

For members of the faculty, many of the factors guiding behavior are internalized standards that are unwritten. For staff members, there are usually formal regulations that state the institution's personnel policies and procedures, and that convey rights to these employees. Department chairs are charged with the responsibility of carrying out these policies. Not only are they held accountable by their institutions, but also, and even more frequently, they are held accountable by arbitrators, external agencies, and the courts. By following a few simple guidelines, you may avoid difficulty and enjoy the benefits of good staff morale.

Know what policies apply to your staff. There may be different rules for professional and clerical staff; technicians may be covered by a union contract, administrative assistants by institutional policy. The rules governing recruitment, interviewing, hiring, probation, transfer, promotion, layoff, discipline, and dismissal may be unique to each category of employee. Department chairs must have a clear understanding of the various policies and procedures governing nonacademic personnel if their departments are to run smoothly and their attention is not to be unnecessarily diverted from academic matters. The office at your institution responsible for staff personnel can be an important resource. Be sure to know whom to call when you have a question or need help.

Although specific policies may differ by institution and by type of employee, there are some basic elements common to all.

RECRUITING AND HIRING STAFF

As is the case with faculty positions, the selection of the best possible support staff is essential to the operation of an effective department. From developing a clear statement of the tasks and responsibilities assigned to a position and the qualifications required or preferred in the successful candidate, to the selection of the person who best meets those criteria, the recruitment and hiring process must meet standards of fairness, job-relatedness, and equal opportunity. There may also be affirmative action hiring goals of which you must be aware.

You may be required to post a position for a minimum length of time before interviewing candidates. There may be a requirement that the position be advertised first to current employees of the institution, or to those in layoff status. It may be necessary to reopen the search if a sufficiently diverse or qualified group of candidates does not apply. Those involved in the interviewing of candidates must be aware of their responsibility to focus on the candidate's suitability for the job and to avoid extraneous, non-job related matters that are inappropriate and can be construed by unsuccessful candidates as discriminatory. Finally, reference-checking is as important for staff positions as for faculty positions.

Once the candidate is appointed, there should be a period of orientation to the department and to the job. It is important that new employees know their duties and responsibilities and their supervisor's expectations, since these will serve as the basis for future evaluations.

DEVELOPING AND EVALUATING STAFF

The "fit" between employees and their jobs must be regularly and carefully monitored. The introduction of new procedures or new technology may require additional training. The errors of an individual employee, or the bad judgment exercised by a supervisor, may indicate the need for special training or coaching. It may also indicate a need to change a job or reassign an employee.

Colleges and universities, committed to the education of students, sometimes neglect the training and development of their own staff employees. Degree programs, continuing education courses, and in-house training classes offered by the personnel office provide employees the opportunity to develop the knowledge and skills necessary to perform well in their current jobs or to prepare for future promotional opportunities. Department chairs normally have the authority to approve time off, with or without pay, to attend classes, or to use department funds to pay all or a portion of course or program fees, or both. Investments in staff development pay dividends in improved performance and morale. The department chair can and should indicate that he or she values and encourages such development.

At all times, but especially in these times of rapid change, decreased budgets, and increased accountability, our effort must be to develop and sustain peak performance. Ongoing evaluation of performance, both formal and informal, is therefore one of the most important responsibilities of every supervisor.

It is especially important to observe, guide, and evaluate an employee during the probationary period. If, after careful assessment of the employee's performance during that period, doubts remain about the individual's ability to succeed in the job, it is better and easier to terminate employment than to permit the employee to continue.

Evaluation must continue beyond probation and throughout an employee's work life. Most institutions require a formal performance appraisal at least annually. Department chairs have the responsibility to conduct these evaluations for staff who report directly to them, and to assure that others in the department who are supervisors also conduct them.

Unlike the faculty evaluation process, which is normally a confidential peer review process, the review of staff employees is the responsibility of immediate supervisors and is not protected from disclosure. Supervisors must, therefore, straightforwardly tell those they supervise that their expectations are being met. Because personnel decisions are based on these assessments (i.e., to continue in employment or to dismiss, to reward or to discipline), they just stand the tests of fairness, job-relatedness, and nondiscrimination. While it is often useful to seek comments from others, including faculty, who have the opportunity to observe the quality of work performed, it is the supervisor who is held accountable for the quality of the evaluation.

Employees who are performing well should be given appropriate recognition. Often a public expression of recognition is appreciated as much as, if not more than, a monetary reward. Department chairs encourage excellence by celebrating excellence.

DISCIPLINING AND TERMINATING STAFF

From time to time it is necessary to recognize that an employee's unwillingness or inability to perform satisfactorily must be addressed. Not to do so is to condone, indeed to encourage, mediocrity and low morale. While the supervisor's first effort must be to correct the problem, it may be necessary to remove the problem employee from the workplace. In either case, the most important thing to remember is that records justifying the action must stand up to scrutiny by external reviewers, such as arbitrators and judges. Most colleges and universities have internal grievance systems that permit employees to appeal actions taken by their supervisors, and all employees have rights under state and federal laws that protect them from arbitrary and capricious acts of their employers. Legitimate acts taken by supervisors today are subject to challenge in a variety of forums and only those that have been carefully documented can hope to withstand such scrutiny. Avoidance of the ill-will, disruption, and negative publicity that can occur as a result of grievances and lawsuits is sufficient reason for department chairs to assure that they and the supervisors (including faculty members) in their departments understand and carry out their responsibilities in these matters. Personnel offices can provide assistance and should be consulted.

CONCLUSION

The role of the department chair as manager of the staff is both difficult and rewarding. The opportunity to select those who will provide the necessary support services carries with it the obligation to set standards and evaluate fairly. The opportunity to reward achievement is combined with the obligation to discipline and remove the nonperformer.

The role of staff supervisor is often foreign to department chairs since for much of their professional life they have operated in a system governed by rules different from those applying to most staff employees they now supervise. However, the effective operation of an excellent department is dependent upon the leadership of the department chair in all areas. The nonacademic support staff is central to this effort and the time and energy the department head devotes to this area will pay important dividends for the department as a whole.

PART THREE

Faculty Development

Attending to the conditions for continued faculty growth and improvement is a major, ongoing responsibility for almost every department chairperson. It is never finished. The task can be time-consuming and difficult, sometimes requiring great personal sensitivity. Its importance is clear, however. Without those conditions that support and enable continued professional growth, faculty are likely to stagnate, lose interest in their teaching and research, and/or develop outside interests in conflict with the time and energy the academy needs.

Department chairpersons are ideally positioned to provide help. The right kind of assistance can return great dividends to them and to the department. No one else in the institution is likely to know as well as the chair the various needs of both the individual faculty and the department. It is the chair who has the day-in, day-out personal contact necessary for detecting and interpreting individual swings in mood and activity. And it is the chair who can coordinate departmental requirements and opportunities with individual strengths and needs. After all, department goals are advanced only through addressing individual needs.

In the first essay, "Chairpersons and Faculty Development," Kenneth Eble reports on the importance of functioning in a caring and supportive role. Administering institutional resources such as sabbaticals, travel monies, and research leaves is surely necessary, but the more basic necessity for chairpersons is a keen observation of human needs and wants, and flexibility in response to them. Some of the specific functions Eble highlights include bringing people together to discuss teaching, creating a stimulating environment by arranging for social and professional interaction, motivating individuals by every means possible, and breaking the patterns of defeat that can trap faculty members.

The developmental needs of faculty frequently differ according to faculty age. Not everyone can create the conditions he or she needs in order to succeed, and these conditions can themselves change. In his essay, "Tactics and Strategies for Faculty Development," Wilbert McKeachie stresses the need for chairs to listen carefully to the faculty in order to identify mutual goals. Then chairs need to create peer support systems in order to advance and nourish the changes underway. McKeachie also argues that regular evaluations can be used constructively to diagnose problems, especially if specific solutions or corrections can be proposed.

"Faculty development" originally referred to ways in which instructional successes could be increased and failures reduced or alleviated. Now it encompasses the broader effort Eble and McKeachie discuss. However, the need to attend specifically to the conditions for instructional success will never leave us. This need is probably greatest at those institutions now experiencing a shift in type of student—from the traditional (18- to 24-year-old) to the nontraditional student.

In her essay, "Teaching the Nontraditional Student," Eileen Rice reviews the challenges this shift creates. It is the rare faculty member who has been trained for the instruction of the nontraditional student—typically a part-time student with a full-time job, often female, perhaps trying to balance family, job, and school. Tactics developed for the instruction of one population will need review and modification for the other. Likewise, systems for the delivery of instruction and advising of the full-time residential student will not work for the nontraditional commuter. The department chairperson must be alert to the need for both changes.

Rice provides a number of concrete suggestions for developing new teaching strategies. Throughout, it is important to recognize the variety of circumstance, experience, and educational objectives existing within the label "nontraditional"—and therefore the variety of motivational techniques and ploys that may be necessary. Department meetings, individual goal-setting sessions, and informal conversations are all contexts in which the department chair can promote specific strategies.

To reflect on teaching leads one to reflect on scholarship. Some faculty do indeed face publishing pressures. The number is probably exaggerated, but it is also certainly growing. Facilitating scholarly writing has been a traditional responsibility (or at least an expectation) of many chairs, especially those at research-oriented institutions. Yet as Boice's first essay indicates, "Chairs as Facilitators of Scholarly Writing," chairs often play a rather passive role in encouraging and enabling scholarly writing within their departments or divisions. This passivity belies the leadership possibilities of the position.

Regardless of the sector of higher education, there are important values associated with scholarship. Imposing discipline upon ideas and information, and forcing concreteness upon vague concepts are demanding and important challenges all educators will recognize. Meeting these demands generates excitement. Successes in writing can increase those in teaching, and vice versa. Other connections between teaching and writing may be more difficult to establish, but the personal satisfactions of modeling to others can certainly contribute to the vitality of a department.

Boice provides a number of suggestions for facilitating scholarly writing. At some institutions, such writing may have only local circulation and still generate the values mentioned above. Indeed, broader publication may cut against the ethos of the college. At other places, though, the familiar pressures to publish in the leading journals will push chairpersons to provide as much assistance as they can.

Again and again in workshops, seminars, and other gatherings of chairpersons, one hears comments on the unpleasantness of working with some colleagues. The aging of the professoriat and the lack of professional mobility appear to have combined to increase the number of discontented faculty on the nation's campuses. The career expectations of their youth have for many faculty proved unrealistic and are now finally recognized by some as unattainable. Morale is diminished accordingly.

In "Coping with Difficult Colleagues" Robert Boice candidly addresses this major source of stress for, and preoccupation of, many chairpersons. Some of these chronic stressors are angry and hostile faculty; others seem to have given up and constitute the more familiar category of "deadwood." Strategies for coping include paying the kind of proactive attention to faculty that periodic casual visits to faculty offices permits and illustrates; setting limits on the amount of hostility to be tolerated; exploration of meaningful alternative activities; and clarification of the department reward structure, emphasizing its stability and consistency.

12

CHAIRPERSONS AND FACULTY DEVELOPMENT

KENNETH E. EBLE

Since 1980, I have been heavily involved in a major faculty development effort funded by the Bush Foundation and affecting virtually all the colleges and universities in Minnesota and North and South Dakota. In 1985, Wilbert McKeachie and I finished a study and evaluation of this project.[1] "It is difficult," we wrote in our conclusions, "to describe just what constitutes effective leadership. Like effective teachers, effective leaders come in all sizes and shapes, and have different styles and different ways of getting their way and helping others get theirs. But clearly within these programs, the presence of individual faculty and administrative leadership was important to a program's success. Where there was little leadership, programs faltered. Where there was imposition of authority or convictions masquerading as leadership, programs had difficulty in getting off the ground."

The specific activities and effectiveness of chairpersons in this group of forty-one colleges varied widely. A few had already taken an interest in faculty development and were promoting specific activities useful to improving faculty performance as both teachers and scholars. The majority gave some unfocused attention to faculty development as one among other administrative responsibilities. Some gave little attention to it, perhaps because it was not necessary to running an efficient organization or because it was too amorphous an activity to work at or because leaving faculty alone to do pretty much as they pleased was an unstated policy.

If chairpersons could provide a high level of motivation for a department's faculty, faculty development as a separate activity might not exist. Traditionally, most support for faculty development comes from a central administration in the form of sabbatical and research leaves, travel, and awards. Departments play some part in competing for such funds, in allocating funds to individuals, and in seeing that such perquisites are fairly awarded. But the lack of travel funds, tangible recognition, or an adequate leave policy is blamed on the institution. In many colleges and universities, these academic perquisites are seen in somewhat the same light as fringe benefits—dental and medical insurance, tuition waivers for family, and the like.

At most, a chairperson might be expected to keep the department faculty informed as to the availability of sabbaticals, travel support, and research opportunities. An energetic chairperson might even encourage faculty members to apply for grants and leaves. But it is a rare chairperson who sees that his or her closeness to the faculty and to the students places a responsibility on him to provide an opportunity for faculty development of a broader and more personal kind.

CHALLENGES TO A BROADER AND MORE PERSONAL KIND OF FACULTY DEVELOPMENT

What I am talking about is the necessary functioning of chairpersons as keen observers of faculty needs and wants and as ingenious providers of motivation, support, and encouragement. Nothing is so necessary to administrators as an understanding of and caring for human beings. Modern business and industrial management has accepted this premise as a key to higher productivity and profits. Herzberg writes, "Without wisdom in management of people today, we find blind alleys for the perplexed and pessimism for the dismayed."[2] If this is so for corporations whose products are foodstuffs and drygoods, how much more so for educational enterprises whose products and producers are human beings.

Getting the most out of people is a demanding and often frustrating job. The demands on academic chairpersons, especially of large departments, are heavy. Pressures come both from above and below, expectations are often ill-defined, and preparation for the job negligible. Faculty members, moreover, vary widely in competence, goals, energy, and general crankiness. There is often little agreement among professors about what they should be doing. Performing the necessary clerical tasks, steering a safe course, conceding to faculty the self-proclaimed right to conduct their business as they see fit may be all that a chairperson can manage. Sufficient as this may be for some minimum level of operation, it clearly is not sufficient if chairpersons are to contribute effectively to faculty development.

Before setting forth some specific ways in which chairpersons can affect faculty development, let me acknowledge some realities that must be faced. First, the motivations of candidates for the chair are curious if not bizarre. Those who want the position are often ruled out precisely because they do. Those who do not want it are often, and unwisely, forced into it. Those who assume the office must face their own disdain for administration and that of many of their colleagues.

Second, few prospective chairpersons have consciously developed skills in administration or have thought seriously about such skills. Few institutions provide chairpersons with much pre- or in-service guidance.

Warren Bennis has lamented the almost total lack of career preparation for academic administrators. "Most of us got into this work adventitiously, and most of us do what we have either observed others do when they were in these roles or emulate, incorrectly, some other shadowy figures of the past, fantasies of Harvard Business School products, General Patton, creatures of fiction or movies, or some atavisms of leadership and authority which never were."[3]

Third, the shift from department heads to chairpersons has shortened the time a chairperson serves and increased the number of faculty who must exercise administrative responsibilities. Rotating chairmanships have reduced the ill-effects of entrenched incompetence, but they exhaust administrative talent rapidly and make too little of skills which might develop over longer periods of service.

Fourth, few administrators at any level recognize sufficiently what Robert Greenleaf calls "servant leadership." And yet, that ability both to lead and serve is fundamental to academic administration. "The great leader is seen as servant first," Greenleaf writes.[4] Seeing no alternatives between an autocratic exercise of power and the exercise of no power at all, chairpersons can end up neither serving, nor leading. College professors are jealous of their independence, proud of their specialized competencies, not easily led, and suspicious of being told what or how they serve. Locked into their disciplines, they may not easily accept the notion, as phrased by Peter Caws that, "Insofar as the university is an institution of its society, its responsibility is to ask itself how it can best serve the people."[5] Nevertheless, faculty members will respond to signs that important services are being rendered—both from their own teaching and research and from the recognition of those services by effective chairpersons. Since a faculty's attention is most often directly focused on teaching and research, faculty members may welcome leadership that gives visibility to the services they render.

Indeed, the most important faculty development function of department chairpersons may be that of affirming the value of the varied services faculty members perform. In a time of low faculty morale and of some floundering among the many expectations placed upon higher education, chairpersons must provide a voice for the faculty that stimulates both personal development and institutional progress.

Finally, chairpersons must confront a reward system meant to serve the pluralistic aims of American higher education that is not merely a chronic source of faculty complaints but a major obstacle to faculty development. The placing of research above teaching—and not just at so called research universities—has had the negative effect of narrowing faculty perspectives. The value of service activities has steadily declined, to a point where no faculty member stands to gain much from being an active citizen of the college or university.

While chairpersons may argue that an institution's values are declared and enforced from the top, they cannot deny the important part that they themselves play. Recommendations for and documentation of retention, promotion, and tenure still begin at the department level in most institutions. A chairperson who holds to a narrow set of professional standards is not likely to develop the kind of varied competencies all departments need. A chairperson who is unwilling to make a case for a faculty member whose merits fall outside such standards will contribute nothing to broadening the perspectives that set standards. A chairperson who does not actively seek to make the reward system more compatible with the actual demands a department makes upon its faculty compromises his or her chances of succeeding at faculty development.

SOME SPECIFIC SUGGESTIONS

These are some of the difficulties institutions face in engaging department chairpersons in faculty development. Difficulties aside, what specific activities might chairpersons engage in? I will single out a cluster of related activities: (1) bringing people together, (2) creating a stimulating environment, (3) motivating individuals by every means possible, (4) identifying wants and needs, (5) targeting objectives and defining goals, (6) providing resources, and (7) picking up those who are down.

BRINGING PEOPLE TOGETHER

My experience with faculty development programs tells me that money is poorly spent if it does not serve both individual and group needs. Meeting individual faculty needs is the easiest way to spend faculty development money, chiefly in the form of travel and research grants, released time, and funds for purchasing instructional and research equipment.

Department chairpersons play a part in fostering such individual activities, but they can play a larger part in relating these activities to department goals and in allotting funds and energy to activities that affect a large part or all of the department faculty and students. Chairpersons should be concerned with how faculty members can be brought together, and not just for transacting department business or assailing each other with reports of their research. Teaching is essentially a process of interaction and one develops teaching skill by exchanging ideas and practices. In a collegial department much of this exchange takes place informally. Where collegiality is missing, as it is in many institutions these days, a department chairperson needs to provide ways of bringing groups of faculty together specifically to improve instruction. What faculty members draw greatly upon the accumulated experience and diversity of teaching practices of their colleagues? What faculty members ever meet any number of students outside the classes in which they are enrolled, or know anything about what affects their learning?

What department chairperson ever acquaints faculty members with research about learning and teaching? Getting faculty together for these purposes is surely as important as holding department seminars where faculty members present their research.

CREATING A STIMULATING ENVIRONMENT

In addition, individual faculty can be stimulated by creating a sense of common purpose that arises from letting faculty know what others are doing, taking an interest in these activities, and recognizing accomplishments in tangible ways. Motivation of this kind is a daily responsibility, not something to be deferred until reviews of promotion, salary, and tenure. The creation of a working environment that in itself provides stimulation is a chairperson's responsibility. Much of this is created by the kind of formal and informal opportunities a department provides for social and professional interaction across the lines created by differences in age, rank, specializations, and interests. Cliques and factions arise when such opportunities are not present.

A favorable climate is also affected by the reminders a chairperson can provide that books are read, ideas are exchanged, that living people as well as dead occupy the often sterile corridors in which faculty spend most of their time. The active demeanor of a chairperson and his or her involvement in a department's diverse activities are in themselves important sources of faculty motivation.

MOTIVATING INDIVIDUALS BY EVERY MEANS POSSIBLE

Third, just as the chairperson is the person with the greatest responsibility for identifying a department's strengths and weaknesses, so is he or she the one most concerned with individual faculty members' wants and needs. Simple-minded maximums like "the squeaky wheel gets the grease" are admissions of failure at the outset. Many institutional efforts at faculty development begin with a needs assessment. What are the chief desires of the faculty with respect to professional development? What are the chief needs among the faculty and within the department? Wise chairpersons have long made it a practice of conferring with every faculty member at least once a year about that person's aims, satisfactions, and frustrations. This kind of information makes it possible to perform many services on behalf of the faculty and to allot even very slender resources in effective and equitable ways.

At the same time, chairpersons who keep themselves informed may have to be tactful, unafraid, open, and tough when necessary. I am speaking here of motivating those who purposely drift, evade, or fudge on their responsibilities. These include the undervalued as well as those who value themselves too much and common goals too little, the lazy who will remain lazy unless they are prodded or coaxed into some purposeful activity, and the dodgers who simply find ways—usually that of being engaged in "their own work"—of avoiding educational responsibilities. I recognize the dangers of either tender- or tough-minded meddling. But I have seen too much leaving well enough alone in which "well enough" is defined by chairpersons as that which best suits their disinclination to exert themselves.

IDENTIFYING NEEDS, WANTS, AND OBJECTIVES

In addition to helping faculty members develop professionally, chairpersons must also identify a department's common needs, and target specific needs that enlist the energies of an entire department. Departments never have enough money to meet pressing needs: for faculty travel, for equipment, for readers or other instructional assistants, for leaves, for speakers and conferences, for clerical staff, for computer time—there is no end of the needs. In most departments spreading resources around so that everyone gets something is an expedient policy. If faculty development were related to specific larger departmental objectives (a more attractive curriculum or a better system of advising students, for example), department chairpersons would necessarily have to target resources to meet such objectives.

DISTRIBUTING RESOURCES

Closely related to targeting objectives and defining goals is the chairperson's function as a distributor, if not provider, of resources. In some respects, this is the easiest demand to avoid. Most faculty members realize that chairpersons have little control over the budget. Individuals may complain about inequities within the department, but most complaints about a lack of resources revert to the institution itself. Chairpersons can and should make the most of the resources that are provided, allocating the majority to the development of faculty. I think chairpersons would do well to argue for discretionary funds that could directly meet small but pressing faculty needs associated with instruction or scholarship. Out-of-pocket grants coming from an office of or committee for faculty development have been conspicuous successes in faculty development programs. It is, of course, always possible that one chairperson can be more persuasive than another in getting a larger share of the college or university budget. But such persuasiveness is likely to come from the presence, not of an individual star or two, but from a department's collective display of strength.

PICKING UP THOSE WHO ARE DOWN

Finally, much concern is manifested in faculty development programs about the deadwood, those faculty members who seemingly are in great need of improvement in their capacities as teachers and scholars or in services to the department or college. Faculty development programs that call for voluntary participation of the faculty are not likely to reach them. For "they" are those people who do not volunteer, do not take advantage of those programs "we" have designed for their specific benefit. "They" do not apply for grants, cannot be trusted with committee assignments, do not win awards. "They" are clearly not "us" and what to do about "them" is a chronic problem.

What a department chairperson might do, at the least, is pick up some of those who are down. By that I simply mean challenging those patterns of defeat which create and confirm some faculty members' poor performance. The reasons are as varied for faculty as for students. Often poor performance relates to personal problems and can be regarded as a temporary decline rather than a confirmed disability. Sometimes it is a matter of ill health, for which recognizing the condition may be a useful form of assistance. Sometimes it is disaffection with colleagues, the department, the college, or the profession itself. Sometimes it is the lack of opportunities, recognition, or encouragement. At all times, some of these faculty members can be helped successfully.

What I am discussing here is probably the most delicate and most frustrating aspect of a chairperson's work. It is an aspect easily neglected, so long as the numbers of the disaffected and dysfunctional do not become too large. And yet, it is work that sharpens a chairperson's skill at dealing with people and situations that affect faculty performance.

My conclusion is that chairpersons could play a much greater part in faculty development than they do. There are easier and safer tasks than trying to motivate faculty, to assist them in their individual development, and to orchestrate their diverse talents and attributes into a department which functions as more than just the aggregate of individual efforts. It is easier to work with things, to monitor teaching loads and class sizes, worry about grade inflation, and watch over the curriculum, and to make sure the faculty is becoming computer literate. And, as specialization works everywhere else in the university, so faculty development can be left to the specialists in that particular line.

I do not think this last position is defensible. Because chairpersons have daily and personal contact with faculty, they are in a key position to further professional development. And professional development involves more than developing specialists or specialized skills. It is, rather, development of whole persons as teachers, scholars, and contributors to the high aims of learning, which alone justify higher education.

NOTES

1. Kenneth E. Eble and Wilbert McKeachie, *Improving Undergraduate Education through Faculty Development*. San Francisco: Jossey-Bass, 1985.

2. Frederick Herzberg, The Managerial Choice: *To Be Efficient and To Be Human*. Homewood, IL: Dow Jones-Irwin, 1976.
3. Warren Bennis, "An O.D. Expert in the Cat Bird's Seat," *Journal of Higher Education*, 1973.
4. Robert K. Greenleaf, *Servant Leadership: A Journey into the Nature of Legitimate Power and Greatness*. Mahwah, NJ: Paulist Press, 1977.
5. Peter Caws, *The Bankruptcy of Academic Policy*. Washington, DC: Acropolis Books, 1972.

13

TACTICS AND STRATEGIES FOR FACULTY DEVELOPMENT

WILBERT J. McKEACHIE

During my service as a department chairman, my chief interest was trying to recruit the very best faculty. If I recruited well, I believed that our recruits would develop well—that they would create the conditions they needed in order to succeed. This is not a bad strategy in times of expansion, but it may be less practical in times of stability or contraction. When the faculty is stable or growing smaller, those who remain may not fit the department's current needs. Our first thought is to encourage early retirement. If that fails, we complain about "dead wood." Our dean, however, is likely to say, What are you doing about faculty development?

The problem with many faculty development programs is that they are based on the assumption that the chair can change people in ways that will make them better, and that the chair must decide what the department needs and how people ought to change to meet those goals. Faculty members readily perceive that the chair has decided to change them, and they resist vigorously. If you start by assuming that you can readily make such changes, you probably come to bat with two strikes against you.

A PROBLEM-SOLVING FRAMEWORK

What can you do? First, rather than devising a faculty development program and pushing people into it, start by *listening* to the faculty. The chances are that few of your colleagues have been asked recently:

1. Where would you like to see our department go in the next few years?
2. How do you think *you* can contribute to the department?
3. What do you see as *your* career pattern and how does it relate to the needs of the department?
4. What can the department, and I, as chair, do to help you to achieve your career goal as well as to help the department work well?

Such an approach enables you to work with your staff in identifying goals that are mutually agreed upon, rather than seeking to impose your own goals, which they may never accept.

When faculty members offer an idea that seems unrealistic, do not reject it. Instead try, "It seems that we would have a problem in carrying out your idea (specify the problem). Would you go and talk to a couple of other people about this and see if you can devise some plan that will help us to cope with the problem which it seems we would run into in pursuing your plan?"

Although this does not *solve* the problem, at least it establishes a problem-solving framework. The chair does not decree that, We cannot do this because it is impossible, or It would never pass the faculty, or The dean would never approve it, and so on. One of the best administrators I ever worked with was Roger Heyns. When you presented him with an idea he was always eager to hear it. He listened very well and would typically say: "Let's see how we can work it out practically." He would frequently make some insightful and helpful suggestions: "Well if you are going to do that, you need to take care of this." Then he would help do it. I would often need to work out some details that I had not yet thought about. Thus he helped me avoid wrecking my own proposal.

Other deans would tend to bargain, saying, "Maybe you could do that if you'll do this." Some would react with an automatic, "No." Then you would have had to return and persuade them to reconsider the answer. Indeed, that is what they *expected* you to do. If you were persistent you would return with a revised proposal for approval. Heyns could turn requests into situations in which issues were realistically assessed and resolved. In faculty development, *start by listening*.

THE NEEDS OF JUNIOR AND SENIOR FACULTY

A faculty member's aspirations are important regardless of his or her age. But some considerations that depend on the age of your staff member may be particularly important. Often administrators ask, "How can senior faculty members be retreaded?" Many senior people are primarily teaching graduate students, but graduate populations are now dropping in many fields. Shrinking funds need to be used chiefly to support undergraduate courses.

How do you get faculty members to readjust to the needed teaching? The simplest solution is to work out new teaching assignments. For younger faculty a new assignment may be a major challenge because new preparation is required. However, this extra work may broaden their experience and thereby enhance their career potential.

For older faculty members, there may be different barriers. Senior people have often become highly specialized. They may not have kept up well with other areas of their discipline, so they may feel, correctly, that they do not have the *breadth of current background* to teach some of the nonspecialized courses. Recently, I reviewed the psychology program at an undergraduate college. Although it has quite an array of psychology courses, it has a relatively small staff whose members have been there from five to ten years. These faculty members want to move out of the introductory areas that they were hired to teach. For instance, of two people in experimental psychology, one wanted to teach clinical courses and environmental psychology. The department decided that it could not make the requested changes because the areas these two faculty members were hired to teach—experimental psychology, learning, and perception—were needed for the psychology major. That posed a problem. In my report I argued that the department ought to make some trade-offs, giving faculty members some choices over what they teach, with a chance to try new things at least every other year or so, in return for commitments to take their turns in teaching traditional courses.

One reason the department insisted on sticking to the old areas was that they felt other members of the department could not teach learning or perception. Although the field has advanced a great deal and there are many recent technical developments, I believe that any reasonably intelligent Ph.D. should be able to keep ahead of the students in an *undergraduate* course. So I argued that in return for an agreement to teach undergraduate courses, they could broaden the expectations of department members as they took turns teaching in some areas that were not currently their specialities. This plan could play a role in faculty development through extending a faculty member's breadth of subject matter competence and ensure that basic courses would be provided.

The second problem is that of *skill*. Some people who have taught only advanced courses lack the rather different teaching skills needed for teaching undergraduate large-enrollment courses. So we must help people prepare to shift roles and develop new skills. Faculty development centers offer workshops designed to help people who seek to develop skills in lecturing, discussion leading, effective speaking, and other skills needed for undergraduate teaching.

Third is the question of *status*. Graduate teaching has traditionally been a higher status activity than teaching introductory courses. So, when we try to get a senior person to shift assignments, it is often viewed as a lowering of status. Fortunately, most departments have some high status faculty members who enjoy undergraduate teaching and can help model the idea that undergraduate teaching is honorable and enjoyable.

One way to sidestep the status problem is to *revise* the curriculum using a committee that includes the people who need to change. As they participate in determining content and sequencing of courses, they are likely to develop some commitment to the revisions.

You may work out a team-teaching plan in which participating faculty members are each scheduled to teach in some course going beyond their own field of specialization. Insist that *all* the members of the team participate in *all* sessions of the class. Although this is relatively expensive the first time through, later—after they have been through it a time or two with other people—participants will feel comfortable, even when teaching alone.

Alternating instructional assignments, such as team teaching, has an additional benefit. It is difficult to develop a faculty member independent of the other departmental activities. If you focus on one individual, that individual may be seen as a prima donna, a deviant, or even a scapegoat. Rather, one key to effective faculty development is to encourage a *team* effort in which people work with other faculty members.

Much as I believe in the importance of faculty development centers, you do not need expertise from such centers for many things. In the area of teaching, the critical skills are often closely tied to subject matter. It is likely that the chief skills—knowledge, and wisdom—already reside in your present faculty. A key to helping people develop skill and confidence in teaching is to encourage them to talk to each other about their teaching. At first this may not happen very naturally, particularly with those who are not doing very well and are afraid to expose that fact. So you need to provide settings which will get faculty members talking to each other about what they are doing. Team teaching or joint planning are ways of stimulating social support for individuals who are trying to change their roles and to develop additional competence.

In summary, the first principle for faculty development is to start with *faculty* members' *needs* rather than with your needs; then try to arrive at a plan that satisfies both the faculty member and the department. The second principle is to develop *peer support* rather than to focus solely on the individual faculty member. The third is to alleviate the status problem by *rotating* assignments.

FACULTY EVALUATION AS A TOOL FOR FACULTY DEVELOPMENT

Some people assume that you cannot develop faculty members without evaluations. To some extent they may be correct. But, more often than not, evaluations may prove to be more harmful than helpful to faculty development. Although all of us could improve, there may be different problems for beginning people than for those who are already skilled. Also, people who are already doing well may want to branch out into new areas. Although different procedures or goals will be appropriate for people at different levels of competence, all of us are suitable candidates for faculty development.

A constructive use of evaluation is as a tool to help an individual identify or diagnose a problem. Sometimes this is very threatening: identifying a particular problem may do more harm than good if the faculty member cannot recognize what can be done about it. If students report that you do not give very clear explanations, but you are doing the best you can to explain things, the evaluation will probably not be very helpful. Or, if students feel you are not really interested in them, that may not be a very helpful report if you think you are already as interested as you can be.

Try to set up an evaluation system that will give some clues about how to deal with difficulties. While on the average student evaluations tend to help faculty members, they are more helpful if the evaluations are discussed with another faculty member or an experienced person who can respond helpfully in two or three ways:

1. One response is to state that, "It's not as bad as it looks; everybody gets some bad ratings from students—so don't get discouraged and give up."

2. Another response might be: "Well, now, let's look more specifically at what the students are saying." Frequently a faculty member who reads ratings allows some negative ones to dominate everything else, particularly if there are several very hostile comments about the teaching. It is hard to believe that anybody sitting could really feel that way. So analyzing *what* the responses *are* and what they *tell* is helpful.

3. A third response another person can offer if complaints focus on one area is to ask, "Have you thought about trying this . . . ?" Or, "Have you tried that . . . ?" Then *more* than one possibility should be suggested, because people are more likely to do something if they have some *choice*. If one has no alternative, he or she is likely to give up and retreat from efforts to improve classroom effectiveness. I think that is actually what happens in the cases of many poor teachers: they received some negative feedback and soon decided that effective teaching was hopeless, so they directed their effort to committee work, research, or something else that does not give them such trauma. Evaluations *can* help to *diagnose* problems.

EVALUATION FOR PERSONNEL PURPOSES

What about evaluations when they are used for personnel purposes (i.e., salary increases, tenure, and promotions)? Here we are looking at evaluations in terms of the goals of the *institution*. It is difficult to weigh all goals equally. Some systems are designed to be overly objective. So there is a certain number of points for each activity: ten points for authoring a book, three more points if it is a *good* book. Five for an article, and five points if you serve on Faculty Committee A. One point if you're a Boy Scout leader, and so on. If you achieve a certain number of points you have made it; if not, you have not. Presumably, there is no chance that individual bias will enter in.

If faculty members are happy with this system, fine. There is, however, a danger that the combination of numbers results in decisions which everyone knows to be irrational. Moreover, a faculty member may work to get points, not to achieve the overall goals of the department and college. Rather, one should consider the wide variety of ways in which people can contribute to the university's goals. We need to think in a more holistic way about faculty contributions. A judgment has to be arrived at in terms of the total contribution of the individual to the institution. I would argue that contributions ultimately be measured in terms of their educational impact upon the students and upon other faculty members. Are we not essentially a community of learners who should look at contributions in terms of teaching, research, and personal influence on colleagues and on curriculum? Individual contributions need to be assessed in terms of how well they achieve institutional goals, not how many points they receive for each activity. *Value* judgments about the *quality* of the activities and their contributions to the *goals* are needed, not a blind summation of points.

REMEMBERING PRIORITIES

Finally, what do you overlook and what do you emphasize? As a department chair, while talking to faculty members, you have to decide what to get exercised about. Sometimes it depends on *how many* things are going wrong. As in rearing children, you can usually straighten a child out on one thing at a time, but you probably cannot reform that child completely if you try to concentrate on everything at once. When kids were getting involved in drugs, drinking, long hair, and much else, my advice to parents was to focus on the drugs and not worry about the long hair. We could survive "hair" no matter how repulsive our children looked, but drugs had more long-lasting effects. I think the same principle applies to faculty members—you need to focus upon what they are doing that has an impact on students. I take very seriously the fulfilling of obligation to students. If an instructor does not meet classes or arrives drunk or poorly prepared, that is serious. If the problem is that he is not turning in some monthly report or has not filled out the latest administrative form, I let the secretary remind him but do not make a big issue of it.

During the sixties many young faculty members showed strong resistance to authority in general. It probably was not worthwhile to make an issue of these efforts to establish that they did not have to kow-tow to authority. We needed to focus on the things that were really important—that contributed to the goals of the institution. We tried to persuade them that it was not simply a question of authority but that what we asked was in the nature of a responsive university—for example, that submitting grades on time had important effects on students— the group with whom they identified.

Faculty members as a group contrast with most others in placing a high value on autonomy, individual responsibility, and intellectual stimulation. So if faculty members feel that an evaluation system cramps their style—is imposed upon them by the administration or even by a faculty committee in which they participate—it is likely that they will resist that system of evaluation. Even if they participate in such evaluations, many of the unique, positive features of the university environment are lost (e.g., the sense of *free* inquiry and curiosity in which people do much good work because they find learning to be an activity that is stimulating in itself). And that is really our goal for both faculty and students.

For *better* evidence you are likely to seek *more* evaluations. I spent much of the 1950s speaking about why teachers *should* use student evaluations. During the 1970s I spent much of the time explaining why you should *not* use them quite as much or that you should *not* use them in stupid ways. The essential point is that student evaluations provide valuable information—the students are there, and they know what is going on. They have some impression as to whether or not they have become interested and involved in a course or have been turned off. That is important information to have. But they do not have the whole picture.

It is unwise to take student evaluations as the final verdict on teaching. It is also important to solicit peer evaluations although it is often a waste of time to have peers sit in on classes. It is more important for peers to look at the goals and content of the courses than at a small sample of teaching performance.

Faculty members are very *unreliable* in their judgments of teaching. An observer must attend class five to eight times during the term to have a reliable indication of what is really going on. Very rarely will a faculty member sit in on a class enough times to become a good judge of the teaching. Although teaching varies from day to day, a single visit may be helpful in answering a specific question or in spotting things being done right or others that might be easily improved. But, if a visit is to be taken seriously as a *judgment* of the teacher's overall effectiveness, a brief sample may be dangerous evidence. However, it may *not* be so dangerous because faculty members are usually quite complimentary of one another's teaching. Such ratings cluster very near the top of the scale, regardless of the scale used. What I think faculty members are essential in judging is whether or not the *goals* and the *content* are appropriate.

Advanced students have some sense of whether the course is what it is supposed to be and whether the information is up-to-date, but there are students in introductory courses who do not. They are unable to judge whether they are covering as much, more, or less than others. They simply do not have the background to judge; for that you need to have the informed judgment of peers. Generally this is better judged by peers through observation of students' products (e.g., final examinations, term papers, what students are doing in a course, and by looking at the course syllabus) to see what the assignments are and what is being covered. Peers have a better notion from that sort of evidence than from sitting in one or two classes that may be atypical.

Students' evaluations *are* good in indicating what the students *think* has happened to them. They are very good in two areas. They indicate what the impact has been upon their *motivation*—a very important outcome of teaching. They show whether or not they are interested and curious and have become excited. Secondly, student evaluations are useful because students know what has actually occurred in class and can probably report better what the teacher is *doing* in class than anybody else. One can be an effective teacher in lots of different ways. Do not worry too much about getting details on whether the teacher verbalizes specific goals or provides summaries, or does this or that which we may think constitutes good teaching. Be more concerned about what the *overall* effect is than how the teacher achieves it.

Good teachers tend to be those whose students learn most. The better-controlled studies of student ratings indicate higher positive correlations than the poor studies done in the past. There is a rather substantial relationship between student ratings and student learning.

If you are concerned about *long-range* goals, *no evaluation* system that *reduces motivation* should be used no matter how good it may look on paper. You should think about the motivational consequences of your evaluation system as much as about its technical characteristics. Psychologists and others can tell you about reliability and such other technical issues. But these are largely irrelevant if the evaluation system does not contribute to teachers feeling a desire to improve.

To sum up, department chairs can do much to make a real difference in the growth and development of their faculty. That difference depends as much upon commitment as upon skill.

NOTES

1. This chapter is based on a talk given to department chairs at The University of Michigan, Flint. Thanks are due to Frank Irish who recorded, transcribed, and suggested its publication.

14

TEACHING THE NONTRADITIONAL STUDENT

SISTER EILEEN RICE

The influx of nontraditional students into the groves of academe is now an accepted fact in most of the nation's universities and four-year colleges. In many instances special programs have been designed for this population and/or accommodations have been made in the scheduling of existing programs. However, sometimes the lion's share of the attention is paid to recruiting these students through attractive packaging. There is a need to look carefully at what goes on behind the classroom door, to look at specific strategies and practices by which department chairs can help college professors be effective teachers with nontraditional students.

This chapter will attempt to address the issue from my dual perspective of twelve years experience teaching in a four-year college where the median undergraduate age is 27, and from my background in teacher education where questions of the effectiveness of the teaching/learning process are always paramount. The suggestions I will make certainly are not foolproof, but they have served to make my own experience teaching nontraditional students one of the most rewarding aspects of my career in higher education.

THE MANY FACES OF NONTRADITIONAL STUDENTS

The first observation is that although much is made in the literature about the differences between traditional and nontraditional students, it is important to recognize the full spectrum that exists within the label "nontraditional." Adults turn/return to the college classroom for a plethora of reasons and each has its implications for effective instruction. A few examples will serve to make my point.

Some nontraditional students started college at the conventional age, dropped out for a variety of reasons, and have come back to complete a degree. Many of them are very bright, with a good sense of their own abilities. This group includes a high percentage of women who had full or partial academic scholarships when they attended college immediately after high school, but left college to marry. Also numbered here are those academically able individuals of both genders who were unable to complete college for financial reasons. On the other hand, there are returning college students who readily acknowledge that they were not motivated to learn when they first entered the ivied halls and are now quite embarrassed at their earlier record. Among both groups of returnees are those whose whole life-focus has changed since they were first enrolled and who now seek to meet completely different goals by earning a college degree, such as the former business major or pre-med student who now wants to be an elementary school teacher.

Another large group of nontraditional students have had no previous college experience, but here again there is as much diversity as similarity. Some are homemakers for whom college was not a real option when they graduated from high school. Others are unemployed workers whose confidence has been severely shaken by the loss of jobs and their inability to find other work with their current repertoire of skills. Some are individuals who simply would not have had a chance to attend college twenty years ago because of their skill level. Others are fairly successful business people who have not heretofore needed a college degree. Now, however, they find themselves on a professional plateau unable to advance further without additional academic credentials. This group is frequently characterized by several competing time commitments. Finally, at least for purposes of this listing, there are the single parents, especially mothers, who are vulnerable about many things, not the least of which is the new experience of attending college.

Of course, the categories described above frequently overlap, and any one classroom is likely to have representatives of several of these subgroups among its students.

The department chair is often in a position to foster awareness of these differences by occasionally including on the agenda of departmental meetings discussions of students' backgrounds and concomitant learning characteristics. Goal-setting and evaluation interviews with individual faculty members offer another opportunity to discuss the variety of students found in that particular professor's classes. A third possibility lies in the initial interviews that search committees, which frequently include department chairs, conduct with candidates for faculty positions. A discussion at that time with the potential new addition to the department's staff about his/her previous experience teaching nontraditional students can be particularly fruitful in determining the match between the candidate and the institution.

Acknowledging this variety is necessary, but not sufficient, for effectively teaching nontraditional students. Strategies must be developed that will allow professors to identify the diversity present in their own classroom and then continuously monitor how these differences are affecting the way students are relating to a given course's content and process. Department chairs can facilitate this process through informal conversations with individual faculty members, by circulating appropriate reading material throughout the department, and discussions with students. All of the above are ways that the chair in his/her leadership position makes clear the department's (and institution's) commitment to welcoming nontraditional students to the halls of academe.

What follows are some relatively painless and highly effective ways for faculty to identify and monitor the variety present among students in their own courses. They are general enough in nature that chairs can adapt them easily to the particular content of the course(s) taught by various members of the department as they meet with them individually or collectively.

FINDING OUT WHO'S IN THE CLASSROOM

It is frequently helpful to incorporate individual interviews into the course structure fairly early in the term (if numbers do not preclude this). Such interviews are generally more effective if they have a somewhat objective starting point directly related to the content of the course, for example, describing the history of one's own education in a History of American Education course or summarizing the main points of a particular chapter in the text used in a biology, mathematics or economics class, or identifying the most relevant concepts discussed thus far in a psychology, business or political science class, and so on. These initial conversations often reveal much about the students' personalities, but the at least semi-objective nature of the topic for the interviews helps reduce the pressure on students to reveal personal information. By scheduling such interviews early in the term, both students and professors have an opportunity to dispel stereotypes at the outset. In addition, the opportunity is provided for students to bring up concerns, questions, and so on, about the course or college in general, in a setting where the student did not have to exercise initiative to make a contact. While student initiative is certainly to be encouraged, for some nontraditional students this requires a fair amount of courage because of their lack of self-confidence—instructors can meet a real need by providing a structure for at least initial communication.

If the class is too large for such individual interviews, it is still possible to achieve some of the same purposes by asking students to fill out a worksheet (e.g., summarizing the main points of a chapter). The more personal dimension of the interview format can then be approximated by including on the sheet follow-up questions such as "What was the most difficult aspect of this chapter for you?" "So far, has this class been what you had expected?" "What's been the most surprising aspect of taking college classes for you?" "What advice would you give me about teaching nontraditional students?" These worksheets can be collected and read for both general insight into nontraditional students as well as specific information that will enable an instructor to meet the needs of a particular nontraditional student more effectively.

To monitor how students are processing their experience in the classroom regularly, consider reserving the last three minutes of class for what a colleague calls "compulsive writing." He asks his students to put pen to paper and to write continuously, without referring to their notes, about what they remember from that class period. They can also indicate areas of uncertainty, ask questions, make suggestions, and so on. He finds that this exercise, which is standard for him in every class session, not only provides feedback on content, but offers students an immediate vehicle for expressing frustration or exhilaration. These student comments can be quickly scanned, even in large classes, and adjustments can be made where necessary in the next meeting's lecture, or personal contact can be made with an individual student.

Although the preceding written communications are not evaluated for students' writing skills, such an assessment is important early in any course. The variety of nontraditional students described at the beginning of this article can span a wide range of writing abilities and instructors need some knowledge of this range at the start of the semester. This can easily be accomplished by giving two writing assignments early in the term. One should be a typical homework assignment requiring those research, interpretive, or problem solving skills that the individual professor considers to be entry level and essential for successful completion of the course. Establishing a minimum competency level for each student with regard to writing skills alerts the instructor to possible problems early enough in the term for the student to receive remedial assistance. (Happily, there is some evidence to suggest that adult students see such skill deficiencies as a challenge, an obstacle to overcome, rather than a discouraging indictment.[1]) Receiving a graded assignment back within the first few meetings of the course also gives students feedback on how an instructor's oral description of his/her grading procedure applies to their specific efforts. Such direct feedback often allays nontraditional students' anxieties about the worth of their work.

In addition to this initial somewhat formal assignment, it is often helpful to plan an early in-class writing task. This on-the-spot assignment allows an instructor to contrast students' native abilities with the level of work they are able to produce with the assistance of additional time, a dictionary or thesaurus, and perhaps a tutor or typist. Such an assessment permits some judgments about the amount of effort required of individual students to produce the more formal homework assignments. This information often provides important insights for both instructor and students regarding the level of extra effort needed to achieve an acceptable level of performance spontaneously.

ENCOURAGING CONVERSATION IN THE CLASSROOM

Feedback of any kind is helpful in relieving the anxiety associated with a new and unfamiliar experience. Sometimes this anxiety is expressed in nontraditional students' reluctance to participate in class discussions, particularly when the group is large. A general rule of thumb is that if the silence barrier can be broken (i.e., if students can hear the sound of their own voices) within the first ten minutes of any class session, the chances that they will contribute to succeeding discussions are greatly increased. The longer an individual or group of students is in a classroom setting without speaking, the less likely it is that they will participate. An efficient and effective way to overcome the tendency of anxiety to produce passivity is to structure a brief interaction exercise at the beginning of each class period. The strategy can be as simple as asking students to turn to the individual on their right and ask him or her which concept, problem, or passage in the chapter to be covered during that class period was the most difficult, or to indicate one question each has about the material assigned, or to ask both to predict what they will learn as the result of the upcoming class session. A multitude of such questions can be generated. Eventually students even ask to provide a question for a particular day! The actual question is not as important as the fact that it be answerable by everyone and that everyone has a chance to answer it in a nonthreatening framework. Paired conversations are especially efficient in this regard.

Sometimes the challenge with non/traditional students is not class participation, but one's own reaction when they do participate. Many nontraditional students are quite confident in the classroom because of their wealth of experience outside of it. Consequently, they may not hesitate to challenge instructors on either specific points or on the general usefulness or relevance of the material being presented or assignment being made. If professors can resist the impulse to become defensive, there is an opportunity in such situations to model for the class as a whole what it means to receive and seriously consider a challenging question. Such an ability is one of the characteristics of a well-educated person, a demonstration of which will probably serve both nontraditional and traditional students far better than any specific content they might receive in a particular class.

EXTENDING THE CHALLENGE: THE MIXED-AGE CLASSROOM

While the above is an example of those aspects of college teaching that are critical regardless of the age of the students, there are some definite and well-documented differences between nontraditional and traditional students. Some of these differences are simply a function of age. Knox, for example, has described the developmental tasks associated with the various stages of an individual's life and their implications for the college classroom.[2] Thus, in the traditional college years (late teens and early twenties), individuals are often concerned with "achieving emotional independence, developing an ethical system, preparing for marriage and family life, and choosing and preparing for an occupation."[3] These concerns are translated into an interest in personal development, career preparation, human relations, and so on. Older students have different foci. In early adulthood (the twenties and thirties) their emphasis is on establishing themselves as citizens, entering the work force, and beginning a family. Thus their educational goals frequently revolve around occupational advancement and specialization, marriage and parenting, and the practical aspects of managing home and civic life. With middle age, concerns shift to second careers, redefining family relationships, and so on. This results in interests in career advancement and transition, stress managements, and values.

Wolfgang and Dowling found that, in general, older students tend to be more motivated by cognitive interest (seeking knowledge for its own sake) than their younger counterparts. Traditional students, on the other hand, acknowledge social relationships (make friends) and external expectations (carrying out the recommendation of some authority) as stronger motivators than adult students.[4] Roelfs, in analyzing the differences between younger and older community college students, found that the latter are "more likely to know what they want out of college, to be challenged rather than bored with their classes, to feel self-confident about their ability to keep up with their studies and to understand what is being taught, to spend more time studying, and to express satisfaction with their classes and their instructors."[5]

Knowles has summarized and synthesized these differences in his concept of andragogy. Although he originally contrasted andragogy ("the art and science of helping adults learn") with pedagogy ("helping children learn"), he later stressed a continuum between the two approaches. To the extent that shifts in learning are gradual and continuous rather than dichotomous, his comparison of the two approaches is useful for highlighting some of the differences between teaching traditional and nontraditional students. Thus he describes the adult learner as increasingly self-directed, problem centered, and interested in learning in a mutually respectful, collaborative and informal climate, in contrast to younger learners who are more dependent (in terms of self-concept), subject centered, and accustomed to at least a somewhat authority-oriented, formal and competitive learning environment.[6]

These differences are certainly cause for concern and accommodation with regard to teaching style when an instructor is faced with an entire class of nontraditional students. However, the situation is further, and interestingly, complicated when both nontraditional and traditional students enroll in the same course. Here again the department chair is in a position to be of assistance by both formally and informally drawing to the attention of faculty the importance of attending to whom, as well as what, they are teaching. Incorporating some of the strategies described below in their own classes (if theirs is both a teaching and an administrative appointment) is a powerful way for chairs to demonstrate their convictions in this regard. Such action also enhances a chair's credibility when he/she offers suggestions to staff members.

A case certainly can be made that many other practices described previously (e.g., the initial interview or the compulsive end-of-session writing) would still benefit both instructor and students in a heterogeneous class. However, a mixed-age class presents its own unique challenge precisely because of the wide range of lived experience presented by the students.

Here, as with nontraditional students, the key is one's attitude toward differences. In a successful mixed-age learning environment, both instructor and students (of all ages) must believe that differences are gifts to be cherished rather than deficits to be corrected. And, of course, the truth is that both groups of students do have something powerful to give to the other. Nontraditional students are living proof to their 18- to 22-year-old counterparts that there is life beyond compulsory education, that there are real-world reasons for wanting an education so badly that one would juggle other commitments, make financial sacrifices, and give up some of the much vaunted adult independence to return to school voluntarily. Traditional students, on the other hand, remind their older peers of what it is like to think one can change the world single-handedly. And it is critical that this memory be reactivated in sometimes shopworn taxpayers who have gotten a bit cynical with age. While stars in one's eyes can sometimes stand in the way of realistic progress, they can also provide the incentive that keeps an individual dissatisfied with the status quo.

DISCOURAGING STEREOTYPING

To capitalize on this sense of "gifts differing," it is critical that stereotypes not develop on the part of either nontraditional or traditional students regarding the abilities, life styles, or interests of the other group. Central to this task are strategies that insure that members of the two groups view one another as individuals, not as members of the "other" group. Fortunately, such strategies are abundant and easily incorporated into most courses, regardless of size or content.

For example, the paired student conversations described earlier as a way to break the silence barrier in a classroom can easily be adapted to this new purpose by pairing traditional and nontraditional students with one another. This may take a bit of direction on the instructor's part, since students with similar backgrounds tend to sit next to one another. Thus a simple charge to turn to one's neighbor on the right often will not suffice. Rather, the instructor may need to notice the geography of the classroom and direct those students on the left side of the room to pair with those on the right. Or it may be worth the few minutes it would take to prepare a list of partners beforehand. This is particularly effective in defusing any tendencies toward stereotyping the instructor may already have noticed. Another approach is simply to direct the students to avoid pairing with those of approximately the same age and/or background. A variation of this technique is to direct students to pair with the individual in the classroom they feel is least like themselves. Of course, alternating between these various approaches is most effective as it reduces the element of predictability and ensures that students will each meet a cross-section of the minds in the room.

Admittedly, an exercise like this takes time, although usually not more than five minutes per class session. And granted, this is five minutes then unavailable for the presentation of new material. However, the benefits such techniques reap in student involvement and active engagement with the course content would alone be sufficient to recommend the practice, even if there were not the added advantage of involving a disparate group of students in establishing a learning community. Once there is evidence of such cohesion, it is not necessary to include such an activity in the lesson plan for every class session. Generally after about four weeks of concerted effort, a dynamic will have taken hold in most groups that will allow less direct attention to be paid to the group-building process.

A logical consequence of this attention to pairing traditional with nontraditional students for these initial conversations would, of course, be to monitor student groupings for laboratory partners, small group discussions, group projects, and so on. Again, given the tendency of "birds of a feather . . ." it may be advantageous for the instructor to exert some leadership in these situations.

Leadership may also need to be exercised in whole class conversations to avoid letting patterns of communication develop based on assumptions held by one group about the other (e.g., that the nontraditional students are "all-wise" because of their experience, or that the traditional students are "smarter" because of the recency of their exposure to related course content in secondary school). Such limiting assumptions may, of course, be held by either group about themselves or the other group. Thus, it may occasionally be necessary to take a nontraditional student aside after class and indicate directly to that individual that comments like "Wait until you've been out in the real world" or "When you've lived/worked as long as I have . . ." are generally not helpful for furthering the learning or understanding of students. On the other hand, the 18- to 22-year-old students sometimes need to be admonished gently (occasionally even within a class session) that characterizing the nontraditional students as "old" (as in "When I'm old like you . . .") is also not productive and the cause of some pain. The key here again is sensitivity, sensitivity to differences as gifts to be cherished, not deficits to be corrected.

MEETING DIVERSE NEEDS THROUGH CLASS ASSIGNMENTS

This sensitivity can also be reflected in the type and structure of assignments given in a course. By attending to variety between and within assignments, it is possible to capitalize on the strengths of both traditional and nontraditional students enrolled in the same class. This can be done by incorporating a combination of theoretical, reflective, practical, and applied components in both assignments and examinations. A theoretical section in which students might be asked to compare and contrast two theories or several literary passages provides the opportunity for those with a more analytical frame of mind (and perhaps the time available to engage in analysis) to excel. A reflective assignment or question might ask students to speculate on the possible outcome of a hypothetical science experiment or the potential influence of a contemporary event on a previous historical period. This type of question does not ask students to regurgitate specific facts but rather to use facts in an imaginative way.

A practical approach asks students to draw on previous experience in solving a problem, for example, reacting to scenarios in a psychology class or discussing the relevance of a particular philosophical concept for the student's life. This approach is often a positive experience for nontraditional students, affirming as it does their out-of-school lives. Even just a question or two from this perspective on an exam or one or two homework assignments from this point of view during the term can do much to validate a nontraditional student's sense of belonging in the college classroom. Related to this practical approach is the applied emphasis. In such an assignment or question students may be asked to take the theoretical concepts presented in class and apply them to a new practical situation, such as a case study in business or original art work. This hands-on approach capitalizes on the strengths nontraditional students often have in translating what they learn in and outside of the classroom into concrete expression.

While it may appear that the applied and practical approaches best serve the needs of nontraditional students, it is important in a heterogeneous class to give traditional students an equal chance at success by including questions or assignments that do not rely on a great deal of lived experience for obtaining an acceptable grade. In addition, even if a class were completely filled with nontraditional students, it would be a mistake to ask students to respond only from perspective that is easiest for them. Granted, it is important to start where students are (from a position of strength), but it is equally important not to stop where students are (to let them be satisfied with where they currently are). Stretching to meet a not easily attainable goal is often one of the most satisfying aspects of learning. The required creativity to do a variety of assignments and examinations is one way to afford every student the opportunity to stretch. In addition, if there is an opportunity for students to compare notes on assignments (perhaps via the initial paired conversation described earlier), they become aware of the variation in degree of difficulty they and their classmates experience with respect to particular approaches to thinking and learning, and develop a healthy respect for the gifts of others.

Of course, one of the interesting by-products of these conversations is that students of, whatever age, often find that more unites them than divides them. A colleague of mine demonstrates this to students quite graphically early in the term by having each one write three worries he/she has about the course in particular, or college in general. In the class discussion ensuing both traditional and nontraditional students find that they share a common concern for understanding course content, time management, financial problems, finding employment, and so on. This discovery does much to meld the group into a cohesive unit whose common purpose, whatever their age, is to "live and learn."

LEARNING: THE COMMON GOAL

Focusing on this common purpose, regardless of the composition of the student body in any particular classroom, is one of the best ways I know to take what is a fact of life on most college campuses, the presence of nontraditional students, and change it from a burden to a challenge. This chapter has described only a few of the ways in which department and division chairs can facilitate this shift in attitude. Because chairs exercise their leadership at the level closest to the individual classroom, they may be one of the most critical factors in the kind of welcome received by nontraditional students in American colleges.

NOTES

1. John H. Clarke, "Adults in the College Setting: Deciding to Develop Skills." *Adult Education* (Winter 1980): 92–100.
2. Alan B. Knox, *Helping Adults Learn.* San Francisco: Jossey-Bass, 1986, 27–28.
3. *Ibid.*
4. Mary E. Wolfgang and William D. Dowling, "Differences in Motivation of Adult and Younger Undergraduates." *Journal of Higher Education* (November/December 1981): 640–48.
5. P. J. Roelfs, "Teaching and Counseling Older College Students." *Findings* (1975: 2 (1)), in K. Patricia Cross, *Adults As Learners.* San Francisco: Jossey-Bass, 1981, 70.
6. Malcom Knowles, *The Adult Learner: A Neglected Species.* Houston: Gulf Publishing, 1978, 110.

15

CHAIRS AS FACILITATORS OF SCHOLARLY WRITING

ROBERT BOICE

As a rule, departmental chairs play an inactive part in facilitating scholarly writing. They may admonish and reward; but only rarely, in my observations, do chairs actually make changes that promote productivity and success in publishing.

Chairs' detachment from scholarly writing does not seem to derive from a disinterest in writing. My surveys of chairs indicate a keen awareness that writing brings greater rewards and more status than any other professional activity. Chairs also agonize over faculty whose lack of scholarly productivity brings rejection in the retention, promotion, tenure processes.

Chairs may assume the role with an expectation that one of the sacrifices they make is a reduction in writing. And many chairs expect faculty to acquire similar adaptive habits of scholarship just as they did—on their own, and by trial and error.

Arguably, the system works. Faculty with the right stuff survive and succeed, but the result brings distress to the majority, the eighty percent of us who publish little or nothing, and the majority of us who feel unfulfilled as professionals.[1] The old habits will be even more inappropriate for an academy where new faculty are increasingly more difficult to recruit.

The recent infusion of new faculty accompanies new and/or increased demands for publication. If new faculty are to flourish, chairs may need to build or remodel department cultures, especially where senior faculty tend to be unproductive as scholars and have a negative attitude toward scholarship. In department cultures where faculty rarely discuss scholarship in positive, sharing ways, new faculty are more likely to be coached on political intrigue than on productivity.[2]

There may be another reason for chairs to take a more active role in promoting scholarly writing. Chairs who are too busy for scholarship tend to apologize for having given up personal interests and professional respectability in the name of altruistic service. So the best reason for a more active role may be the most selfish. Chairs who remain active in publishing report the highest levels of satisfaction with chairing and acceptance by faculty.

This chapter outlines practical means by which chairs can facilitate writing. None of the strategies is original. What novelty there is lies in providing chairs with methods for initiating and maintaining writing programs and in selecting program components on the basis of empirical tests.

STRATEGIES FOR FACILITATING SCHOLARLY WRITING

Instituting Regular Discussion Groups

This strategy is the most familiar and easiest to manage of the approaches presented here. Still, its use is not widespread. In one sampling of 100 social science departments, I found fewer than 25 percent of doctoral programs and fewer than 8 percent of master's level programs where such groups met at least once a semester.

I also found indications, especially in more direct observations and follow-ups, that effectiveness varies dramatically among discussion groups. Groups rated as beneficial by faculty were more likely to show the following components, ranked in order of apparent importance:

1. Group generates and shares writing ideas.
2. Group meets at least once a month.
3. Group shares practical knowledge about finishing and publishing scholarly work.
4. Group builds cultural acceptance and support for scholarly writing.

Curiously, these faculty reports about their discussion groups did not correlate well with actual increases in pages written and articles accepted by refereed journals. The factors that did relate more substantially to improved productivity were:

1. Group expects each member to bring samples of ongoing writing projects to meetings and to share those samples with colleagues.
2. Group openly discusses maladaptive notions about writing (e.g., it is best done in binges).
3. Group regularly includes department chair.
4. Group helps arrange collaborative writing.

Getting a Few Faculty to Model Ideal Writing Habits

Chairs can, in my experience, increase the power of modeling scholarly activity themselves by enlisting one or a few willing colleagues to join them in regular regimens of writing and in open discussion of that experience with colleagues. Extensive testing shows that a single regimen of writing, in brief (30–60 minute) and daily sessions, produces the most output in the long run. It improves productivity for already active writers, most of whom write in binges:[3]

Outcome Measure	Binge Writing	Brief, Daily Writing (next 3 months)
X pp. written and/or re-written per week	2.0	12.3

Brief, daily sessions are also more likely to work with currently unproductive faculty, particularly those who suppose themselves too busy for writing.

Making Brief, Casual Visits to Faculty Offices

In my experience, many chairs acquire a habit that helps maintain inactive roles vis-à-vis scholarship; they prefer to leave their office doors open for substantial parts of each work day, holding nearly unlimited audience for faculty and students. While this tradition demonstrates admirable accessibility and patience, it may undermine some aspects of departmental functioning. It surely helps constrain the scholarship of chairs. It apparently encourages selectivity about who interacts with chairs (e.g., by encouraging the isolation of more asocial faculty) and what happens in interactions (e.g., by encouraging content consisting largely of complaints and requests). And it rarely helps model or reinforce scholarly writing among faculty.

I encourage chairs to make brief (10–15 minute), biweekly visits to faculty. These interactions not only foster improved communication between faculty and chairs, but they also help enlist faculty, especially isolates, to participate more fully in departmental activities and goals. When one of those activities is scholarly writing, regular visits by a chairperson make a dramatic difference in faculty writing output:

Long-Term Productivity and Satisfaction of Twenty-Four Faculty with and without Field Contacts after Agreeing to Write Regularly

	Writing Productivity (written pgs. per wk)		Self-Satisfaction (10 points max.) with writing	
	1 mon.	*2 yr.*	*1 mon.*	*2 yr.*
With field contacts	10.2	7.1	7.8	7.9
Without field contacts	6.5	1.5	7.8	6.1

Holding Workshops on Better Writing Habits

Chairs, more than any other people on campus, can influence the adoption of good writing habits.[4] They can do this by leading or collaborating in workshops that promote better writing habits. The examples that follow require no special expertise; all of the components have proven successful on several campuses with a variety of chairs as presenters or co-presenters.

Step 1. Demystification of the writing process. This workshop proceeds around discussion of a handout like the one abstracted here:

Common Misconceptions About Writing

1. Writing is inherently difficult. In fact, good writing is not much more difficult than collegial conversation. Both writing and conversation carry the risk of being criticized; and both, when not practiced, carry the potential that faculty will be isolated and unheard.

2. Good writing must be original. In fact, little, if any, of what we think or write is truly original. Much of what we cherish bears repeating, especially in new perspectives.

3. Good writing must be perfect. This is no more true for writing than for social conversation. Successful authors are more likely to realize that perfect manuscripts are unattainable, perhaps even undesirable.

4. Good writing must be spontaneous, and good writers await inspiration before beginning. In fact, writers work best by beginning before they feel completely ready. Writers who await inspiration court writer's block.

5. Good writing proceeds quickly. The same writers who procrastinate often believe that writing, once under way, should occur effortlessly and that manuscripts should be finished in one or a few marathon sessions.

6. Writing is done best in binges. Many writers believe that writing requires large blocks of undisrupted time—at least whole mornings, better yet, whole days, whole vacations, whole sabbaticals, or retirement.

Step 2. Helping writers get started. This workshop helps faculty find efficient ways of generating momentum and ideas for writing. It consists of acquainting participants with a simple technique known as free writing. The workshop begins with a minimum of discussion. Participants are asked to move quickly into the task described in the instructions at the top of an otherwise blank sheet.[5]

Generating Writing Sheet

Pause just long enough to recall an experience from your school years that helped or hindered your writing. Then, before you have had a chance to think it all out, begin writing spontaneously. Stick to the story, but do not stop for anything. Go quickly without rushing. Do not struggle over form or correctness. Just get something down. Keep it up for ten minutes.

Faculty, in my experience, may look a bit surprised, but even the most blocked among them join the group in writing. The experience becomes even more curious as the group proceeds. Everyone writes furiously—most will write at least a page. This result is a useful demonstration for faculty who believe that writing requires substantial warm-up time and pre-planning. When they are asked to stop, many faculty show disgruntlement; they dislike stopping once they are on a roll.

Their reluctance to stop points out a reason why many faculty write in binges. Writers may fear that they will never again find momentum and/or ideas for writing.

The final surprise comes when writers read their writing aloud. Not only is the quantity remarkable, given the brief investment in time, but so is the quality. When they abandon their self-consciousness, many faculty produce admirably simple, direct, and readable sentences.

Step 3. Helping writers establish discipline. Establishing momentum and generating useful material is relatively easy. The more difficult step is to write regularly, to the point of completing and submitting manuscripts. This workshop consists largely of sharing information about ways of establishing a regimen. As I typically conduct it, the workshop focuses on a handout like the one abstracted here:

An Outline of Control Principles for Writing

1. Establish one or a few regular places for writing, places where you do nothing but write. Make writing sites sacred by removing temptations (such as magazines) for not writing.

2. Limit social interruptions during writing session by: closing your office door, posting a writing schedule, unplugging your phone, and enlisting others to help you observe your schedule.

3. Find another writer to join you for quiet periods of writing, preferably in surroundings with few distractions, such as the library.

4. Make more valued activities (e.g., newspaper reading) contingent on writing first for a minimum period of time. Write while you are fresh (in the morning, if possible), in brief and regular daily sessions.

5. Plan to work on specific finishable units of writing in each session. Plan beyond daily goals, scheduling stages of manuscript completion over weeks.

6. Share your writing in its most formative stages, while constructive critics can still offer advice that you can use.

7. Write in brief, daily sessions whether or not you feel ready.

Step 4. Arranging workshops around local talent. On campuses where programs like the one described above are put into action, the inspiration typically continues in other, related workshops. One consists of assembling successful publishers for advice about publishing. Another involves discussing published advice on ways of coping with editorial systems.[6]

Helping Arrange Mentoring and Collaboration

This strategy follows from those just discussed. Faculty who discuss writing problems and writing ideas in workshops often collaborate. As a rule, faculty with complementary needs seek each other out. One person may have a great deal of unanalyzed data and another may like analyzing data. Or one may have a surfeit of ideas and another may feel that he or she has none. Chairs can play a particularly valuable role in fostering these interactions by asking faculty to suggest possibilities for collaboration and then encouraging faculty to follow through on them. Even where needs and benefits are obvious, faculty may require prodding to become more sociable about writing.

Becoming an Active Model for Good Writing Habits

Many chairs with whom I have worked, even those who planned to implement the strategies described above, have resisted doing so. Whatever else, they assure me, chairs are too busy to manage much writing themselves.

Once involved in helping promote the writing of others, however, chairs invariably discover that the individual who benefits most is the facilitator. For a variety of reasons, the act of teaching strategies for generating ideas, productivity, and cooperation in writing leads to practicing what is taught. In an earlier article in *The Department Advisor*, I presented an example of data showing the gains, including scholarly productivity, made by chairs who had taken an active role in facilitating faculty changes.[7]

Chairs who become beneficiaries of such systems also help build other circular benefits, most notably in modeling good habits of scholarship for faculty. A recent study of new faculty at a regional university demonstrated the power of chairs as models.[8] Chairs who demonstrated increased levels of scholarship and collegiality were linked to the new faculty who were writing at rates sufficient for eventual promoting. In contrast, where chairs claimed to be too busy for scholarship, most of their new faculty were quick to adopt similar excuses.

Preparing for Resistance and Frustration

Despite the accounts of success already mentioned, such ventures are nonetheless difficult. In my experience, chairs who undertake the project with realistic expectations of resistance and frustration fare better.

The topic of writing, especially of being remiss in getting published, generates defensiveness among faculty. This resistance exceeds the usual excuses for not writing such as being too busy. Discussion of writing often elicits a variety of comments that can undermine the efforts of colleagues and chairs. The list that follows orders by rank, the frequency of comments made by faculty in my many years of doing workshops:

1. Negativism expressed about writing and publishing (e.g., "Most of what gets published is crap, so why should I add to that pile?")
2. Beliefs that scholarship grows at the expense of good teaching
3. Statements about writing being beyond the scope of one's responsibilities (e.g., "When I was hired, writing wasn't required;

I'm just doing what I was hired to do and that doesn't include writing")

4. Self-doubt expressed about writing (e.g., "I have nothing significant to say," or "I'm afraid that if I try to publish, people will discover I'm a fraud.")

5. Participants who engage in excessive display of confidence (i.e., some workshop participants who already publish offer comments that make nonproductive participants feel even more insecure or unprepared)

Each of these forms of resistance can be handled with positive responses. At least the first four contain elements of truth. These "yes-but" objections to presentations are less frustrating when the leader finds cheerful ways to agree with some aspect of the criticism. At the least the leader can begin by saying, "I can see how you might feel that way. Including other workshop participants in the discussion also helps.

In essence, advice about dealing with resistance confirms what we already know about faculty: they like to scrutinize reasons for doing things, especially things valued by administrators; they want their objections to be heard, no matter now unoriginal; and they need to be presented with ideas for scholarly productivity in ways that encourage them to adopt or reject them as they see fit. Several chairs have told me that learning to interact with faculty over the pressure to publish is excellent training for exercising leadership on less sensitive issues.

NOTES

1. Robert Boice and F. Joines, "Why Academicians Don't Write." *Journal of Higher Education* 55 (1984): 567–582.
2. Jim L. Turner and Robert Boice, "Starting at the Beginning: The Concerns and Needs of New Faculty." *To Improve the Academy* 6 (1987): 41–55.
3. Robert Boice and Patricia E. Myers, "Stresses and Satisfactions of Chairing in Psychology." *Professional Psychology: Research and Practice* 3 (1986): 200–204.
4. G. A. Kimble, *A Departmental Chairperson's Survival Manual.* New York: Wiley, 1979.
5. Robert Boice, *Professors as Writers.* Stillwater, OK: New Forms Press, 1989.
6. S. Scarr, "An Editor Looks for the Perfect Manuscript," in *Understanding the Manuscript Review Process: Increasing the Participation of Women,* D. Loeffler ed. Washington, DC: American Psychological Association, 1982.
7. Robert Boice, "Coping with Difficult Colleagues." *The Department Advisor* (Spring 1987).
8. Turner and Boice, "Concerns and Needs," 41–55.

16

COPING WITH DIFFICULT COLLEAGUES

ROBERT BOICE

Working with chairpeople, as I have done for the past decade, produces inevitable reflections about why being a chair is so difficult. At first hearing, too little time and too much paper work seem like leading candidates. Later, when chairs get past concerns about admitting possible failures, emphasis turns to fellow faculty members. Difficult colleagues, far more than busyness or bureaucracies, produce sleepless nights.

I confirmed that impression in a national, anonymous survey of chairpeople.[1] All four of their most highly rated stressors involved faculty: "faculty misbehaviors" (e.g., loud arguments at faculty meetings, refusal to cooperate) ranked just above "giving faculty evaluative feedback," "dealing with faculty complaints," and "faculty politics."

That validation of what chairs already suspected led to other inquiries. What characteristics cause chairs to label faculty difficult? How should chairs cope with difficult faculty?

THE NATURE OF DIFFICULT FACULTY: THE CHAIRS' VIEW

The first question, about experiences with difficult faculty, raises the same issues as those about difficult students. Difficult colleagues (or difficult students) are so rarely discussed with peers that chairs (or teachers) may see their own experiences as unique. Moreover, much like victims of terrorism, chairs (or teachers) afflicted with especially disruptive and intimidating colleagues (or students) may blame themselves. So sharing information about difficult colleagues helps alleviate guilt and prepare chairs for coping strategies.

Once again surveys provide a starting place for analyzing experiences. In one series of surveys where I had already established rapport with chairs, I asked for open-ended recollections about colleagues who were chronic sources of stress and/or disruptive to the department. Two kinds of descriptions emerged. The strongest, most detailed descriptions recalled one or a few especially angry, almost intimidating colleagues who, like "classroom terrorists," sometimes ruined the mood of departmental meetings and other interactions. Other descriptions recalled colleagues seen as difficult but not impossible. The single most frequent descriptor for this group was "deadwood."

In one series of surveys with chairs already in my developmental programs, categories generated in earlier work were used to provide more quantitative information.[2] Thirty-two chairs from a research / doctoral university and twenty-eight chairs from a regional university made the following estimates about their own departmental faculty:

	Estimates of post-Ph.D. faculty	
	less than 12 years	more than 12 years
inactive as scholars	42%	71%
shirk responsibilities re: committees and advising	32%	49%
socially isolated from colleagues	16%	34%
frequent source of student complaints	16%	22%
explosive with students and colleagues	11%	22%
regularly unfriendly toward chair	5%	24%
actively paranoid	5%	12%

Some aspects of this survey on difficult faculty confirm the obvious. Faculty described as deadwood tend to be social isolates and inactive scholars, and older faculty are more likely to be seen as problematic. But other results surprised respondents. They did not expect the phenomenon of explosive, unfriendly faculty to occur much beyond their own departments. And they began to wonder, when they saw how extensive the problems raised by deadwood faculty were, what could be done to help.

THE NATURE OF DIFFICULT FACULTY: MY VIEW

I collected two final pieces of information about difficult colleagues before applying intervention strategies with chairs. In one survey, I suggested chairs ask "difficult" faculty what had contributed to their sense of disillusionment and helplessness. The strongest replies were about perceived unfairness and bias in reward procedures, about colleagues rewarded for self-promotion rather than teaching or research, and about vague and untrustworthy administrators.

In the other survey, I compared academicians with a matched and stratified sample of peers who had left academe for applied work.[3] The nonacademics reported being significantly healthier and happier, more than anything else because they were not regularly bothered by the feeling that they had not done enough. Academic life seems to undermine the contentment and cooperativeness of faculty (especially inactive scholars) who rarely leave the office without a sense that more scholar-ship and more writing should be done.

LOOKING FOR COPING STRATEGIES

I relied on other faculty developers, colleagues who had worked on similar problems, for actual strategies. The value of this source of infor-mation can be seen in two prior issues of *The Department Advisor*.

Bennett condenses his experience in working with chairs into the following advice: (1) dealing with negativity is both essential to survival and time-consuming; (2) interacting with faculty on issues such as eval-uations can disrupt friendship and personal well-being; (3) trying to isolate other responsibilities of chairing from assisting the growth of colleagues is fruitless; (4) growth contracts help facilitate individual re-sponsibility and initiative; and (5) evaluations properly done help pre-vent problems, help identify problems not prevented, and help reduce the dysphoria of chairing.[4]

Eble makes related observations: (1) chairpeople are ideally suited to facilitate faculty growth and professional improvement; (2) chairs can help by bringing faculty together for exchange of ideas and practices, by creating a stimulating environment and common purpose, and by pro-viding tangible recognition of mutually desired behaviors; (3) chairs can help by breaking into the patterns of defeat that help make and maintain difficult faculty; and (4) chairs can help by learning to be tough with faculty who purposefully drift or shirk responsibility.[5]

The following scheme for coping with difficult colleagues provides additional specification and validation of these strategies.

A SCHEME FOR COPING

Step 1: Casual Visits to Faculty's Offices

Few chairpeople (less than 11 percent in my own observations of chairs in graduate departments across the country) make a regular practice of visiting their faculty's offices. Fewer still regularly visit *all* their faculty's offices.

This is based on the belief passed from chair to chair that the essence of good chairing is remaining in one's office with the door open. One reason for this style is the concern about academic freedom; that is, actively seeking out and admonishing faculty might be seen as Machi-avellian in approach. Eble has an excellent response to such reserva-tions: "I recognize the dangers of either tender- or tough-minded meddling. But I have seen too much of leaving well enough alone in which 'well enough' is defined by chairpersons as that which best suits their disinclination to exert themselves very strenuously."[6]

Once I have helped convince chairs that their reservations may not be adaptive, I advise them to try this incremental approach:

1. Establish the habit of visiting the offices of *all* departmental faculty, at least once a semester.
2. Make the visits brief (e.g., 5–10 minutes). Always begin with small talk. Show faculty that not all of your interactions need to be directed at business.
3. Avoid the temptation to make guilt-inducing statements (e.g., pointing out the individual's obvious lack of professionalism in not attending faculty meetings during the past three years). Avoid the temptation to respond in kind to faculty's guilt-inducing statements.
4. Try to induce changes in faculty behavior by asking faculty to help you. So, for example, someone who no longer says hello, even in response to your friendly greetings, can be told this: "While the ritual of saying hello may be unimportant to you, I'd feel better if you indulged my silly need by responding to my greetings." Similarly, a request for attendance at faculty meetings can be based on your need to worry less about a colleague.

   While faculty see the transparent motives in these visits and requests, they almost always go along with the process. Despite impressions to the contrary, difficult colleagues may not know face-saving ways of overcoming the inertia of isolation and unfriendliness. And they usually appreciate the unaccustomed role of being asked for help and advice, once requests for help assume more substantial dimensions.
5. Think of the programmatic visits as a research project; the prospect of visiting difficult, sometimes intimidating, colleagues as a somewhat detached observer and data collector helps make the process more tolerable.

   Chairs with whom I have worked typically chart various events over periods of many weeks. Complaints per visit and obvious displays of anger or anxiety typically decrease in frequency; initiation by the faculty member of small talk, of scholarly interests and teaching, of inquiries about the chair typically increase in frequency.
6. Be prepared, especially with difficult faculty, to agree to some extent with the content of their complaints and criticisms. At the least, chairs can agree that they understand the colleague's perspective, and display willingness to listen. By trying to agree, understand, and ask for clarification, the chair tends to remain calmer (and so, too, the colleague).
7. Rehearse scenarios for establishing contacts in advance. Things worth practicing include avoidance of guilt-inducing statements, listening skills, and placing clear limits on the amount of hostility to be tolerated.

In my experience most faculty who resort to overt hostility either feel that they will not be taken seriously if they remain calm, or that they will lose control once frustration sets in. Chairs faced with such outbursts can help themselves and difficult colleagues by doing a few, simple things. Plan a calm refusal to continue an unpleasant interaction (e.g., say, "I have a rule about putting off conversations that make me tense—for at least a day. That way I can calm down and think clearly!") Let the faculty member know that some things (e.g., agitated calls to the chair's home late in the evening) are unacceptable, and not open to discussion or explanation. Then follow up with more meetings in which a clear expectation of calm interchanges is communicated. Unlikely as it seems, many difficult colleagues welcome limit-setting because it helps them exercise self-control.

Step 2: Finding Meaningful Activities

Once rapport and trust are established, difficult faculty typically make an interesting disclosure. They admit disliking their reputations as unproductive or as undermining to colleagues. Difficult colleagues usually report general anxiety and discomfort about coming to their offices or facing colleagues. And, above all, they express apprehension about becoming overly emotional during interactions or meetings.

With this new information, the chair can take the initiative in arranging responsibilities for difficult faculty. Typical outcomes include enlistment of colleagues as instructors of workshops for staff members, as coordinators of undergraduate advising, and as coordinators of off-campus internships for students.

In my experience, many chairs doubt that difficult colleagues can be trusted with such responsibilities. Conversely, difficult colleagues doubt that they will be asked to do anything worthwhile. The result of traditional standoffs is maintenance of tension and the waste of potential, including careers. I have found that the mere act of communicating with formerly isolated colleagues generates a surprising array of possibilities.

Step 3: Renegotiating for Meaningful Incentives

While steps one and two work, they lack the external incentives that favored colleagues have been getting all along. Without realistic prospects of earning some of the same rewards, difficult colleagues eventually begin to feel that they will never receive equitable treatment.

One difficulty in making rewards just is that most campuses rarely make reward processes specific, objective, and public. The usual process resembles Social Darwinism; survivors have the "right stuff," while failures do not. The code of survival is not a polite subject for discussion. The result of an unwritten code is suspiciousness that standards change capriciously and that success may depend primarily on political skill.

A second set of difficulties in democratizing the academic reward process follows from the first. Administrators expect that difficult colleagues cannot change, that enough rewards will not be available if most faculty are eligible, and that difficult colleagues will try to distort a system that offers them access to rewards. Difficult faculty, similarly, doubt that administrators who make growth contracts with them will keep their promises.[7]

Despite this mutual suspicion, such programs can work nicely, given a few precautions:

1. The growth contracts should begin with steps 1 and 2, where difficult faculty are communicating real needs, plans, trust, and reengagement in responsible activities.

2. These programs should be initiated, as tentative proposals, by faculty who indicate a plan of professional growth (e.g., coteaching, collaborating in scholarly writing) and expected rewards (e.g., discretionary merit raise, promotion, and a small account to buy books at the campus store)

3. These programs require more than traditional contracting. Measurable success, in my experience, depends heavily on regular follow-up visits by chairs to participants' offices to check on progress and reinforce motivations.[8]

4. These programs require negotiation. The chair can act as a mediator between the colleague who is proposing a plan of reengagement and administrators or committees who help make decisions about rewards. The point is not to get promises of rewards from administrators and committees, just guidelines about what levels of quantity and quality are sufficient to merit a positive recommendation.

Faculty, be they middle-aged and difficult or new and untenured, deserve clear and stable indications about "what is enough." Without these assurances and guidelines they have what my research indicates as the single best reason for becoming inactive, isolated, and difficult.

THE BIGGEST CHALLENGE: CONVINCING SKEPTICAL CHAIRS

When I have outlined this approach on various campuses, I have been fascinated by the creativity of listeners who generate reasons why the scheme will not work. The most difficult part of my mission is to turn those creative energies into ways to making the scheme work.

Chairs are swayed, I have found, by data showing the success of programs where chairs persisted in systematic efforts. This is a typical example. Of forty-five targeted faculty, thirty-eight were judged successes in reestablishing both social communication and involvement in departmental activities, thirty-one negotiated mutually agreeable growth contracts and sustained regular activity toward goals over a semester, and twenty-six made significant and measurable progress toward public rewards. Twelve of the participants in this ongoing program have already earned substantial public rewards such as promotion, research or released-time grants, and discretionary salary increases.[9]

Information showing that the beneficiaries of these programs include the chairs who help implement them also convince skeptics. This sample of data from seven chairs contrasts their attitudes and habits after their first month as facilitators with those after a year.

	first month	after a year
Feeling significantly more comfortable interacting with all departmental colleagues	43%	100%
Frequently wishing they were not chairpeople	72%	29%
Finding regular, weekly times for scholarly writing	0%	57%
Making significant progress toward manuscript completion/publication	29%	57%
Often worried about lack of faculty approval/appreciation	58%	14%
Saw faculty evaluations as one of the most difficult aspects of chairing	100%	43%

These changes seemed to have happened because, as one chair put it, "You can't expect the faculty to take you seriously if you aren't practicing what you preach."

NOTES

1. Robert Boice and Patricia E. Myers, "Stresses and Satisfactions of Chairing in Psychology." *Professional Psychology: Research and Practice* 3 (1986): 200–204.
2. Robert Boice, "Faculty Development Via Field Programs for Middle-aged, Disillusioned Faculty." *Research in Higher Education* 25 (1986): 115–135.
3. Robert Boice and Patricia E. Myers, "Which Setting Is Healthier and Happier, Academe or Private Practice?" *Professional Psychology: Research and Practice* 18 (1987): 526–529.
4. John B. Bennett, "Faculty Evaluation: The Roles of the Department Chair." *The Department Advisor* (Spring 1985).
5. Kenneth E. Eble, "Chairpersons and Faculty Development." *The Department Advisor* (Winter 1986).
6. *Ibid.*, 4.
7. Boice, "Faculty Development."
8. Robert Boice, "Faculty Development Programs Based Around Scholarly Writing." In K. G. Lewis and J. T. Poulacs (eds.), *Face to Face: A Sourcebook of Individual Consultation Techniques for Faculty/Instructional Developers.* Stillwater, OK: New Forums Press, 1988, 217–36.
9. *Ibid.*

PART FOUR

Legal Issues

To many chairpersons the introduction of legal regulations and the threat of lawsuits in the academic environment is an offensive obstacle to the exercise of seasoned academic judgment. The perturbations of the law and lawyers appear to be arrayed with unrelenting force against traditional collegial understandings and modes of operation. Too often, the perceived legal assault is resisted or avoided in the hope that time will remove the torment. A more considered approach, however, leads to the conclusion that the complexities of the law have become a constant of academic life and must be understood and managed.

In the first chapter, "Legal Liability: Reducing the Risks," David Figuli provides a road map through tort, contract, and civil rights theories of liability—the most frequent sources of claims against chairs. He also explores several risk management devices—immunity, indemnification, and insurance. The conclusion of the chapter offers some hope of relief, suggesting that the most effective method of managing the legal risks is through the exercise of sound judgment— implementing clearly established policies and procedures with fair and reasoned judgment.

One recurring legal problem that requires a depth of understanding and exercise of the chair's best judgment is sexual harassment. Its most troubling aspect is its frequent impact upon intense interpersonal relationships between faculty and students and other employees of the university. The chair's ability to deal with this problem is also hampered by the ambiguous definition of the conduct that constitutes sexual harassment. Typically, it is defined as unwelcome sexual advances that are made as part of a person's pursuit of employment or educational opportunities, or actions or practices that create an intimidating, hostile, or offensive working or educational environment. Chairpersons are placed in a critical position of administering the institution's obligations to eliminate this conduct or responding to complaints that it has occurred. Often personal liability is an attendant risk. It behooves chairs to gain an understanding of the issues and risks involved and the appropriate preventive techniques for dealing with this problem.

In his chapter, "Sex in the Department," Mark Hurtubise provides basic information about how to deal with the problem of sexual harassment and other gender-related issues that frequently arise in academic departments. In addition to exposing the risks, he offers legally sound and practical responses.

Often enough, many chairpersons report, problems of chemical dependency emerge with the occasional faculty member or with the support staff. Such problems are always significant and solutions may seem quite distant. In his chapter, "Dealing with the Chemically Dependent Employee," David Figuli provides a pathway through several of the legal and management issues. The important definitional distinctions that separate protected handicaps from actionable performance deficiencies not only dictate the nature of the response by the chairperson, but may also place constraints on the amount of personal care the chair can display toward the affected individual.

Potential liability for false information either given or received in hiring has surfaced as a specific concern for chairs. In "The Chairperson's Dilemma: Bad Apples in the Department," Lois Vander Waerdt provides a variety of suggestions for minimizing liability. Central to her analysis is the need to strike a balance between the development of information required to make an informed judgment concerning future colleagues and the protection of individual rights to privacy and good reputation. While personal employment references, whether given or received, provide an easy source of information about a candidate for employment, blind faith in the accuracy or completeness of this information may at times be misplaced.

17

LEGAL LIABILITY: REDUCING THE RISK

DAVID J. FIGULI

The wave of litigiousness that has swept American society and inundated its legal system has also overwhelmed higher education. The immunity that previously acted as a barrier to student suits has been withdrawn and the sanctity of the collegial process has lost its influence over many faculty who now perceive resort to the legal process more expedient. Contentiousness has also been introduced into the academy with the advent of collective bargaining and its focus on employee rights and introduction of quasi-judicial processes as a means of securing those rights.

Department chairs have found their roles to be dramatically affected by these events. Increasingly, the focus of their day-to-day activities is on the formulation of responses to legal claims or threats. Decisions once made with only academic principles and collegial understanding in mind, are now burdened with issues of law that are often at odds with the former.

The reaction of chairs has been mixed. Some have attempted to fight against the intrusion of the legal menace. Others, ostrichlike, have ignored the issues with the hope that they will evaporate or be handled elsewhere. Most have recognized that the intrusion cannot be repulsed and have sought to equip themselves with knowledge and necessary advice.

The best interests of the institution and of the individual dictate the latter course. Legal liability cannot be administered solely out of the president's office or once a lawsuit or claim has been filed. By then it is often too late and the only alternative is to reverse the action that led to the suit or claim. From a personal standpoint, a chair cannot avoid liability simply by avoiding the issue. Liability is often predicated upon what should have been done or known. To avoid liability, chairs need to know the areas of potential difficulty.

This chapter will provide the reader with basic information about those legal theories frequently the source of liability claims against chairs. Those theories fall into three general categories of law: tort, contract and civil rights.

TORT

A *tort* is a civil wrong, other than a breach of contract, for which society recognizes a right of the injured party to recover compensation from the perpetrator. Not all wrongs, however, give rise to a right to recover. In some cases, society has deemed certain relationships or functions to be so important that it has accorded them immunity from suit. In other circumstances, the wrong is of such a limited degree or insignificant impact when viewed in light of the objective of achieving a structured and orderly society that it has not been accorded judicial protection. Also, certain acts or omissions which cause injury to an individual's person or property may, nevertheless, be consistent with the achievement of societal objectives and therefore be left unrestrained by law. For example, highly aggressive competitive actions may destroy the business and value of property held by another, but because they are consistent with a free economy and market place, the law does not redress the injury or damage.

This chapter will address torts that are a prevalent source of potential liability for department chairs. There are, to be sure, other tort actions than those that will be discussed below. The reader is also advised that the principles presented are subject to variations and nuances from one jurisdiction to the next.

Negligence

The most common and generic form of tort action is negligence. It is the basis for such familiar law suits as those arising from automobile collisions, automobile-pedestrian collisions, slip and fall, and professional malpractice. It operates from generalized principles and concepts which may, through repeated application, lead to the identification of certain types of behavior that have uniformly been recognized as negligent.

A negligence case requires that the party bringing the lawsuit (plaintiff) establish four essential elements. First, he/she must show that the defendant was under a legal obligation to act or not to act under the circumstances; second, that the defendant breached that duty, that is, failed to act in the manner that a reasonably prudent person would have acted under like or similar circumstances; third, that the injury for which compensation is sought was caused as a proximate result of the defendant's breach of duty; and fourth, that the plaintiff has suffered compensable damages as a result of the injury.

The first element of the negligence action is predicated upon a societal determination of norms and standards as reflected in the decisions of judges and juries. Not all obligations or undertakings of an individual rise to the level of a legally recognizable duty. While the duty of a person to operate a motor vehicle within the prescriptive standards of state law and the duty of a physician practicing a medical specialty to conduct his practice within the standards of that specialty are universally recognized, not all individual or professional undertakings can be so precisely defined from a negligence standpoint. For example, in the mid and early 1970s a spate of lawsuits occurred that were popularly referred to as "educational malpractice" cases. The plaintiffs in these cases alleged that certain educators had breached a duty to them as students since they had failed to inculcate a sufficient degree of knowledge or develop an acceptable level of proficiency in order for the student to succeed in the marketplace. These arguments were uniformly rejected by judges and juries on the grounds that the educator could not be held responsible for results in the same way that other professionals could.[1]

This example may provide educators solace, but there are other circumstances where claims of negligence may be successfully lodged against chairs. Most frequently such claims involve charges of inadequate supervision over programs which require hazardous, or at least risky, activities to be performed by students. Supervision over physical education, chemistry laboratory, and industrial arts classes is frequently the focus of negligence claims.[2] Somewhat surprising is the number of claims presented as a result of injuries sustained during the course of activities in theater arts programs. Students involved in handling or rigging stage props have been seriously injured and have alleged negligence in the supervision of their activity by faculty and chairs.[3] For chairs who supervise off-campus courses or programs, attention should be paid to the standard premises-liability issues such as slip-and-fall, fire, and security.

Defamation

In the last decade faculty members have frequently resorted to the law of defamation as a means of challenging the substance of judgments made by department chairs concerning their professional performance or status. Claims of libel and slander have been made against chairs because promotions, tenure, renewal of probationary employment, and salary increases have been denied. Such actions have been used as an alternative to a direct challenge of the basis for those decisions because the courts, in most cases, have refused to engage in second-guessing the professional judgment of chairs on academic and professional issues.

The law of defamation is a composite of the common law actions for libel and slander. Both involve allegations that the defendant has made false statements about the plaintiff that have caused damage to the reputation or good name of the plaintiff. Libel formerly referred to statements that were published in some form of writing or other tangible form, whereas slander referred to oral communications. The evolution of the mass media, including radio, television, and other forms of electronic communications, has virtually obliterated the basis for distinguishing between libel and slander.

The essence of an action for defamation is a claim that an expression made by another has damaged the reputation of the plaintiff. Since truth is an absolute defense, in order to succeed, the plaintiff must show that the substance of the expression is false. The plaintiff must also show that the expression was disseminated or published by the defendant. What constitutes a sufficient publication of a defamatory expression is largely dependant upon the context. The general rule is that the dissemination of a defamatory expression to one other person is sufficient, and the defendant is thereafter liable for all reiterations of the expression. In other circumstances involving privileged conduct, such as an employer's evaluation of its employees, a defamatory expression must exceed the bounds of legitimate communication, given the nature of the privileged activity, before it can be made the basis of an action for defamation. The proof of damages likewise turns upon subject-matter distinctions. While damages are technically a required element in a case of defamation, in certain circumstances damage is presumed and actual damage need not be proved. Such circumstances include statements made that are injurious to a person's professional reputation, accuse one of criminal behavior, unchastity, or affliction with a loathsome disease.

There are two defenses against the defamation actions that are of particular import to department chairs. As noted above, such actions are commonly used to attack evaluative decisions made by chairs about faculty members. The law recognizes the right of an employer to evaluate its employees and allows a qualified privilege to the employer in conducting such activity free of legal challenge, even if the evaluative judgments made are arguably defamatory, unless the plaintiff can show that the defamatory statements were made with actual malice, that is, with an improper motive or ill will, or were published beyond the reasonable bounds necessary to further the protected interest. In one case, the evaluation of a faculty member was communicated to consultants hired to evaluate the effectiveness and appropriateness of the departmental structure. The court held that a communication of the evaluation to the consultants, even if false, was not actionable since an evaluation of the department by the consultants necessarily included a review of the effectiveness of the faculty.[4]

A further pertinent defense is encompassed within the evolving law concerning opinions. As the law presently stands, an individual may express an opinion about another and be held harmless from charges of defamation if the basis for the opinion is fully disclosed and the communicator does not act with actual malice. It is necessary that the expression of opinion be clothed with the facts upon which it is based, since under the law the opinion is only protected if those to whom it is communicated can assess the basis upon which it is made and render independent judgment as to its accuracy or appropriateness.[5] Thus, the statement that a person is a "liar" or is a "crook" or other pejorative statements may be protected as opinion if proper disclosure of the basis for the opinion is made.[6]

Misrepresentation

In virtually all jurisdictions this type of case is a hybrid. It encompasses both an intentional tort—fraud—and a negligence form commonly referred to as "negligent misrepresentation." It requires proof of the following elements:

1. A false representation made by the defendant
2. Knowledge or belief by the defendant that the representation is false, or a reckless disregard for its truth or falsity
3. An intention by the defendant to induce reliance by the plaintiff on the representation
4. Reasonable reliance by the plaintiff on the representation in taking or refraining from action
5. Damage to the plaintiff as a result of such reliance

This type of action is particularly adaptable to what is commonly referred to as "student consumer" claims. It has been used in cases where students have challenged the accuracy of representations made in catalogs or other institutional documents concerning the content of courses, the adequacy of courses to prepare them for certifications or licensures, the accuracy of academic advice, accreditation status, success of graduates in obtaining jobs, and representations made concerning admissions requirements and practices.[7] The success of students in bringing misrepresentation suits is sufficient cause for chairs to beware of overselling courses or programs of study in order to attract larger enrollments. In some jurisdictions punitive or exemplary damages, that is, damages designed to punish or make an example of the defendant, may be awarded for particularly egregious misrepresentations.

Assault or Battery

Assault and battery are civil tort actions, although the terms are more frequently employed to describe related criminal charges. Battery occurs when an individual intends to contact and does contact the body of another without consent. A person may sue for and recover nominal damages, even where the battery has caused no actual harm. An assault is the inchoate form of a battery. It is generally defined as a reasonable apprehension of battery. A claim of assault may also succeed without proof of actual harm. Punitive or exemplary damages may be awarded upon proof of an assault or battery.

The torts of assault and battery have acquired special prominence with attention recently given to claims of sexual harassment. Nonconsensual sexual or amorous contact or the reasonable apprehension of such contact, fit well within the definitions of assault and battery. Indeed, those actions have frequently been utilized by plaintiffs offended by sexual harassment that occurs in the workplace.[8] It should be noted that the use of these tort claims is generally in addition to the pursuit of statutory remedies under state and federal nondiscrimination laws.

Intentional Infliction of Emotional Distress

Recovery of damages may be sought by an individual for emotional distress suffered by actions of another that violate the conscience or exceed the bounds of proper conduct usually tolerated by society. The tort action that allows such a claim is presently in a state of flux. Its acceptance is still diminished by an early fear that such claims were easily feigned and difficult to prove. In some states such a claim cannot stand alone; it must be supported by the existence of a contemporaneous independent tort (e.g., an action for negligence). The increased acceptance of psychiatric and psychological medical evidence, however, has allowed inroads to be made in other states where the tort has been recognized as an independent cause of action.

Claims for intentional infliction of emotional distress most frequently involve circumstances where one individual has engaged in a prolonged course of harassment or hounding of another. In higher education such a claim will frequently accompany a claim for defamation, wrongful discharge, violation of civil rights, assault, or battery. Often, the perceived intractability of tenure causes chairs and departmental faculty to engage in a course of conduct designed to force out an undesirable colleague. Such action can form the basis for a claim of intentional infliction of emotional distress.

Invasion of Privacy

The expectation of individuals that the private concerns of their lives will not be exposed to public scrutiny is protected against nonconsensual invasion. The law prohibits one individual from intruding into the affairs of another in a manner offensive or objectionable to a reasonable person. Further, one may not publicly disclose the private facts of another's life if such disclosure would be offensive or objectionable to a person of ordinary sensibilities. Unreasonable activities that are precluded by this tort action are: eavesdropping, invasion of physical premises or personal possessions, dissemination of personal facts to public media such as radio, TV or newspaper, or other unwarranted disclosure of personal facts concerning an individual's life.

Department chairs should pay careful attention to the use and disclosure of information concerning faculty members or students that comes into the possession of the chair even if the information is legitimately obtained. Nonconsensual disclosure of information concerning a faculty member's private life to a potential employer, where such information is not solicited or related to the legitimate interests of the future employer, can give rise to liability. Eavesdropping on conversations of faculty members or surreptitious inspection of a faculty member's private files, whether maintained on institutional property or not, may constitute an unlawful invasion of privacy if conducted in an unreasonable manner or without legitimate pertinence to the interests of the institution. Similar claims may be raised by students arising out of improper statements made during the course of graduate school or employment references, or as a result of an improper release of information from student records. (It should also be noted that improper disclosure of student records may also constitute a violation of the Family Educational Rights and Privacy Act.[9])

CONTRACT

The liability of chairs for claims of breach of contract is not a common problem. Since in entering into contracts chairs are acting as agents of the institution and not on their own behalf, the institution is liable for performance of the contract and not the chair. Nevertheless, a chair may be held liable for breach of a contract where the chair has acted in excess of his or her scope of authority. In such circumstances both the third party with whom the contract is made and the institution may seek to hold the chair liable for any damage that results.

Even when a contract is never made, a chair may be held liable for representations or commitments made to a potential contracting party where the representation of commitments is beyond the chair's authority. Thus a court may enforce an obligation against the chair and the institution if the third party has acted in reliance on the chair's representations or commitments and as a result of said reliance has suffered pecuniary loss.

Claims for breach of contract may arise if a chair undertakes to make purchases of equipment or supplies in the name of the institution when such purchases have not been properly authorized in accordance with institutional policy. When the institution refuses to honor the purchase contract, the chair may be held liable for performance in lieu of the institution or, if the institution is forced to honor the contract, it may in turn seek indemnification from the chair. Liability may also be imposed in situations where the chair, in recruiting employees or students, makes representations of a contractual nature concerning terms or conditions of employment or of matriculation that the institution refuses to honor and that are beyond the scope of the chair's authority.

CIVIL RIGHTS

The civil rights laws of the state and federal governments provide one of the severest forms of potential liability for chairs. The laws affect chairs employed at public institutions or institutions that have been determined by law to be involved in state action. The determination of whether a private institution is involved in state action is a highly complex and technical one. Chairs employed in private institutions that receive some public support should inquire as to the "state action" status of their institution.

The civil rights laws and the liability potential that arises from them emanate from a variety of federal and state statutes as well as constitutional provisions. Nondiscrimination laws provide one portion of the subject-matter proscriptions. The First and Fourteenth Amendments to the U.S. Constitution as well as parallel provisions in state constitutions provide another portion. A third component is established by section 1983 of Title 42 of the United States Code. It, and companion provisions of the code, prohibit any state officer or agent or anyone acting under color of state authority from denying any individual's civil rights guaranteed under nondiscrimination laws and state and federal constitutional provisions. It allows for the institution of lawsuits in state or federal courts in order to seek remedies for civil rights violations. The remedies available include compensatory and punitive damages, attorney's fees, and injunctive relief.

Recent decisions of the U.S. Supreme Court have provided some shelter for defendants. A qualified immunity has been interposed in those circumstances where the defendant's actions were taken in a good faith belief that they were in compliance with the law.[10] The immunity may be lost, however, if it is proven that the defendant violated clearly established constitutional rights of which a reasonable person should have been aware. In order to take advantage of this immunity, department chairs should be cognizant of the laws governing nondiscrimination as well as the First and Fourteenth Amendment rights of individuals. They should understand the rights and limitations of freedom of speech and association, freedom of religion, equal protection, and due process.

REDUCING THE RISKS

In order to reduce the risk of liability that the preceding laws impose, chairs should take advantage of three risk management devices—immunity, indemnification and insurance. The benefits available from these three sources, if any, should be analyzed and coordinated so that the broad array of potential risks is reduced to a level where personal liability is as small as possible. The following discussion will provide a foundation from which the chair may determine what assistance is necessary as well as the quality of assistance obtained.

Immunity

Immunity is a creature of state law, established either by statute or by court decision. Historically, government agencies and charitable institutions were uniformly and extensively clothed with immunity from suit based particularly on tort claims. Today, such immunities have largely dissolved. In the process of dissolution the law of immunities has followed a rather tortuous path.

It is rare to find blanket immunity for either governmental or charitable institutions any more. In some states the extent of immunity depends upon the type of function of the entity being challenged by the tort claim. Recently, governmental immunity statutes have taken a new turn. States have enacted immunity statutes with dollar amount limitations. For example, some state laws waive immunity to the extent of any insurance coverage available, while others set a specific dollar limit beyond which the state cannot be held liable. Often where immunity is provided, coverage for employees is excluded when the employee acts willfully, wantonly, or in excess of his or her authority.

A word of caution is in order. Even if a chair researches and determines that immunity is provided under state law, frequent review should be made of the status of that law. Both legislative and judicial activity in this area has been frenetic in recent times. Most often, legislatures have worked to institute broader immunity while the judiciary has acted to strike down or restrict laws.

Indemnification

Indemnification may be provided by law or by contract. Laws or contract provisions providing indemnification generally cover litigation expenses, including attorney's fees, and payment of any damages adjudged. Willful, wanton, bad faith, reckless and intentional acts of employees are usually excluded from indemnification coverage. Consequently, punitive or exemplary damage judgments are almost never paid under indemnification agreements or laws.

Often in order to take advantage of indemnification, the employee must surrender defense of the lawsuit to the state or the employer providing the coverage. This likely will reduce the control the chair can exercise over the representation of his or her interests. Whether a case is settled or compromised or a judgment appealed may as a result be influenced by financial or other considerations that may cause the chair considerable discomfort.

Nevertheless, indemnification is generally to be desired. If it is not provided by statute, chairs should seek to include it in their employment agreements.

Insurance

The final element of risk management is insurance. It should be used to provide comprehensive protection to fill the gaps that immunity and indemnity do not. In order to use insurance most effectively a chair must understand the variety of coverages and limits available within the industry and within particular companies. Unfortunately, insurance policies have yet to be written in a manner which facilitates comprehension by laypeople.

Insurance can be obtained from a variety of sources. Chairs are almost always covered by some type of employer-paid liability insurance. In addition, most homeowners policies can be expanded to provide professional liability coverage for a reasonable additional premium. Liability insurance is frequently available through disciplinary or professional associations for a modest group fee.

Although insurance is readily available, the real problem is coverage. Most liability or errors and omissions policies exclude coverage for such torts as assault and battery, defamation and civil rights claims. It is also unlikely that coverage will be extended to willful, wanton, or reckless acts. Unfortunately, these are also areas which usually are not covered in indemnification agreements.

Competent professional advice should be obtained to conduct a risk management analysis of the chair's personal liability. Frequently, this assistance can be obtained through an existing insurance carrier. Such assistance may also be obtained from competent legal counsel or an insurance consultant. Each of the risk reduction techniques discussed in this article should be addressed in any such analysis.

The best insulation for chairs against legal liability, however, is their own good judgment and common sense. The tort and civil rights actions previously discussed revolve around standards of good faith and reasonableness. Chairs who diligently undertake to understand the liability potential inherent in their roles and undertake to perform them in a reasonable manner and in good faith are their own best insurance against legal liability.

NOTES

1. See Perry A. Zirkel, "Educational Malpractice: Cracks in the Door?" *West's Education Law Reporter* 23 (1985): 453.
2. See *Perkins v. State Board of Education,* 364 So. 2d 183 (La. 1978); *Butler v. Louisiana State Board of Education,* 331 So. 2d 192 (Ct. App. La. 1976); *Kiser v. Snyder,* 205 S.E. 2d 619 (Ct. App. N.C. 1974); *Wells v. Colorado College,* 478 F. 2d 158 (10th Cir. 1973).
3. See *Christilles v. Southwest Texas State Univ.,* 639 S.W. 2d 38 (Ct. App. Tx. 1982); *Potter v. North Carolina School of the Arts,* 245 S.E. 2d 188 (Ct. App. N.C. 1978); *Erwine v. Gamble, Pownal & Gilroy, et al.,* 343 So. 2d 859 (Ct. App. Fla. 1976).
4. *Keddie v. Pennsylvania State Univ.,* 412 F. Supp. 1264 (M.D. Pa. 1976).
5. *Gertz v. Robert Welch, Inc.,* 418 U.S. 323 (1974).
6. See *Lauderback v. American Broadcasting Company,* 741 F. 2d 193 (8th Cir. 1984); *Orr v. Argus-Press Company,* 586 F. 2d 1108 (6th Cir. 1978).
7. See *Idrees v. American University of the Caribbean,* 546 F. Supp. 1342 (S.D. N.Y. 1982); *Dizick v. Umpgua Community College,* 599 P. 2d 444 (Or. 1979); *Steinberg v. Chicago Medical School,* 371 N.E. 2d 634 (Ill. 1977); *Zumbrum v. University of Southern California,* 25 Cal. App. 3d 1, 101 Cal. Rptr. 499 (1972).
8. See *Skousen v. Nidy,* 367 P. 2d 248 (Ariz. 1960); State v. Allen, 95 S.E. 2d 526 (N.C. 1956).
9. 20 U.S.C. 1232 (g).
10. *Harlow v. Fitzgerald* 457 U.S. 800 (1982); *Scheur v. Rhodes,* 416 U.S. 232 (1974).

18

SEX IN THE DEPARTMENT

MARK HURTUBISE

After it became known to Louisiana State University at Baton Rouge (LSU) that a twenty-nine-year-old female graduate assistant was having an intimate relationship with a seventeen-year-old female freshman, LSU reassigned the graduate assistant to duties that did not include teaching undergraduates. The graduate assistant brought legal action against LSU alleging that LSU had violated her Equal Protection rights under the Fourteenth Amendment, her right to privacy, and her First Amendment right of association.[1]

When a female instructor at Muhlenberg College in Allentown, Pennsylvania was denied a promotion and tenure, she elected to sue the institution as well as the president and two deans alleging sex discrimination. During her employment at Muhlenberg, three male faculty members in the same department, who were similarly situated, had been granted tenure. The instructor not only sought an injunction prohibiting the alleged discrimination, but reinstatement at a higher rank, tenure, back pay, costs and attorney's fees.[2]

Two female students reported to the president at Whitman College in the state of Washington that a male tenured professor had made sexual advances toward them. After hearing testimony from twenty persons, an advisory investigatory committee composed of five senior faculty members at Whitman College recommended dismissal of the tenured professor based upon evidence of sexual advances not only toward the female students, but female staff and faculty members, and wives of faculty and staff members. After the professor was dismissed from his tenured position, he and his wife sued for reinstatement and for $2 million in damages for libel and damage to his professional standing.[3]

Within the academic department, the rights and responsibilities of faculty and students can be gleaned from a labyrinth of federal, state and local laws, administrative regulations, and internal policies and procedures. Often there is duplication and conflict, confusion, and lack of direction for the department chair. In addition, the chair may be perceived as savior or persecutor.

The laws pertaining to sex-related issues in higher education are complex. One of the most confusing areas is determining which laws apply to independent institutions and which laws fall under the "state action" doctrine. Federal constitutional principles such as the First

Amendment requirements of due process (e.g., notice of a regulation and an opportunity to be heard if there is an alleged violation of a regulation) apply only to state agencies, which include state-sponsored public institutions of higher education. Independent institutions, on the other hand, generally are not bound by constitutional mandates, but by state court interpretation of contract law.[4] Through their contractual agreements, independent institutions do incorporate many of the basic rights found in the Federal Constitution. For example, most independent institutions include a due process provision in their faculty handbooks.

Within the past two decades, a patchwork of federal and state statutes has evolved that applies both to public and private post-secondary institutions with the purpose of promoting equal employment opportunities and protecting individuals from discrimination based on sex and other categories. This chapter will review some of the most important and at times most controversial sex-related issues as they pertain to the academic department.

SEX DISCRIMINATION

The federal government has at least eight major discrimination laws and one executive order that apply to public and private higher education. Each one has its own comprehensive set of administrative guidelines. Many states, furthermore, have state civil rights laws that may apply to postsecondary institutions and overlap federal statutes.

At the federal level, sex discrimination is covered by Title VII of the Civil Rights Act of 1964, by Title IX of the Education Amendments of 1972, by the Equal Pay Act, and by Executive Order 11246.

Executive Order 11246, which was signed by President Lyndon Johnson in 1965, was amended in 1973 by Executive Order 11375 to include sex on the list of prohibited discriminations. The executive orders apply to educational institutions that have federal contracts. By signing a contract, the institution promises to take affirmative action to eliminate discrimination. The Department of Labor has exclusive authority to enforce compliance with Executive Orders 11246 and 11375.

Since July 1, 1979, the Equal Pay Act has been administered by the Equal Employment Opportunity Commission (EEOC), a federal agency. The guiding principle of the Equal Pay Act is "equal pay for equal work." Although women have been the primary beneficiaries of this Act, men have also been beneficiaries. For instance, in the early 1970s the University of Nebraska had a numerical formula for computing the average salary for male faculty.[5] It was determined that ninety-two male faculty members received less salary than female faculty members who held substantially similar positions. The court held that this practice violated the Equal Pay Act which prohibits public and private institutions from discrimination on the basis of sex in wages paid for equal work on jobs which require "equal skill, effort and responsibility and which are performed under similar working conditions."[6] There are exceptions to this rule (e.g., a seniority system or a merit system). The department chair should note that if the institution believes it is potentially in violation of the Equal Pay Act, wages cannot be reduced, only raised.

Although used primarily by students alleging sex discrimination, Title IX of the Education Amendments of 1972 has been extended to prohibit sex discrimination in employment within those programs at an educational institution that receive financial aid. The Supreme Court has held that student financial aid constitutes aid to the institution. If sex discrimination is pervasive or persists within the federally funded program or activity, or if the institution refuses to comply with Title IX regulations, the Education Department could terminate student aid.[7]

The cornerstone that protects employees against sex discrimination is Title VII of the Civil Rights Act of 1964.[8] In 1972, Title VII was extended to cover public and private educational institutions. The EEOC, which administers Title VII, has the power to adjudicate issues of sex discrimination at no cost to the employee. A complaint alleging discrimination must be filed with the EEOC or a state human rights agency *before* it can be taken to court. There are three statutory exceptions to Title VII, all of which are narrowly construed, but which are of particular interest to higher education:

1. Bona Fide Occupational Qualifications (BFOQ). Title VII permits employment discrimination where the consideration of sex can be shown to be a BFOQ. It does not apply to such areas as refusing to hire women because of the belief that women have a higher turnover rate than men. The EEOC will consider sex to be a BFOQ when it genuinely is necessary for an employee to be a man or woman, as in the case of an actor, actress or model.

2. Religiously-Affiliated Institutions. This exception generally applies to institutions that are primarily religious in character. Nevertheless, the discriminatory hiring practice must be exercised only to maintain the institution's religious character. For example, a seminary that offers degrees only in theology, religious education, and church music, would be permitted to hire faculty that "fit the definition of ministers."[9]

3. Seniority Systems. For example, "last hired, first fired."

Although Title VI broadly prohibits sex discrimination against male and female job applicants or employees in connection with hiring, lay off, firing, promotion, compensation, and all terms, conditions, and privileges of employment, it does not prohibit institutions from hiring faculty on the basis of job qualifications or recognizing faculty members on the basis of seniority, scholarship, teaching ability, or service.

Courts have been reluctant to construe the restrictions against sex discrimination to encompass discrimination based on sexual preference or orientation. Title VII forbids discrimination in employment practices on the basis of race, color, religion, national origin, or sex, but not sexual preference. Discrimination on the basis of sexual orientation is often challenged on First Amendment grounds of freedom of speech or association. Alternatively, some homosexuals find protection in collective bargaining agreements and faculty handbooks that ban discrimination based on sexual orientation (preference). In both cases, the faculty member who believes he or she is discriminated against could allege breach of contract. Additionally, a few municipalities, counties, and states have statutes banning such discrimination.[10]

How to Prove Discrimination

Today, courts recognize three tests an employee must pass before a ruling will be made against a college or university for sex discrimination.[11] The tests customarily begin when a female faculty member is denied promotion or tenure.

1. The first test requires the faculty member to show that:
   a. she belongs to one of the protected classes;
   b. she applied for the position or promotion;
   c. despite her qualifications she was rejected.

2. Once test number one is passed, the burden shifts to the institution to show "some legitimate non-discriminatory reason for the employee's rejection."

3. If a justifiable reason is shown by the institution (e.g., lack of scholarship or service), the burden shifts back to the faculty member to prove that the reason purported is simply a facade for unlawful sex discrimination.

Remedies

Ms. Connie Rae Kunda, the instructor at Muhlenberg College referred to at the beginning of this chapter, was awarded back pay, reinstatement to her previous position with the rank of assistant professor, costs and attorney's fees, and tenure if she completed her Master's degree within two years. The institution claimed Kunda was denied promotion because she lacked the requisite Master's degree. Kunda proved that she was denied tenure because Muhlenberg discriminated against her on the basis of sex. She met with the president and department chair, both of whom told her she was not given tenure because she lacked a Master's degree. This was the first time she was informed of such a prerequisite. Yet three male faculty members similarly situated had been promoted during Kunda's employment. The Court concluded that discrimination was the reason for the denial.

An important lesson can be learned by department chairs in the Muhlenberg College case. Courts are beginning to flex their muscles in the area of promotions and tenure in higher education, where traditionally they would have limited themselves to back pay and reinstatement.

The department chair should recognize that Ms. Kunda could have asserted not only sex discrimination, but a violation of the Equal Pay Act and breach of contract. She also could have sought damages for emotional distress. Muhlenberg had salaried male employees whose job qualifications and responsibilities were substantially similar to Kunda's. The college, furthermore, failed to follow its own procedures in granting promotion and tenure which could be construed as a breach of contract.

Promotion and tenure in academe are treasured in a faculty member's professional career. The chair should encourage a review process that grants or denies promotion or tenure on non-sexist bases and standards. The criteria should be written, well-publicized, and justifiably academic, regarding, for example, teaching ability, professional stature, scholarship, and service. If the institution needs to take into consideration such factors as available resources or enrollment, these factors should be stated clearly in the promotion and tenure guidelines. Any denial should be supported by relevant and available documentation and independent judgment by an *ad hoc* or standing committee.

If a faculty member is denied promotion or tenure, an independent appeals process should be available. Any evaluation that supports promotion or tenure should be taken seriously, for such endorsement may be introduced as evidence against an institution that denies promotion or tenure. In any event, win or lose in court, the institution loses. It is an expensive process, both financially and emotionally. Thus, internal preventative techniques are usually preferable.

SEXUAL HARASSMENT

Most definitions of sexual harassment focus upon unequal power in faculty member–student, department chair–faculty member, or faculty member–secretary relationships. Sexual harassment occurs when the power relationship is exploited and sustained at the expense of another person. Persistent ogling, continuous sexual innuendoes, unsolicited touching, or outright physical assault can be sexual harassment. What sometimes may be difficult is to distinguish between sexual harassment and a consenting relationship.

A faculty member need not prove loss of any tangible benefit, such as employment termination or denial of promotion, to prevail against an institution under Title VII. Although harassment in the work place most frequently occurs where submission to unwelcome sexual advances becomes a condition of employment or employment opportunities, it is sufficient to prove that unsolicited sexual advances "unreasonably" interfered with job performance or created an "intimidating, hostile, or offensive working environment."[12]

A department chair should understand further that the chair and the institution could be liable for the sexual harassment (sex discrimination) committed on campus, at an off-campus site, or anywhere within the community. The perpetrator may be a department chair, a faculty member, or even people not employed in the department (e.g., students sexually harassing the departmental secretary). If the department chair knew or should have known that a faculty or staff member was being sexually intimidated, the chair has an affirmative duty under the Civil Rights Act to investigate the matter and correct any violation under the law. By refusing to carry this responsibility, the chair, as an agent of the institution, exposes the institution and all involved parties to a great deal of liability.

In addition to actions under Title VII and the state fair employment practice laws, a person alleging sexual harassment could also bring charges in state court under various criminal, tort, and contract statutes. The recovery for assault, intentional or negligent infliction of emotional distress, fraud and deceit, breach of contract, interference with contractual relations, or wrongful discharge may include embarrassment, probation, termination, a fine, or even imprisonment for the offender and emotional distress, back wages, reinstatement, promotion, punitive damages, and costs and attorney's fees for the harassed party. On the other hand, if the charges prove to be fabricated and the institution was negligent in its handling of the matter, the alleged offender might sue under such legal theories as breach of contract, emotional distress, slander, libel, and so on.

The responsibilities of a department chair toward student sexual harassment are similar to those as outlined above with respect to employees. One major distinction is that students alleging sexual harassment look to Title IX of the 1972 Education Amendments for protection. The published Title IX regulations *require* all institutions within the jurisdiction of the regulations to adopt and publish procedures providing for prompt and equitable resolutions of student complaints.[13]

Whether or not a grievance procedure exists within the university, students may take complaints of sexual harassment directly to the Office for Civil Rights in the U.S. Department of Education, or press charges in a private lawsuit. The literature of educational institutions has nondiscriminatory policies which, if violated, could constitute a breach of contract. In addition, economic losses incurred by the harassed student as a result of the breach may be recoverable against the institution and the offender (e.g., attorney's fees, court costs, expenses for doctors and transferring to another institution, unrefunded tuition, and room and board charges). The student, as in the case of the employee, could also seek damages for emotional distress.

Sexual harassment can encompass verbal, physical, and visual harassment. Given the magnitude of the problem and the multifaceted issues involved, it is advisable for the institution and department chair to take preventative measures to save everyone unnecessary expense, time, and humiliation, and to foster an environment of mutual respect in which students, faculty, and staff can work together harmoniously.

A written policy should be adopted that not only defines sexual harassment, but also provides for an internal grievance procedure with appropriate sanctions. This will assist the department chair immensely in taking immediate corrective action to prevent or remedy the harassment of an innocent victim. This policy must be fair to both parties and could be publicly announced and explained at an in-service workshop. A good place to publish the policy is in faculty, staff, and student handbooks.

Department chairs should remain sensitive to the volatile nature of the predicament in which the alleged victim and harasser have been placed. Confidentiality in an atmosphere of understanding and professionalism should be the pillars of the chair's behavioral pattern. The names of outside counselors could be made available to both parties. The chair should also give serious consideration to having an individual of the same sex as the victim present when discussing the matter. This may provide an atmosphere for discussing a sensitive and highly personal matter freely.

If the final decision is adverse to the harasser, any sanction should only be enforced through established disciplinary procedures, with the right to appeal the decision. Complainants who do not prevail should be provided a reasonable explanation that is supported by the evidence.

Professor Lehmann, who was discharged from Whitman College (referenced earlier), is a dramatic example of the multiple issues surrounding sexual harassment. Though it was time consuming and costly, he and his wife lost their $2 million lawsuit against the college. Whitman College had reacted judiciously by following proper procedures in gathering relevant evidence, soliciting testimony, and protecting the rights of all the parties involved.

OTHER SEXUAL AFFAIRS

Are romance, marriage, pregnancy, hiring whomever one pleases inalienable rights that human beings are entitled to enjoy without interference?

Romance
Intimate relationships between professors and students traditionally have been held suspect because they appear to conflict with a faculty member's primary role, which is to teach students.

When LSU transferred Ms. Kristine Naragon, a graduate assistant, out of the undergraduate classroom for having an intimate relationship with a seventeen-year-old female undergraduate, the Court agreed with LSU that there was a "breach of professional ethics" which "undermined the proper position and effectiveness of the teacher." The Court stated further that her homosexual tendency was not the motivating factor in deciding to transfer her, but rather the romantic relationship with a student that she had encouraged, which outraged the student's parents and which put the institution at great risk with the public and other parents.

Becoming intimately involved with a student is a foolish gamble for a faculty member. Not only is there a detrimental effect upon the student, but one's career and reputation could be jeopardized if the liaison were to fall into the lap of an administrative disciplinary committee. Although it might appear in the mind of the parties intimately involved that it is "no one's business," faculty members are considered by the public, parents, and students as role models. Professors are relied upon to carry out their proper role as mentor and counselor and should avoid any suggestion of exploitation of students for their own private advantage.[14]

If such a relationship is brought to the attention of the department chair, the chair should review first the policies within the faculty and student handbooks to determine if there is a written procedure to be followed. Before making allegations, the chair should protect both parties until it can be determined that the facts are incriminating. Action becomes arbitrary if solid facts do not support the conclusion.

After seeking appropriate advice and support within the institution, the chair can proceed by implementing the proper steps established by the university or college. Remember that the private conduct of a faculty member is the proper concern of the chair when it can potentially scar the institution's reputation and disrupt the lives of community members.

One of the main reasons institutions and the courts are so concerned with the faculty–student relationship is because "mutual choice" between individuals of equal status does not exist. When give and take are based on mutual consent, the chair should be reluctant to interfere. This is usually the case between faculty members. When there is no fear or coercion, then the privacy of two individuals should not be invaded. Only when the relationship interferes with the faculty member's performance within the department should the chair even consider discussing the issue.

Should the affair include the chair and a faculty member within the department, caution should be exercised. The power relationship shifts and if the faculty member is not promoted or tenured a complaint of sex discrimination or sexual harassment could arise.

Marital Status and Antinepotism

Title VII of the Civil Rights Act of 1964 does not prohibit discrimination based on marital status, but upon sex. Nevertheless, if an institution discriminates against married women in its hiring, promoting, or terminating policies, the same rules must apply equally to men; if not, such action constitutes sex discrimination.[15] In other words, if the institution does not promote married women, it also must not promote married men.

As a general rule, the department chair must realize that the marital status of any employee or the marital status between employees should not influence any decision regarding employment responsibilities, privileges, or benefits. But the chair should be cognizant of one exception.

There are "no spouse" or "close relative" rules (typically, immediate family members, spouse, parent or child, or individuals related by marriage or blood), that are very limited in their application. Generally, the university or college may prohibit both spouses from working within the *same department* or having one spouse under the direct supervision of the other. Preclusion of spouses or close relatives is reasonable when its purpose is to avoid conflicts that might affect job performance, supervision, or employee morale. Such a policy must be "sex neutral" (i.e., apply to all employees regardless of sex). A rule that uniformly requires the female to resign or transfer would constitute unlawful sex discrimination. If co-workers marry and are employed in the same department, a valid requirement would be to allow the spouses to determine which one is to be transferred or terminated. Finally, the word "spouse" has been interpreted to include cohabitation without being legally married.[16]

Pregnancy

In 1978, President Carter signed into law an amendment to Title VII known as the Pregnancy Discrimination Act.[17] As a result, discrimination based on pregnancy, childbirth, or related medical conditions constitutes unlawful sex discrimination under Title VII. The law states clearly that pregnant women who can and want to must be allowed to work. Forced maternity leave will not be tolerated. Also, women disabled by pregnancy, before and after birth, must be treated as other employees who are temporarily disabled by a short-term medical disability. When on disability, the institution must hold her position open with no loss of seniority, as though she were on any other short-term disability.

Moreover, an institution of higher learning may not refuse to hire, promote, or deprive a pregnant woman of any employment benefits. If the university or college has a health program, it must include pregnancy coverage for female employees as well as the wives of male employees. Under Title VII, it also appears to be unlawful to deny employment opportunities to females with children unless there is a rule that applies equally to men with children.

The real challenge for a department chair is the pregnancy of an unwed faculty member. When addressing the issue related to "state action," the United States Supreme Court has stated that "where a decision as fundamental as that whether to bear or beget a child is involved, regulations imposing a burden on it may be justified only by compelling state interests, and must be narrowly drawn to express only those interests."[18]

A Delaware federal district court held that a director of residence halls at a state college who bore a child out of wedlock was entitled to reinstatement because the state college would most likely not be able to establish a compelling state interest to justify invasion into the director's decision to bear a child.[19] Other courts have rejected arguments from state supported institutions that a pregnant unwed parent is "per se immoral" because any such categorizing would violate an individual's equal protection rights under the Federal Constitution, since it excludes unwed pregnant women from the same rights and privileges available to married pregnant women or unwed fathers.

With respect to a private institution, any policy terminating an unmarried pregnant employee arguably violates Title VII because it discriminates against unwed pregnant women and not all pregnant women or unwed fathers. "Pregnancy is a condition unique to women, so that termination of employment because of pregnancy has a disparate and invidious impact upon the female gender."[20]

AVOIDING THE CROSS FIRE

Full understanding of and compliance with all the laws and regulations of discrimination can be confusing. Statutory protections overlap and individuals who believe they have been discriminated against may seek redress under several statutes simultaneously. Retaliation of any kind against anyone who opposes an unlawful practice is forbidden by law.

The safest way for a department chair to avoid a fracas is to establish a sense of fair play by adhering to the written guidelines of the institution, seeking appropriate advice, encouraging discussion on such discrimination issues as sexual harassment, publicly stating that discrimination will not be tolerated, and by being patient and honest with all involved parties. But most of all, it is important to remember that prevention, common sense, and being a good role model are the best ingredients for longevity as a chair and for avoiding being singed by the cross fire between disputing parties.

POSTSCRIPT

On June 19, 1986, the Supreme Court in its *first* sexual harassment case reaffirmed the belief that Title VII of the Civil Rights Act of 1964 extends not only to discrimination based on sex, but also to sexual harassment.[21] Furthermore, Justice Rehnquist was explicit in stating that an employee need not prove loss of any tangible benefit such as employment or a promotion to prevail on a Title VII claim. It is enough to prove that *unwelcomed* sexual advances created an "intimidating, hostile, or offensive environment."[22]

What is clearly evident from this case is that although the facts may have supported a conclusion that a female bank employee and her immediate supervisor "voluntarily" participated in or consented to the claimed sexual escapades, the critical inquiry was whether the sexual advances were *unwelcomed*. When there is a question of sexual harassment, the department chair should not focus exclusively on the "voluntariness" of the participation in a claimed sexual act. It is the *unwelcomed* advance that creates an offensive atmosphere.

This decision is very important to the department chair, for it highlights once again the serious nature and consequences of sexual harassment. Academicians must respond affirmatively by establishing clear, written policies that define sexual harassment and provide for an internal grievance procedure with appropriate sanctions. Inasmuch as a grievance procedure will assist in protecting the institution and its community members, an allegation or knowledge of possible harassment should be acted upon swiftly and judiciously because the complainant has the option of bypassing the collegial hierarchy and filing a complaint with the Equal Employment Opportunity Commission ("EEOC"). Implicit in the Supreme Court's decision is that there should be a procedure that allows the grievant or any third party to report any alleged harassment to someone other than his/her immediate supervisor or instructor. This will encourage victims of harassment to come forward and avoid the time and expense of having the issue resolved outside the institution.

Sexual harassment can encompass verbal, physical, and visual harassment. Given the multifaceted nature of the issues involved, the institution and department chair should take steps to prevent sexual harassment from occurring. Moreover, when a department chair believes harassment may have occurred, the chair cannot shut his/her eyes and hope it will go away. There must be an immediate and appropriate response that initiates corrective action.[23]

NOTES

1. *Naragon v. Wharton,* 737 F.2d 1403 (5th Cir. 1984).
2. *Kunda v. Muhlenberg College,* 621 F.2d 532 (3rd Cir. 1980).
3. *Lehmann v. Board of Trustees of Whitman College,* 576 P.2d 397 (Wash. 1978).
4. See *Rendell-Baker v. Kohn,* 102 S. Ct. 2764 (1982), a major U.S. Supreme Court case where neither government funding nor government regulations were sufficient to classify a private school's discharge of teachers as "state action."
5. *Board of Regents of University of Nebraska v. Dawes,* 522 F.2d 380 (8th Cir. 1975).
6. 29 U.S.C. sec. 206 (d)(l).
7. *Grove City College v. Bell,* 104 S. Ct. 1211 (1984).
8. 42 U.S.C. sec. 2000e et seq. The EEOC has issued sex discrimination guidelines which can be found in the Code of Federal Regulations (29 C.F.R. secs. 1600 through 1610).

9. *Equal Employment Opportunity Commission v. Southwestern Baptist Theological Seminary,* 651 F.2d 277 (5th Cir. 1981).
10. For example, Detroit, Minneapolis, Tucson, San Francisco, Seattle, New York, Iowa City, and the State of Wisconsin.
11. *McDonnell Douglas Corp. v. Green,* 411 U.S. 792 (1973).
12. See 29 C.F.R. sec. 1604.11.
13. See 34 C.F.R. sec. 106.8.
14. *Korf v. Ball State University,* 726 F.2d 1222 (7th Cir. 1984). See also, *Board of Trustees of Compton J. Col. Distr. v. Stubblefield,* 16 Cal.App.3d 820, 825 (1971): "It would seem that, as a minimum, responsible conduct upon the part of a teacher, even at the college level, excludes meretricious relationships with his students . . ."
15. 29 C.F.R. sec. 1604.4.
16. *Espinoza v. Thoma,* 580 F.2d 346 (8th Cir. 1978).
17. 42 U.S.C. sec 2000e-(k).
18. *Carey v. Population Services International,* 431 U.S. 678, 686 (1977).
19. *Avery v. Homewood City Board of Education,* 674 F.2d 337 (5th Cir. 1982).
20. *Jacobs v. Martin Sweets Co., Inc.,* 550 F.2d 364, 370 (6th Cir.), cert. denied, 431 U.S. 917 (1977).
21. *Meritor Savings Bank, FSB v. Vinson,* 106 S. Ct. 2399 (1986).
22. See 29 C.F.R. sec. 1604.11.
23. In Decision No. 86-6, the Equal Employment Opportunity Commission recently identified some reasonable procedures employers can follow when confronted with a sexual harassment issue.

SUGGESTED READINGS

Brandenburg, Judith Berman. "Sexual Harassment in the University: Guidelines for Establishing a Grievance Procedure." *Signs: Journal of Women in Culture and Society* 8 (No. 2, 1982): 320–336.

Dziech, Billie Wright and Weiner, Linda. *The Lecherous Professor.* Boston: Beacon Press, 1984.

Figuli, David J. "Legal Liability: Reducing the Risk." *The Department Advisor* 1 (No. 1, 1985): 6–10.

Fubin, David. *The Rights of Teachers, The Basic ACLU Guide to a Teacher's Constitutional Rights.* New York: Bantam Books, 1983.

Goldstein, Leslie Friedman. *The Constitutional Rights of Women: Cases in Law and Social Change.* Madison: University of Wisconsin Press, 1988.

Guthrie, R. Claire. "Sexual Harassment and Preventative Planning." *Lex Collegii* 5 (No. 2, 1981): 1–5.

Kaplin, William A. *The Law of Higher Education.* San Francisco: Jossey-Bass, 1985.

Larson, Arthur. *Employment Discrimination. Volumes 1–4.* New York: Mathew Bender, 1984.

McCaghy, M. Dawn. *Sexual Harassment: A Guide to Resources.* Boston: G. K. Hall & Co., 1985.

Simeone, Angela. *Academic Women: Working Toward Equality.* South Hadley, MA: Bergen and Garvey Publishers, 1987.

Stoddard, Thomas B. *The Rights of Gay People, The Basic ACLU Guide to a Gay Person's Rights.* New York: Bantam Books, 1983.

Tepker, H. "Title VII, Equal Employment Opportunity and Academic Autonomy: Toward a Principled Deference." 16 *University of California Law Review* 1047 (1983).

Weeks, Kent M. *Legal Deskbook for Administrators of Independent Colleges and Universities.* Atlanta: Center for Constitutional Studies, Mercer University, 1983.

19

DEALING WITH THE CHEMICALLY DEPENDENT EMPLOYEE

DAVID J. FIGULI

The problems of drug and alcohol abuse in American society have been well publicized. The dimensions of the problem transcend geographical and socioeconomic boundaries. There are sociological, political, medical, and economic ramifications.

Employers in both industrial and professional settings have recognized and dealt with the problems of alcohol and drug abuse by their employees for a number of years. Epidemiological and economic studies have calculated the prevalence of substance abuse in the work force and the resultant costs to the employer, and ultimately to the consumer of goods and services. On an operational level the manifestations are performance deficiencies, absenteeism, tardiness, illness, increased insurance and benefit costs due to a rise in alcohol and drug-related illnesses and accidents, and higher incidence of conflicts, including grievances and lawsuits, and the costs associated with resolving them.[1] It is estimated that fifty percent of all "problem" employees are alcoholics.[2]

To date, there are no hard data documenting the extent of the problem in academe. There is, however, anecdotal evidence of a serious problem with alcohol and drug abuse among the professoriat. Furthermore, conclusions that have been validated elsewhere concerning the factors influencing chemical abuse give ample reason to suspect that the incidence of alcohol and drug abuse in academe is at least as significant as that found in other sectors of the work force.[3]

First, there is a high correlation between professional and educational achievement and alcohol abuse. Approximately 45 percent of alcohol abusers in this country are in the professional or managerial ranks; 50 percent have attended or graduated from college.[4]

Second, additional evidence is generated from the application of adult development theory to academic life. The problems associated with establishing one's position in professional life, and then later experiencing diminishing aspirations and lessened expectations of meeting one's earlier hopes are highly stressful events for all professionals and especially for academics. The pursuit of tenure is particularly difficult, being intellectually demanding, highly visible, and precipitously climactic. Tenured or not, the highly unstructured yet stable existence of the middle-aged professor, combined with low salaries, little opportunity for perceptible advancement, and diminishing public esteem create greater frustration and higher susceptivity to chemical dependency than that experienced by other professionals in parallel developmental stages.[5]

Finally, it is regrettable and ironic that the cherished characteristics of academic life create an environment that is ideal for the development of chemical dependency. Thoreson identifies seven environmental factors that lead to this conclusion:

1. low visibility and minimal supervision of the academician,

2. myths about the academic as a Renaissance scholar, unfettered by performance demands, inscrutable, and undaunted by the problems of mere mortals,

3. a quasi-indentured employment status in an environment that provides maximum security and minimum opportunity for advancement for both academic and nonacademic employees,

4. collegial relationships within departments, minimizing social distance between academic supervisors and their academician-employees, which severely limits the capacity of the supervisor to manage,

5. tenure, which seriously diminishes the threat of job loss as a motivator—*a sine qua non* in successful industrial alcoholism programs,

6. a remarkably unchanging and stable work force, accompanied by boredom and the frustration of slowly but inexorably eroding salaries and status, and

7. an aging professoriat now concentrated in the forty-five to sixty-five age range where mid-stage alcoholism predominates.[6]

He concludes that the academic environment is "ideally constructed to nurture both the wellspring of creativity requisite to a community of scholars and the development of alcohol abuse."[7] The accuracy of Thoreson's perceptions appear to be confirmable by the limited anecdotal experience available.[8]

For the department chair, theoretical projections can quickly devolve into practical complexities. A chemically dependent department member, or nonacademic employee for that matter, creates a managerial conundrum that defies conventional academic management wisdom. When collegiality is frustrated by a colleague whose professionalism and academic principles are held hostage to chemical rogues, what, if any, resources does a department manager have available to effect a liberation? Inevitably the chair will be faced with countervailing motivations: humanitarian impulses that are expressed in a personal concern for the individual, and professional ethics that will be manifested in efforts to assure performance accountability.

Injected into this balance of concerns are technical requirements that only serve to make the accommodation more difficult. Treatment of chemical dependency as a "handicap" or "disability" under federal, state, and local nondiscrimination laws must be taken into account. This chapter will provide the framework within which to analyze these concerns as well as to provide practical guidance to assist the department manager in pursuing a humane yet professionally responsible solution.

CHEMICAL DEPENDENCY AS A "HANDICAP"

"Handicap" or "disability" nondiscrimination laws exist at the federal, state, and local levels. The federal enactment was passed as part of the Rehabilitation Act of 1973.[9] All fifty states have some type of legislation regulating discrimination against handicapped or disabled persons, although the scope of coverage varies from state to state.[10] In some states only physical handicaps or disabilities are covered; in others those with both physical and mental disabilities receive protection. Whether termed "handicapped" or "disability" the state laws generally parallel the federal law in defining the extent of their coverage.

Section 706(7)(B) of Title 29 of the United States Code defines the term "handicapped individual." The definition is embellished in regulations but reads essentially as follows:

> . . . any person who (i) has a physical or mental impairment which substantially limits one or more of such person's major life activities, (ii) has a record of such an impairment, or (iii) is regarded as having such an impairment.

Many of the operative terms in the foregoing definition have been defined by regulation.[11] Specifically, "physical or mental impairment" has been defined to mean:

> . . . (A) any physiological disorder or condition, cosmetic disfigurement, or anatomical loss affecting one or more of the following body systems: neurological; musculoskeletal; special sense organs; respiratory, including speech organs; cardiovascular; reproductive; digestive; genito-urinary; hemic and lymphatic; skin; and endocrine; or (B) any mental or psychological disorder, such as mental retardation, organic brain syndrome, emotional or mental illness, and specific learning disabilities.

Further, "major life activities" has been defined as "functions such as caring for oneself, performing manual tasks, walking, seeing, hearing, speaking, breathing, learning, and working." State laws, depending upon the extent of their coverage, generally closely track the physical or mental dimensions of these definitions, or both.

Handicap nondiscrimination laws have both prohibitory and mandatory components. The laws prohibit discrimination in employment against handicapped persons who are "qualified." A handicapped individual is qualified in an employment setting if he or she can perform the essential functions of the job in question with "reasonable accommodation." It is this latter term that gives rise to the mandatory aspects of the law. An employer must provide a "reasonable accommodation" to a handicapped individual if that "reasonable accommodation" will allow the individual to become qualified, that is, capable of performing the essential functions of the job in question. The "reasonableness" of accommodations that employers are required to make under the law has been the subject of a great deal of litigation and commentary. The most that can be said at this point is that a determination of what is reasonable is fact-specific, generally taking into account programmatic, economic, and safety considerations.[12]

Alcoholism and drug addiction have been defined as "handicaps" under virtually every law that includes mental or physical impairments within its scope. In 1977 the Secretary of the then Department of Health, Education and Welfare determined that alcoholism and drug addiction were "physical or mental impairments" within the meaning of the Rehabilitation Act of 1973 based upon a legal opinion received from the U.S. Attorney General. The Secretary was able to conclude decisively that alcohol and drug addiction were diseases but was unable to conclude whether they were primarily mental or physical.[13] Since that time the courts have reached the same conclusion, both in interpreting the federal legislation,[14] and in state laws.[15] These decisions demonstrate a dramatic turnaround in both medical and judicial understanding of alcoholism and drug addiction as diseases.[16]

The inclusion of alcoholism and drug addiction as protected handicaps under the federal law, and the Secretary's decision in 1977, quickly led to a reconsideration and amendment in 1978 due to the episodic nature of the impairments caused by these diseases. Although an alcoholic or drug abuser may in a state of sobriety be qualified to perform the essential functions of a job, at unpredictable times of intoxication he or she is decidedly unable to perform the same functions. In 1978, the definition of the term "handicapped individual" under the Rehabilitation Act was amended to exclude from the scope of that term:

> any individual who is an alcoholic or drug abuser whose current use of alcohol or drugs prevents such individual from performing the duties of the job in question or whose employment, by reason of such current alcohol or drug abuse, would constitute a direct threat to property or the safety of others.[17]

With this change, and similar adjustments to state laws, the treatment of alcohol and drug abuse under nondiscrimination laws was materially distinguished from other protected "handicaps," by removing protection in cases of performance deficiencies caused by current alcohol or drug abuse.

For the academic manager, the current state of the law creates two requirements with respect to chemically dependent employees, with the line of demarcation significantly blurred. First, chemically dependent employees are protected as handicapped individuals against discrimination in employment so long as their condition does not create current performance or safety problems. Consequently, they are required to be treated without regard to their handicap, as long as they are qualified to perform the essential functions of the job. If in order to attain "qualification" they require a reasonable accommodation, it must be provided. Reasonable accommodations include leave for counseling or therapy, extensions beyond the accrued leaves available to other employees under the employer's personnel policies. On the other hand, if the employee's current use of alcohol or drugs prevents the individual from performing the functions of the job or constitutes a direct threat to the property or safety of others, then the employee is not a protected "handicapped individual" and the employer may take adverse action based upon performance deficiencies or safety concerns.

Ambiguity arises, however, where the employee's current use of alcohol or drugs creates performance or safety problems but the employee is undertaking good-faith efforts to obtain help. Recent decisions by arbitrators suggest that forbearance from adverse job actions are required, as long as good-faith efforts are pursued. Indeed, continued participation in assistance programs may be made a condition of continued employment, or of the continued suspension of a disciplinary sanction. Arbitrators do not appear to be as disposed to require accommodation even where rehabilitation is being pursued in good faith if the nature of the deficiencies support the adverse personnel actions taken.[19] Nevertheless, it would seem prudent for an employer to accommodate a chemically dependent employee who is pursuing a treatment program, even in the face of performance deficiencies, so long as those deficiencies do not put the employer in a position of breaching duties or obligations to others.

OTHER LEGAL ISSUES

There are other legal issues that the department administrator is cautioned to consider in dealing with a chemically dependent employee. First, protection is also afforded to alcohol or drug abusers under the Equal Protection Clause of the United States Constitution and parallel provisions in state constitutions.[20] That is, a public employer is prohibited from discriminating against alcohol or drug abusers as a class unless there is a rational basis for the discrimination based on principles of sound public policy or public personnel administration. Compliance with the nondiscrimination laws should amply protect the departmental administrator against constitutional violations as well. Second, liability for defamation should be avoided. Department chairs should not refer to employees as drug addicts or alcoholics in conversations with outsiders (i.e., persons who are not involved in administering aspects of the employment relation with the affected employee), unless there has been a clear clinical diagnosis of the employee's condition. Even in the face of such a diagnosis, the chair should be reluctant to disclose that information to outsiders for fear of invading the privacy of the employee. Further, colleagues are wise to focus only on performance issues in providing references for fellow employees with chemical dependency conditions.[21]

A final issue concerns the use of drug or alcohol testing as a prophylactic against abuse. Testing techniques have been widely used in the industrial sector and have been judicially upheld. While such concepts seem Orwellian in an academic context, they have been applied in educational settings, including testing of student athletes and teachers. In private institutions it is possible to institute a testing program that will pass legal muster, as a condition of employment. At public institutions, however, such procedures would likely be ruled a violation of the Fourth Amendment prohibition against unlawful search and seizure.[22]

MANAGEMENT GUIDELINES

In dealing with chemically dependent employees department managers must take into account legal and psychological prescriptions. It is infrequent that the dictates of the law and human concerns are harmonious. Fortunately, this is one circumstance where they are. Both focus on the manifestations of the employee's condition in his or her work performance and seek to obtain the employee's recognition of the problem and pursuit of assistance in controlling or removing the cause.

The following guidelines are recommended for department chairs who deal with chemically dependent employees:

- *Put the problems in writing.* Stick to specific, work-related problems, such as missed classes, sick days, incomplete assignments, reduced productivity, and relationships with co-workers and supervisors. Give a confidential memorandum to the professor.

- *Be supportive and express concern.* Indicate that you have valued the professor's performance in the past, but that you have noticed changes in the quality of his or her work. Be empathetic but do not try to solve everyone's problem yourself.

- *Do not diagnose the professor's problem as alcoholism.* You could be wrong, and you could be liable in a lawsuit. Instead, if you have reports of alcohol abuse on the job, say, "You seem to have problems managing alcohol."

- *Suggest that the faculty member seek help.* Be able to recommend places to go, such as a campus employee-assistance program, counseling service, personnel office, or community mental health agency. If possible, suggest a particular person to see.
- *Outline a plan of improvement.* Explain where change is expected, such as completing research reports, maintaining regular office hours, or improving teaching quality.
- *Set a date for another review.* Check the faculty member's progress within six weeks to six months. If the person is seeking treatment, he or she will need more time. After the second review, give the professor another memorandum summarizing the meeting.
- *Keep your expectations realistic.* Alcohol problems can take seven to ten years to develop. Do not expect them to disappear magically after six weeks.[23]

These guidelines are legally sufficient and also practically appropriate.

A necessary adjunct to the department chair's efforts is an employee assistance program. Whether staffed by the institution or organized as a referral source, it provides the chair with a referral outlet to which he or she may be directed to obtain assistance in dealing with the problems of chemical dependency. It allows the chair to divide the issues. While the chair focuses on the performance-related concerns, humanitarian considerations can be accommodated by an employee assistance center.[24]

Ultimately, in dealing with chemically dependent employees it is important not to become entangled in a web of legalism or blinded by humanitarian passion. Attention to the principles and practices discussed above ensure that management responsibilities are fulfilled, individual rights protected, and a colleague assisted in a responsible, caring way.

NOTES

1. S. Cohen, "Drugs in the Workplace," *Drug Abuse & Alcoholism Newsletter* (August 1983).
2. G. C. Pati and J. I. Adkins, Jr., "The Employer's Role in Alcoholism Assistance," *Personnel Journal* (July 1983): 568–572.
3. R. W. Thoreson, "The Professor at Risk: Alcohol Abuse in Academe," *Journal of Higher Education* 55 (1984): 56–72.
4. Pati and Adkins, "The Employer's Role in Alcoholism Assistance," 568.
5. Thoreson, "The Professor at Risk: Alcohol Abuse in Academe," 60–61.
6. *Ibid.*, 62.
7. *Ibid.*, 56.
8. L. McMillen, "The Alcoholic Professor: Campus Ideal Environment for a Hidden Problem," *The Chronicle of Higher Education* (October 9, 1985): 26–27.

9. 29 U.S.C. Section 794.
10. L. F. Rothstein, "Section 504 of the Rehabilitation Act: Emerging Issues for Colleges and Universities," *Journal of College and University Law* 13 (Winter 1986): 234–35, n. 33.
11. 45 C.F.R. Part 84.
12. 45 C.F.R. Section 84.12.
13. 42 Fed. Reg. 22686 (May 4, 1977).
14. *Whitlock v. Donovan*, 598 F. Supp. 126 (D.D.C.1984); *Davis v. Bucher*, 451 F.Supp. 791 (E.D. Pa. 1978).
15. *Hazlett v. Martin Chevrolet, Inc.*, 496 N.E.2d 478 (Ohio 1986); *Consolidated Freightways, Inc., v. Cedar Rapids Civil Rights Commission*, 366 N.W.2d 522 (Iowa 1985); *Squires v. Labor and Industry Review Commission*, 1980 CCH EPD Paragraph 31,044.
16. *See for example, Powell v. State of Texas*, 392 U.S. 514, 20 L.Ed.2d 1254, 88 S. Ct. 2145 (1968) (U.S. Supreme Court found that there was "no agreement among the members of the medical profession" as to the meaning of "alcoholism" as a disease.)
17. 29 U.S.C. Section 706A(7)(B).
18. Marmo, M., "Arbitrators View Alcoholic Employees," *The Arbitration Journal* 37 (March 1982): 17–27.
19. Rothstein, *ibid.*, 260, n. 196.
20. *Davis v. Bucher*, 451 F.Supp. 791, 799 (E.D. Pa. 1978).
21. For further information on the legal theories of defamation and invasion of privacy, see chapter 17 of this book.
22. *See for example, Patchogue-Medford Congress v. Board of Education*, 505 N.Y.S.2d 888 (S. Ct. 1986).
23. McMillen, L., "Guidelines to Help Chairmen Deal With Alcoholic Professors," *The Chronicle of Higher Education* (October 9, 1985): 27.
24. Pati and Adkins, "The Employer's Role in Alcoholism Assistance," 568.

20

THE DEPARTMENT CHAIR'S DILEMMA: BAD APPLES IN THE DEPARTMENT

LOIS VANDER WAERDT

Department chair Tom Frederick has received several complaints from students about Bill Jones and his sexist treatment of the women in his classes. Last year, one student made a formal complaint and a grievance hearing was held. The committee found in the student's favor, recommending a written reprimand for Bill. Tom had prepared that document, discussed it with Bill, and placed the reprimand in Bill's file.

Yesterday, Helen Murray, a colleague from another institution, called Tom and asked him for information about Bill, who had applied for a faculty position at Helen's institution—a golden opportunity to rid the department of a continuing problem! Tom, however, is uneasy about passing on a department member who has shown a reluctance to change his behavior and a gross insensitivity to female students. If he ever has to call Helen in return, he would appreciate honesty from her!

Helen also faces a problem common to department chairs who are hiring new faculty members. She wants to hire people with appropriate academic credentials who will fit in with departmental colleagues and not cause unwanted problems. She is particularly sensitive to the importance of accurate references ever since the history department at her institution hired a new professor whose alcoholism made it impossible for him to meet his classes. None of his references had mentioned a problem with drinking. A few after-the-fact phone calls, however, revealed that his problem was well known by previous academic employers.

THE ISSUE OF LIABILITY

Tom and Helen face the classic problems of hiring—how to receive and offer accurate references without facing a libel suit from the problem faculty member who is the subject of the adverse reference. Helen's dilemma is exacerbated by the emergence of a new legal cause of action, a tort called negligent hiring. Over the past decade, the liability of employers, including institutions of higher education, has expanded so

172

that employers are now held liable for actions their employees took prior to being hired.

In Prince George's County, Maryland, a young boy was murdered by a prison inmate who was employed by the county in a work-release program. The convict's record included a conviction for second degree murder. He was responsible for guarding the work-site against vandalism and had been overheard remarking that he would kill the next person he caught spraying graffiti. The boy was that person. His parents are presently suing the county for $10 million. An appellate court decision recently remanded the case to the trial court, holding that the foreseeability of the convict's action by the employer was a relevant issue of fact.

Avis Rent-A-Car hired a car-washer who had a prison record as a rapist. The employee raped a secretary in Avis' office during working hours. The court awarded her $750,000 in damages. Avis had not done a background check on the employee and the Court ruled that the employer has a duty to other employees to investigate applicants before they are hired.

Although these cases arose outside of academe, higher education is not immune from negligent hiring suits, and, indeed, will be treated by the courts just like any other employer. With only a little imagination, we can envision discovering that a faculty member who sexually harasses a student was terminated from his previous institution for a similar offense. The institutional liability in that case was enormous, assuming that the hiring department would not have hired the faculty member had this information been gathered as part of the hiring process.

The sins of omission or commission on vitae, past job performance, or in society at large provide compelling reasons for department chairs to check thoroughly the backgrounds of prospective faculty members.

GATHERING DATA

Most applicants have not committed crimes that would result in lawsuits by co-workers or colleagues. Most do not distort their backgrounds in a way that results in the hiring of a large number of unqualified people, although one estimate is that 80 percent of vitae contain false information about unearned degrees, job titles, responsibilities, or salaries. Frankly, a basic background check is a good management practice. Here are a number of steps department chairs can take to gather adequate data for making informed employment decisions about prospective colleagues:

- Require that all candidates fill out a brief application form as a means of gathering uniform data in a usable format. The form should include a position and educational chronology that highlights missing years of education or employment.

- Look for gaps in a candidate's employment record, such as a foreshortened military career or an unusual career path. If any of these appear on the job application or vitae, ask the candidate about them. One candidate had been injured in an automobile accident and had spent two years in therapy and rehabilitation. Another had remained at home with her children when they were pre-schoolers. Another had taken a year to sail around the world. Many times the explanation is both interesting and unrelated to why an applicant would not make a good faculty or staff member.
- Ask finalists to sign waivers for transcript request forms for all educational institutions they have attended. Each form should request that the receiving institution bill the applicant and should provide a place for the applicant's signature. Mail the transcript requests directly to the registrars of the appropriate institutions. Request that experienced personnel—perhaps someone from the admissions office—scrutinize all transcripts and confer with issuing institutions regarding any irregularities.
- Check the references yourself. The new colleague will report to you; even though a department chair is a quasi-administrative position, no one else has a larger or more personal stake in hiring competent faculty members for the department.
- If the person must start work immediately, limit the background check to the person being offered the job, perhaps making the job offer contingent upon the background check. If you have time during the interviewing process, check several finalists before making the job offer.
- Call colleagues and administrators at the applicant's former institutions to gather information about work history and performance. If those sources will not give you substantive information because of their personnel policy, make a note of this so that your records will show that you made a good-faith effort to check out the applicant.
- Remember, the best source of accurate information about a prospective colleague or employee is someone you already know at the applicant's present or former institution. Use your contacts.

A complete reference check also involves hiring a consumer agency to investigate the character, general reputation, personal characteristics and credit history of the finalists and requiring that all applicants request a criminal record check. Such a check falls far outside academic tradition and few institutions are likely to investigate a prospective colleague's background so thoroughly.

THE LIKELIHOOD OF LIABILITY

Helen Murray's search for quality faculty members can be aided by careful reference checks, validation of educational credentials and discussions with colleagues at other institutions such as Tom Frederick's. She will also minimize the likelihood of charges of negligent hiring by practicing good management during the hiring process.

Tom's dilemma, on the other hand, is both legal and ethical. His sense of integrity urges an honest response to Helen's inquiry, but he is concerned that if he gives an honest reference about Bill, he may be open to a defamation suit if Bill does not get the job. This concern has become more prevalent as administrators try to avoid litigation.

Over the past several years, we have seen more and more campuses adopt policies against substantive references regarding present or former faculty, staff, or administrators. Because they fear defamation actions, many campuses have adopted the most conservative position possible, limiting the information they provide to employees' job titles and dates of employment. In so doing, they prevent other institutions from gathering information about applicants' job histories, work performance, and any undesirable work-related characteristics—key data in making thoughtful hiring decisions.

When department chairs are asked for references for faculty or staff members who have performed poorly, who have drug or alcohol problems, who conduct themselves inappropriately in class, or who are sexual harassers, the risk of liability is minimal if they follow the guidelines at the end of this article.

Of course department chairs can be sued by colleagues who believe they were given bad references. The fear of a defamation suit is neither frivolous nor foolhardy, but the likelihood of such suits has been greatly exaggerated. Since the highly publicized failure of the libel cases brought by Ariel Sharon against *Time* magazine and by General Westmoreland against CBS, the number of newly filed libel suits has dwindled.

Although one-third of all defamation cases that reach a verdict are now filed by discharged employees, the plaintiffs have won only when the statements made by employers have been inaccurate and outrageous. One winning plaintiff, for example, was described by his former employer as ruthless, disliked by his colleagues, and a failure. His award of $1.9 million was upheld by the Supreme Court. Another plaintiff collected nearly $2 million in damages from an employer who called him a "Jekyll and Hyde" and a sociopath.

The common law of defamation was transplanted from England to the United States with the thirteenth-century edict that one who tarnished the good name of another would have his or her tongue cut out. Penalties today are less dramatic, but the underlying interest in redressing attacks upon reputation is the same. Generally speaking, defamatory works harm a person's reputation, lower them in the estimation of the community, and deter others from dealing with them. There are some variations from state to state, but in general, to recover for defamation, a plaintiff must prove publication, falsity, malice, and resulting injury. Oral defamation is called *slander*; written defamation is called *libel*.

RECENT LITIGATION

Several defamation cases in recent years have involved institutions of higher education. In one recent case, when Professor John Connally of the University of Nebraska Medical Center evaluated a doctor's performance as "well below average" in a reference letter, the case hinged on technicalities and finally was dropped when the plaintiff ran out of money to pay his lawyers.

In another case, the Court held that the alleged libelous statement, contained in a letter sent by the defendants to the president of the college at which the plaintiff was employed, was not actionable because the president did not think less of the plaintiff academically and the plaintiff did not suffer humiliation or a lowering of his reputation as a scholar.

Wayne State University won a case brought by a student who, failing to get into medical school because of a letter questioning his "personal integrity," brought a libel action. The court held that the letter was the committee's opinion based on true and undisputed facts. Another court in a different case held that opinions—no matter how insidious—are not actionable under the law of defamation.

Defamation actions can be brought against faculty members and department chairs, but the risk is substantially less than popular wisdom would lead one to believe. It is difficult for candidates to determine why they were turned down for a faculty position. The plaintiff also faces the often insurmountable burden of proving that the statements were false or that they were made carelessly, recklessly, or maliciously.

In addition, many state courts are recognizing a qualified privilege among employers for employment references, reasoning that accurate and substantive information about employees' work histories is essential to proper decision-making by prospective employers. These courts recognize a public concern that employers who respond to requests for employment references should not have their speech inhibited by fear of defamation actions. Their ruling show judicial recognition of the fact that the quality of an institution can suffer if bad apples get jobs because their former employers are afraid to say they are rotten. In many jurisdictions, the courts' major concern is the fairness of imposing liability when the defendant, in this case the employer, can show a justification for its acts.

GUIDELINES

By following these guidelines, department chairs can protect themselves from liability for defamation and minimize the likelihood that such an action will be brought against them:

- Be sure the request for a reference is legitimate. If it is by telephone and you do not know the caller, call the person back so that you can verify the caller's identity. Keep a written record of dates and details of such requests.

- Communicate only with proper parties such as someone from the personnel office of the inquiring institution, the administrator to whom the employee would report on the new job, the chairperson of the hiring department, or a member of the search committee.
- If the request is in writing, be sure it is accompanied by a consent form signed by the candidate. Even so, avoid being specific in writing about the person's deficiencies. Suggest, instead, that the reference-seeker call you for further information.
- Limit the information you provide to the actual inquiry and to job-related data.
  - Avoid medical diagnoses such as "I think Sam is an alcoholic."
  - Avoid statements pertaining to the exercise of legal rights such as "We thought Mary was a good colleague until she filed that charge with the Equal Employment Opportunity Commission." (Mary will have a charge of retaliation under Title VII of the Civil Rights Act if she does not get the job.)
  - Avoid general statements like this: "Sally performed well below average" or "Ed just didn't fit into the department."
- Limit references to factual statements for which you have documentation, such as Sam's pattern of not meeting his afternoon classes or Ed's refusal to advise students. Tom could mention the letter of reprimand that was placed in Bill Jones' files subsequent to the grievance filed against him. Focusing on documentation, of course, is a strong argument for an effective departmental program of performance evaluation and appraisal.
- Remember, if you give damaging information about a present or former colleague, the information you give must be true to the best of your knowledge. If you do not know the answer to a question, simply say so.

CONCLUSION

Like all department chairs, Tom Frederick and Helen Murray have an interest in informed decision-making. This means gathering accurate references for colleagues and in turn providing accurate information about former or current colleagues. Informed decision-making also calls for department chairs to take seriously the case law that has developed outside of higher education, because these defamation cases do apply to academe. We should not, however, immobilize our conduits of information because of an unrealistic fear of lawsuits.

To stay within the law, be sure that references you give are not motivated by personal animosity; that they are factual, accurate, and job-related; and that they are given from your personal experience or from clear, written documentation. This will provide concrete and useful decision-making information for institutions hiring faculty, staff, or administrators.

Another version of this chapter appeared in *The Chronicle of Higher Education*, copyright 1987. Reprinted with permission.

SUGGESTED READING

Ralph Brown, "Can They Sue Me? Liability Risks from Unfavorable Letters of Reference." *Academe* (September–October 1986).

Lawrence Duke, "Employment References and The Law." *Personnel Journal* (February 1986).

"Misrepresentation in the Marketplace and Recognizing Fraudulent Credentials," 1987, *American Association of Collegiate Registrars and Admissions Officers*.

Michael Silver, "Negligent Hiring Claims Take Off," *ABA Journal* (May, 1987).

PART FIVE

Determining Departmental Priorities and Direction

The immediate context of the department is the school or college of which it is a part. There may or may not be a university beyond the college. In either case, directions taken at the department level will influence those of other departments and of the institution as a whole. Influence flows both ways, of course, and it is the wise department chairperson who stays alert for new developments and opportunities.

Today's "buzzword" associated with planning of all types seems to be "strategic." In his chapter, "The Department Chair's Transforming Role in 'Strategic' Academic Planning," Robert Cope offers helpful clarification of the term and provides several pointers for department chairpersons. Too often "strategic" planning has hindered rather than facilitated the department's need to review its strengths, examine developing external opportunities, and relate the strengths to the emerging opportunities. The department chair can play a transforming role in this process, making sure that common academic values are protected and enhanced. Properly understood, strategic or contextual academic planning is not a solution, but rather a means of arriving at one.

Program vitality is affected by a variety of factors. Periodic departmental review of these factors can be an effective way of securing and maintaining viability and vigor. In "Five Indices of Program Vitality," Thomas Emmet and John Bennett explore critical points of program evaluation. Distinctions are drawn among criteria, standards of accomplishment, and sources of evidence for measuring accomplishments. Accreditation requirements and financial crises can provoke intense scrutiny of program accomplishment and vitality. The benefits of regular, ongoing self-study, however, call for long-term evaluation of department congruence with the institutional mission and with changing societal needs and student interests. Similarly, departments need to determine their status vis-à-vis competing departments and institutions in terms of quality and cost on a regular basis. There are various ways of conducting these reviews.

The two exercises that follow provide specific help in clarifying department priorities and in positioning the department for stability or growth. John Minter's exercise is private and for the chair's eyes only. "Positioning the Department for Survival and Growth" involves a listing of current and desired department objectives, an enumeration of relevant internal and external changes, an inventory of departmental capabilities and the resources to which the department has access, and an analysis of how the changes and capabilities interact to affect the likelihood of achieving the objective. Identifying peer or competitive departments within and without the institution is an important step in positioning the department to advantage.

Elwood Ehrle's exercise can be used by the department as a whole in clarifying how the individual faculty members assess and value the competing choices before them. In "Clarifying Priorities Through Paired Choices" the objective is to determine the relative importance of items and in a manner in which each person's judgments are weighted equally. Accordingly, the exercise can be used to lay bare the composite ordering of current and desired departmental objectives—against which the chair can then compare his or her sense of things and make appropriate adjustments.

Two other matters related to planning can be important for department chairs: monitoring enrollment and establishing community based programs. Concerns about departmental enrollments are common and are frequent topics of conversation among chairs. After all, the most basic index of departmental financial health is the student credit hours generated. Expecting the admissions office to be solely responsible for department enrollments is both shortsighted and unprofessional. It is shortsighted because the department faculty has the most to lose if enrollments drop. Responsible educators know most intimately the values of the inquiries they conduct and so are best situated to communicate their importance to the uninitiated.

In her chapter, "The Department Chair and Enrollment Management: Some Strategies," Antoinette Iadarola reviews several enrollment-related issues for department chairpersons and provides a number of concrete suggestions about ways to proceed. Central concepts include developing a clear departmental mission, one that is appropriately related to the broader institutional mission; securing needed data on recruitment, retention, course evaluations, and advising; developing faculty commitment to specific recruitment and retention plans and activities; and forging new relationships with area businesses.

Establishing and nurturing relationships with community and regional agencies and industries is becoming increasingly important for a number of department chairpersons. At some institutions such external relationships are becoming actual ways of getting the departments' business done—as important to them as the more traditional classroom offerings are for the traditional institutions.

In his chapter, "A Prescription for Success: Developing Successful Community-Based Programs," Anthony Zeiss reviews the accomplishments of Pueblo Community College in establishing public-private partnerships. Whether the objective is providing management assistance to small businesses or career assessment services to the community or region, successful community-based programs are usually planned around clearly identified community needs—answers to which seem to fit within the institution's mission and capability. Zeiss provides a helpful list of the steps necessary for success in this area.

21

THE DEPARTMENT CHAIR'S TRANSFORMING ROLE IN "STRATEGIC" ACADEMIC PLANNING: HOW TO WORK IN CONCERT WITH THE FACULTY

ROBERT G. COPE

At the great majority of colleges and universities, the term *strategic*, usually associated with *planning*, has been applied to virtually every administrative action over the past six years or so. Many, perhaps most, faculty believe the term has been over-used and misused. The term has been over-used by administrators because it is applied to anything that a central administration, trustees, or a state agency wants others to think is important. It has been misused as well. Most of those applying the strategy concept fail to understand its conceptual foundations or the fundamentals of applying the concept in ways consistent with the values of the academy.

The concept, however, has substantial value for academic planning. It is, and always has been, an important way of looking, listening, and thinking about how to achieve a mission. And for most faculty, achieving a mission is synonymous with achieving quality.

This chapter will explain why the concept has been adopted so quickly by many administrations across the country, clarify the appropriateness of its use from a faculty perspective, and outline the role a chairperson can play in concert with the faculty in using the concept effectively. There are several short examples of colleges that follow the strategic concept and one case example of a department, to illustrate ideas that may be useful at any college for a nearly ideal strategic planning process.

It should be clear that strategic academic planning is less a solution than a means of arriving at one. This chapter is written to be shared and read by any or all members of a department.

WHY WAS THE STRATEGY CONCEPT ADOPTED?

During the late 1970s most states were allocating fewer dollars to higher education; some state and regional economies were floundering; and a drastic decline of graduates from high schools was forecasted. These were (and are) times of more rapid change, decreased budgets, and increased accountability. Both private and public institutions were affected. The administrators of our institutions were looking for a management solution when George Keller, an experienced academic administrator and gifted writer, wrote *Academic Strategy: The Management Revolution in American Higher Education*. Published in 1983, it is the largest-selling book ever printed about management in the academy. It carried the message that colleges could adapt to change, manage resources better, and respond to the changing external environment if they planned strategically. The book has been reprinted six times. Enough copies have been sold to have more than five copies on every college campus. It is still recommended as essential reading for any chairperson or faculty member.

When the book was discovered, usually by well-intending presidents, vice presidents and other administrators, who are frequently desperate for solutions to administrative problems, they grasped at the "solution" by setting up all-campus strategic planning committees, establishing administrative task forces, and sometimes writing the strategic plan themselves.

The results have been mixed. Some institutions such as Drake University and Centre College report that they were saved by strategic planning. Other institutions, such as Memphis State University, report that strategic planning was a dismal failure (it was imposed upon them) or that they went through the process with substantial faculty resistance, such as at Bradley University. Some visible cases—notably at the University of Minnesota and Iowa State University—are still struggling.

WHAT IS STRATEGIC PLANNING EXACTLY?

Strategic planning is planning in context. It is first seeing the interests of the department in its larger context. It is then shaping and maneuvering the department—shaping it to be an able competitor for resources and maneuvering it to a favorable position within a larger context. This larger context reflects demographic changes, value shifts, economic trends, new technologies, the politics of the situation, and entities competing for the same resources. Strategy concerns context. It is about adjusting to and even shaping the context that provides favorable conditions in which teaching and scholarship can take place.

"Strategy is a simple idea but not for that reason easy," said the Prussian general Clausewitz. Planning in context, however, is, if done well, a thoroughly engaging intellectual process.

WHAT HAVE BEEN THE MAJOR MISTAKES WITH STRATEGIC PLANNING?

The first mistake has been an attempt to do strategic planning without understanding its origins and its limits. Although strategic planning is widely assumed to have started in the business community in the 1960s and in higher education in the early 1980s, the foundations of the strategic concept can be traced to the writing of Sun Tzu as long ago as 500 B.C. Its conceptual origins are deeply imbedded in the mathematical, the sociological, the geopolitical, and the biological disciplines.

Because of the resulting richness of the concept, it has been linked to many other concepts of management. If it is everything, perhaps it is nothing. And if its interpretation is too shallow—and it usually is—little is obtained from its use. If its interpretation is too extreme—and it frequently is—its application can do harm. The concept is properly and clearly related only to the ways in which an entity (college, department, or program) achieves its mission and acquires resources to carry out that mission as it responds to changes in its external environment.

Even with this limited purpose—achieving a mission and acquiring resources—not all entities are equally able to apply the concept. The application of the concept depends upon the degree to which an institution or department has control over "price" (tuition and overhead charges), range of "products" (programs and degrees), and "location" (where and how it offers services and attracts resources). Thus, not all entities are equally able to shape themselves and maneuver. A department that cannot control its budget, cannot decide on its curriculum, cannot decide on who shall be educated and how, and cannot independently attract resources can plan strategically about as well as the Walla Walla prison.

Another mistake has been to plan strategically from a marketing perspective, often with the assistance of consultants and firms, thus frequently ignoring the common academic values rooted in the faculty members' shared experiences and guiding behaviors, internalized, frequently without written standards, but understood tacitly.

Sometimes the concept has been used deceptively for program review when the administration wanted to close or reorganize departments. This has given the concept a tarnished reputation on some campuses.

Even if the concept has been understood and applied ethically, departments mistakenly become involved in a lengthy information-gathering process. The strategy process should be simple, informed and driven by ideas, not by data and paper.

The final mistake is to write something called a strategic plan. The process should result in shared expectations, common understandings, and a shared sense of direction. If a plan is written at all, it should be about how to implement the common understanding of the department's or institution's direction.

Correcting these mistakes depends on understanding a few key points about the content of contextual planning. Notice that *strategic* is no longer the modifier here. The warlike term *strategic* is not consistent with the dominant values of the academy. From now on the discussion will be about planning in context or contextual planning. Contextual planning might well, however, result in strategizing, and risk-taking on the assumption that certain future states will exist.

HOW TO DO CONTEXTUAL PLANNING: CASE ILLUSTRATIONS

The key to planning contextually is to look outside the department or college. Observe what is happening or likely to happen. Planners call this "environmental scanning." Some planners place great stock in "futures studies." I do not. As the case examples illustrate, what really matters is seeing today's reality. Today's reality shapes the future.

Institutions planning within their context regularly and passively assess changes occurring in their environments at two levels: institution or college and department. The institution assesses megatrends or forces; departments assess trends/forces in their discipline, profession, or program. Most scanning is passive; most of the information needed to make strategic choices is already in the minds of the participants. *Contextual* planning—which I suggest as a synonym for *strategic*—can be, and should be, done quickly and with little expense. To do this it is important to separate planning from implementation and finding direction from management. To be certain the values of the academy are expressed realistically, departmental faculty must play a key role in direction finding.

In order for a department or college within a university to apply this concept, the institution must provide guidelines. For example, Dean Ann Morey of the College of Education at San Diego State University, after conducting a participatory process in which the faculty decided what should be emphasized in the years ahead, directed her departments to emphasize serving the needs of multicultural learners, extend educational services beyond schools in and around San Diego, and focus scholarly inquiry on the connection between theory and application. Department budgets, faculty leaves, new hires, research funds, equipment, and so on, are now directly determined by the extent to which the request coincides with these college-level aims. Strategic planning will mean little if it is not tied to the budget.

Millikin University of Illinois has been very successful in a difficult competitive environment because it knows its niche. Contextual planning helps identify a favorable niche. Nearly failing Centre College of Kentucky has set out to be the best liberal arts college with less than 1000 students in the United States. Centre has found its niche and, even better, has a vision.

Carnegie Mellon University, Northwestern University, and the University of Minnesota have made or are making commitments to focus on selected themes and on particular departments that reflect these institutions' strengths, special circumstances, and the anticipated changes in their worlds. Departments not joining in institutional level plans will discover that plans have already been made for them.

ARE THERE IMPORTANT GUIDELINES TO FOLLOW?

It will be useful to separate planning from implementation, and strategy from tactics (i.e., determining goals or directions from how to attain them). Planning "where to go" should be limited to decisions associated with the external environment so that the efficiency and effectiveness of resource acquisition is enhanced. The strategy concept for management limits it to decisions about how to implement plans and how to make efficient use of resources. One important distinction—seldom made—is that between the "where" and the "how." Deciding where to go is strategizing. This is where the faculty should play the key role. How to get there is the work of the administration. Our administrators will feel the challenge is adequate if they follow Napoleon's dictate, "Strategy is a simple art, it is just a matter of execution."

Strategizing, however, is a demanding intellectual art because it properly addresses issues in areas where an institution does not have control—in its external environment. The external environment presents both opportunities and threats. Management is appropriate where an institution does have control over its own resources, structures, personnel, information systems, and so on. Most planning activities do not make the important distinction between where and how and therefore the results of the planning activity are less satisfying to the participants and less successful in increasing resources.

For example, during the 1970s Seattle's City University decided to move statewide with centers in all the major communities of Washington state. This was clearly a strategic move having important implications for resource acquisition or depletion within City University's geographic, demographic, and political context. On the other hand, Gonzaga University's decision to increase flexibility for students transferring between its five colleges in Spokane, Washington, did not lead directly to more resource acquisition from the external environment; this choice made better use of resources (i.e., the students and tuitions) already acquired; therefore, carrying out the decision requires improved management rather than increased acquisitions. In both instances, however, the faculty's role is to assure quality.

THE DEPARTMENT OF HOME ECONOMICS: A CASE HISTORY

Abstract
This is a hypothetical case drawn from several real situations. The case illustrates a simplified strategic planning process in a field of study we may all understand. The process is recommended for any academic department, college, or educational organization.

Context
The Department of Home Economics at Midwestern State University (MSU) must review its curriculum. MSU's central administration has asked that the review be completed during the next four months. The review is to involve all the department's faculty and any other stakeholder the faculty feels might contribute ideas.

With costs zooming and declines in the number of high school graduates forecasted until the late 1990s, the university's trustees are considering the possibility of reorganizing or closing several departments. The president of the board of trustees, Mr. Safeguard, an insurance executive, is on record as having said, "There is probably no need for a department specializing in cooking and sewing, family finance, and clothing design, given that the university's new emphasis is on applied research aimed at reviving the state's rapidly declining economy." The state's economy is largely based on raising sheep for wool, on wheat, corn, and livestock farming, and on the insurance industry. The report from the department's review will be submitted to the faculty senate's Curriculum Policy Committee, which will make its independent recommendation directly to the administration. The administration will then make a recommendation to the trustees.

The Department
The Home Economics Department in the College of Arts and Sciences has thirty faculty members and 525 students in three programs of about equal size—Home and Family Living; Textiles and Fashion Design; and Foods. The College of Arts and Sciences has not endorsed any particular strategic planning process and has not provided any direction.

Because only a few new positions have been available over the past fifteen years and because there has been very little turnover among the faculty, the majority of faculty are within five years of fifty-five years of age. Six of the faculty are men.

Most of the students are undergraduates (90 percent) and most of these students are in teacher education degree programs. The market for teachers of home economics is declining but the department has an excellent placement record. Nearly all the students are women. The department has maintained a strong connection to its graduates. While the alumni contribute very little money to the department or the university, they are unusually loyal followers of department affairs and are the main source of contacts in the placement of graduates, which has been excellent in several midwestern states. Several of the alumni are also married to prominent attorneys, a point the department chair mentions in her negotiations with the central administration.

Mission
The broad mission of the department states that it is primarily concerned with helping families and individuals attain and sustain self-reliance and control of their destiny through family and individual well-being.

Departmental Issues
Most of the faculty in the department are especially concerned about the growing importance of "nonhuman factors" in the determination of university decisions; most of the faculty in the Home and Family Program are fearful about the possibility that their department will be closed entirely or merged with agriculture. Some of the faculty in Textiles are pleased about the review and the possibility of reorganization because they have been unsuccessful in making their case before the chairperson, whose background is in foods. They want to align themselves with the department of chemistry and the school of engineering and emphasize chemical research on new textiles and the establishment of small manufacturing businesses to produce new artificial fabrics that could compete with imported clothing from Asia. The Food Program has not indicated any concern with the review, feeling the chairperson will take care of its interests. The Food Program faculty are certain that their curriculum design, which has served them well for the past twenty years, is adequate.

A major home economics educator recently published a highly-regarded article in a leading journal about how the profession is dying because other professions are moving in on its turf. The author cites specific examples easily found throughout North America.

Her article calls attention to numerous examples—taken from journals in her field and other professions—of nurses researching the relationship between family health and nutrition and studying such matters as the effect of divorce on raising children; of business schools giving advice on family investment alternatives; departments of building and design offering courses and doing research on home construction and family sociology; departments of natural resources emphasizing the "blue" revolution—fish farming, and fish-based diets; chemistry departments researching food preservation techniques; and a department of continuing education, in cooperation with a business school, developing adult education courses for delivery into homes via telephone and video screens.

Some of her examples are even from MSU. The Department of Sociology and the newly established Medical School are cooperating on research funded by the National Hospice Organization on how to treat the family-related effects of care for cancer and AIDS patients. She points out the MSU's Computer Engineering department is building experimental R2D2s to do housework; the Transportation Department in the Business School is studying the effect on home life of two-earner families when one commutes to work two states away via airplane; Procter and Gamble Foods, the Campbell Soup Company, Nabisco Cookies, and Pepperidge Farm have contracts with the College of Agriculture for a variety of projects related to the packaging and sale of frozen foods, and finally, the giant candy-making firms (Hershey, Nestle, and Mars) have market research contracts with members of the Marketing Department in the College of Business.

Her article concludes that "the handwriting is on the wall." She adds, "If the profession of home economics cannot establish firmer footing on defensible turf within five years, what is known as home economics today will be history."

Strategic Planning

MSU's president, who would like the home economics department to set a good example, has suggested the department engage in a newer approach to determining its future direction, an approach known as strategic planning. From her alumni-supported Excellence Fund, she allocated $10,000 for planning expenses. The money would go for luncheon meetings and a retreat.

She said, "Strategic planning seems suited to helping a department make transitions in a changing world. When done well, the planning process will be powered by the basic need of the faculty to reexamine, to refocus, and to seek creative new ways for accomplishing their purposes."

She suggested that the starting point might be to examine what it has already done well (i.e., its salient strengths). Then the department should examine economic, demographic, political, and technological changes to identify opportunities. Next, she suggested, the faculty needed to relate the strengths to emerging opportunities.

She summarized the strategic planning as an idea-driven, creative way to link present strengths to emerging opportunity. The result should be a collective sense or vision of what the department needs to do to become outstanding.

She recommended a simplified, four-step process—each step to take about one month. She was of the opinion that too many strategic planning processes lasted too long and were too often driven by unnecessary paperwork. She suggested the process should be simplified and driven by ideas.

Step One: Look Inside the Department. First, an emphasis should be placed on identifying salient strengths: what can the department build upon? To find the department's greatest strengths, she suggested those involved in the planning process think about location, reputation, values, connections to knowledge, technology, finances, physical plant, and so on. Anything the department could use as "leverage" should be considered a salient strength.

She suggested the department conduct a series of luncheon meetings involving department faculty, alumni, and invited professors from other departments to determine its strengths. Each participant should read George Keller's book and one or more of the references she found helpful. The participants, however, should not forget that strategic planning is a simple idea: relate strengths to opportunity. She did not think they should get carried away with technique. Strategic planning is common sense.

She also thought that most planning efforts made a serious mistake in addressing weaknesses early, during the direction-finding phase. She thought weaknesses were addressed best later, when the plan was being implemented. If addressed early, discussion of weaknesses leads to discord. It was more important to build trust and confidence.

She was also of the opinion that the process should not begin with a review of a mission statement. She had seen too many groups get bogged down early. It was better to assume a satisfactory mission existed, whether stated well or not. A vision of a future condition for the department should emerge later in the process. At that time it could be revised or a new one created.

Step Two: Look Outside the Department. During the second month, the same groups should meet—again over lunch—to look beyond the department. This is called environmental scanning. They are to look for new opportunities created by changes that are occurring. Before the luncheons, the participants should read, but not take too seriously, futurist books and articles by Harlan Cleveland, Willis Harman, John Naisbitt, Alvin Toffler, Robert Theobald, and so on.

Step Three: Propose Directions of Travel. During the third month, the same groups connect the strengths to opportunities and recommend "directions of travel." Directions of travel might be thought of in terms of a compass. Given the many changes that cannot be controlled by the department or university, it is better to think of following a path determined by a compass. She pointed out that plans with goals and objectives are useful, but only pertain to those elements that can be controlled. Strategizing is only about what cannot be controlled.

Step Four: Develop a Vision. Vision provides conceptual glue, momentum, illuminates shared purpose, and provides meaning.

During the fourth month—at a retreat setting—all those participating in the luncheon meetings compare their "directions of travel." Everyone then works in small groups to synthesize strengths, opportunities, and the directions of travel into a viable/visible future.

The president suggests using the five R's of vision to determine direction and to shape purpose: redirect, reshape, renew, risk, reaffirm. Using the five Rs for guidance, each group is to propose a strategic plan based upon a few directions of travel.

All participants then vote to determine the best strategic plan to pro-pose to the university's Curriculum Review Committee. The strategic plan should identify how the strengths are related to the opportunities and how the resulting directions of travel come together in a vision. She says that a good plan would help her, as president, and the board, to see what the department looks like and should be doing in five years.

While she was convinced that every college or department finds itself in a unique situation, from the results of a strategic planning work-shop among over 150 participants held at the Joint AAHE-NCAHE Con-ference in San Francisco in 1987, she thought a strategic plan might have directions of travel that could include elements such as:

1. A redirection: a shift in emphasis from serving individuals in their roles as homemakers to assisting individuals in career prep-aration.
2. A redirection: a shift from consumer protection to a preventative approach in teaching, service, and research
3. A reaffirmation: an emphasis on the importance of the multi-disciplinary character of home economics
4. A reshaping: a revision of the home economics curriculum to make it more useful in health matters, especially where it relates to the growing proportion of elderly dependents.

She thought this set of directions would result in a renewed multi-disciplinary emphasis, shift resources toward health and careers, and encourage a more proactive approach.

After the administration had an opportunity to review the draft strategic plan, which should probably be no longer than five or six pages in length, the next stage of planning would be implementation. Each of the four elements of strategic direction involve annual choices, time lines, and resources.

She concluded her advice by stressing that after the review of strat-egy by the board and the administration, explicit annual plans should be formulated with specific goals and objectives. That is where the administration—always in consultation with the faculty—does its work.

WHAT CONCEPT OF DEPARTMENT LEADERSHIP IS MOST BENEFICIAL IN CONTEXTUAL PLANNING?

Appropriate leadership provides the continuity between the "where" and the "how." With leadership appropriate to the context, a depart-ment or an institution will develop a staff with the capability to think strategically and thereby able to compete for resources in future envi-ronments. Thus, transformational leadership is a process of assessing changes in the environment, and providing assistance to faculty mem-bers in working through change.

It is central to the effectiveness of the contextual concept that it be driven by ideas, not by data and paper. An important result of a contextual planning process is the development of a broad approach to thinking contextually, and a vision. The vision must go beyond desired enrollment, faculty, and financial indicators. It is necessary to create within the faculty a deep sense of the department's goals and mission. There should be a glimmer of something improbable, surely difficult, and maybe even remote.

SUGGESTED READINGS

Bennis, Warren and Burt Nanus. *Leaders: The Strategies for Taking Charge.* New York: Harper & Row, 1985.

Chaffee, Ellen and William Tierney. *Collegiate Cultures and Leadership Strategies.* New York: American Council on Education/Macmillan, 1988.

Cleveland, Harlan. *The Knowledge Executive.* New York: E. P. Dutton, 1985.

Cope, Robert C. *Enterprise and Environment: How to do Strategic Planning When People and Their Ideas Matter.* London: Basil Blackwell, 1989.

Keller, George. *Academic Strategy.* Maryland: Johns Hopkins Press, 1983.

Peterson, Marvin and Lisa Mets, eds. *Key Resources on Governance, Management and Leadership.* San Francisco: Jossey-Bass, 1987.

Seymour, Daniel. *Developing Academic Programs.* Washington, DC: Association for the Study of Higher Education, 1989.

22

FIVE INDICES OF PROGRAM VITALITY

THOMAS A. EMMET
JOHN B. BENNETT

Accreditation requirements and looming financial distress provide two good occasions for departments and chairs to assess program accomplishment and vitality. However, the first is infrequent, and everyone hopes that the second will never develop. In any case, there are sufficient benefits to suggest that program evaluation ought to be a regular, ongoing practice—not one reserved for the unusual or extreme condition.

One large dividend that periodic program evaluation can pay is greatly improved clarity and direction in departmental activities. Rather than remaining an episodic and quickly forgotten affair, the clarity generated and shared in an evaluation can produce further improvement in program quality. Vitality will then be both recognized and increased. Faculty involved with the programs can only be helped, the students better served, and the department's role within the institution itself strengthened.

Program evaluation is in fact an indispensable part of broader departmental planning. The data generated are essential for identifying appropriate and viable future directions. Especially in more complex departments, it is a good idea to take a holistic view of activities periodically and to determine, for instance, how coherently the graduate offerings are related to the undergraduate courses, and how both fare in the larger institutional environment. The very activity of program evaluation establishes and reinforces the attitudes necessary for coping productively with the future.

Of course for these benefits to occur, the activity must be properly conducted. Otherwise, the positive returns can quickly be outweighed by the negative. And program evaluation must be considered important in the eyes of key institutional officers, otherwise the sense may quickly develop among the faculty that it is only a ritual or ceremony, as often happens when the results of the evaluation seem unconnected with subsequent institutional decisions.

There are at least five indices chairpersons can use in gauging program vitality. Each index involves both a standard of accomplishment and a range of evidence for measuring that accomplishment. Naturally, the specific content of the elements will vary according to the program at hand. But awareness of these common features can help the chairperson to structure and conduct the evaluation with both objectivity and productivity.

CONGRUENCE WITH MISSION

The most important index or criterion is the degree of congruence a program has with the institutional mission. Public perceptions of an institution start to blur in proportion to the number of activities unrelated to its central calling. Consonance of the department programs with the broader mission is essential if the institution is to maintain a clear identity and to allocate its resources with efficiency.

The standard, therefore, is that program mission and objectives be appropriately congruent with institutional mission and objectives. Each department needs to determine for itself its specific program expectations. There will be a range of possibilities. The program could be so congruent that it is virtually essential to the mission of the institution. One thinks, for instance, of the central role of various agricultural programs within a land grant institution in a region known for farming and ranching. Another example would be the role of a finance program within a business school.

Alternatively, the program could be somewhat removed from the essential mission of the institution but be central to the operation or support of other programs that are themselves essential. An example would be programs of instructional remediation in those institutions which stress access for individuals not traditionally associated with higher education.

Often the institutional mission will itself be recognized to be in a process of change, as the environing society and/or governance structure changes. All institutions are characterized by such an evolutionary process. Of course a few will be *relatively* unchanging, especially those with an historic mission at the heart of their identity—as is the case with some religious or single-sex institutions. But even here the pertinence of some programs, and the relevancy of the ways others are presented, will change. Hence the necessity for a periodic review of department program congruence with institutional mission.

The evidence for program centrality is ordinarily found in several places. Institutions will have mission statements somewhere—in accreditation self-study materials, charter documents, and so on. (There may, in fact, be too many, and conflicting, statements.) Public institutions will often be governed by a state master plan or a role and scope document. The evidence for individual program missions may be more difficult to locate or identify. Sometimes one must work backward—from accepted outcomes to the isolation of presupposed program objectives.

SOCIETAL NEEDS

The second index or criterion for program evaluation is consonance with the needs of society. Departments at many institutions, especially ones with public governance structures, will find this second criterion to be of key importance. State authorities are showing less reluctance to convey changing societal trends and expectations to public institutions. Funding and political pressures often assure reception. Likewise, most private colleges and universities will have interest in the new funding possibilities that changing societal interests, attitudes, and technologies present. Department chairpersons should be paying attention.

The ability to serve the educational needs of the region requires that departments be aware of those needs as they develop and change. Mechanisms must be established for securing information both about these changes (the current buzzword for this activity is "environmental scanning") and about regional perceptions of the adequacy of institutional responses. Community colleges with their many advisory committees seem especially well-equipped in this respect. Baccalaureate and graduate institutions are starting to take notice.

Of course, the mission of some institutions is deliberately independent of immediate, local community needs. Traditional liberal arts institutions are examples. But even in these cases some programs will have to be carefully assessed, based on the standards of societal need. Many liberal arts institutions are moving toward greater societal responsiveness as measured by such matters as curricular relevance to student career objectives, linkages with regional businesses and industries, or greater emphasis upon foreign languages and computer applications.

The specific location of most institutions will function importantly in providing departments with some opportunities and in eliminating others. Institutions located near military bases have certain obvious possibilities for continuing as well as nontraditional education. The same potential holds for many urban—as opposed to rural—institutions. Similar considerations hold with regard to cultural particularities and strengths, as well as with distinctive economic climates.

Evidence of the need for evaluating programs with respect to this criterion will come from various sources. General national reports and studies can play a role in the determination of unmet needs. The report of the Commission on Excellence in Education identified a number of deficiencies in secondary education, and by implication also in postsecondary education. Inadequacies in scientific and technological literacy stand high on the list. Other commissions have reminded us of the need for substantially increased foreign language instruction. Doubtless, basic academic skills and civic competencies will remain important, as the Newman report suggests.

At the regional and local level, departments can secure indications of societal need through careful environmental scans and through marketing studies. Technological advances will be relevant. Local demographic data will be important, as will data from the regional labor bureau and chamber of commerce. Special commissions or committees may have identified future area needs and/or plans.

STUDENT INTEREST

The third criterion for program evaluation is the character of student demand. Some may be tempted to place this index first. Such an impulse is natural but mistaken, as it could easily yield imbalance in curricular offerings and may in fact promote programs completely out of line with the institutional mission and resources.

The standards against which to measure demand for departmental programs and services are several. Obvious traditional ones are overall student credit hour generation as well as numbers of majors. Other benchmarks include retention rates and applicant flow rates. No less important than number is the comparative quality of applicants and students—as measured against other years and/or against other programs. Student demand will also bear some relationship to the current market opportunity for graduates, though this standard will vary widely depending upon the program. Special institutional relationships can also pose standards against which program success can be appraised. Examples are linkages with local or regional business, industry, or government. Various cooperative arrangements are another illustration, as are consortial undertakings and agreements.

The types of evidence by which programs are to be assessed are typically quantitative in character. The offices of the registrar and the director of institutional research will have the data concerning the various credit relationships. However, other sources should be surveyed as well. Alumni can provide valuable information about the quality, adequacy, and relevance of program content. Exit interviews of graduating or withdrawing students can also provide significant information about participant perceptions.

QUALITY

As an essential criterion of program vitality, considerations of quality are now in the public eye and must be joined to those of student demand and of program relevance to mission and to society.

Quality has to be determined in the context of institutional mission and from the perspective of different constituencies. Students often assess program quality in terms of substantially new skills, abilities, or bodies of knowledge acquired. These factors might be called the outcomes of their learning. Faculty are likely to look at resources committed or inputs (library holdings, equipment, salaries, staff support, and credentials held) as well as such outcomes as grants and research awards received, publications, and other evidences of knowledge advanced or services performed. They may also look at student performance on national tests, licensing examinations, or placement results. There are, therefore, multiple perspectives and multiple outcomes regarding quality. As a result, measurement of effective performance is not easy.

In general, though, relevant standards of quality will include past department records and accomplishments of both students and faculty, and appropriate comparisons with other campus programs as well as with competitive programs at other institutions. Programs that are truly competitive must be selected, otherwise judgments will be skewed. In making comparative judgments several factors should be examined.

The relative capability of applicants (as assessed by scores on national tests as well as by other common measures) and of students should be determined. Similar judgments can be made concerning career patterns and successes of graduates (such as the percentage who pass licensing examinations on first attempt). Faculty should also be compared with respect to academic and experiential accomplishments, as well as with an eye toward balance among the skills and areas of expertise presented.

Of course, the adequacy of the library holdings and of other supporting facilities, equipment and services should be monitored and appropriate levels maintained. The evidence of such adequacy is available through various internal institutional data pools as well as from the reports of specialized accrediting agencies or external visitors or evaluators. Annual reports are another source of information, as are relevant sections of grant proposals. Various alumni surveys and student output studies can provide helpful information. The occasional ranking of departments nationally provides additional information, although sometimes hotly disputed. Disciplinary organizations and associations can sometimes provide additional normative information.

COST

Inevitably, cost is a major criterion in program evaluation. By no means ought it ever to be first in priority, but it certainly plays an essential function. Some activities, no matter how excellent, simply cannot be afforded. And some levels of other activities, no matter how desirable, are just too expensive. Too many courses can dilute and weaken department expertise, not strengthen it. Any procedure for systematic program evaluation must pay careful attention to cost, recognizing that it may well be different from price—what the institution chooses to charge.

Certain traditional standards readily come to mind. Among them are institutionally specified faculty–student ratios and cost per hour of instruction, calculated in terms both of salary and support facilities and equipment. Comparisons with similar programs both within the institution and at selected other institutions are appropriate. Likewise, the degree to which available external funding has been secured is an important consideration, although funding availability should not drive program desirability, without regard to the first criterion of compatibility with institutional mission. The expense required to bring a particular program to the next level of quality is also an important consideration.

The information for determining program costs resides in the office of institutional research, the registrar's office, and other institutional data repositories. Departments whose institutions are members of various consortia and/or state systems may have access to cost data at other member institutions. Likewise, peer departments and/or institutions may swap data periodically. Such exchanges can also occur at regional or even national disciplinary meetings. And specialized accrediting associations often provide extensive cost and resource recommendations.

CONCLUSION

Quite often chairs can acquire information on these five areas of program review informally in the course of doing other things. In that sense program review is an ongoing activity, not one that must be done with great fanfare and noise every five or seven years. But when this information does come along, do not let it escape or fade from memory. Special attention periodically paid to program effectiveness and relevance is the best way of assuring that the department remains vital and vigorous.

23

POSITIONING THE DEPARTMENT FOR SURVIVAL AND GROWTH: AN EXERCISE

JOHN MINTER

Whether new to the job or an old hand, a department chair obviously wishes to maintain, if not improve the department's position. What follows is an initial exercise that can give you a clearer picture of your department.

Each department has a de facto position. It is the result of its own beginnings, what it is trying to accomplish, the changes that are now shaping higher education, comparable trends in its field of knowledge, and its relationship to other departments in the institution, as well as to other departments in other institutions.

What you need is a framework for identifying your current position. This exercise will do just that. Only when you understand clearly your current position will you be able to work toward maintaining this position and move toward an even more beneficial one.

List on a sheet of paper, in a column on the left, the *objectives* your department is currently pursuing and those you hope to achieve during your administration.

The sequence of the items on this list is not important at this point. Some topics that you might note are: instruction, research, academic support including library resources, computing resources, facilities, student services, and student financial aid. Be as specific as possible. Name the courses and programs you want to establish or phase out. Set a target figure for research funding.

Making your list may take longer than a few minutes. Take your time. Do not worry about approval by the dean or faculty. No one else need ever see this list. Mixing short- and long-term objectives is perfectly all right. Later, when you understand more about your position, you can take time to assess whether a specific goal can be achieved quickly or not. You may be surprised. For now, just put them down on paper.

Next, take a separate sheet of paper and make a second list. In this list include the *changes* within the department and outside it that are going on right now that are likely to have a significant influence on the department.

Again, the sequence is not important and do not worry about how someone else might react to your choice. This is for your eyes only. After you have the list, you will have time to weigh the relative importance of each change.

Think about possible changes in personnel, funding, regulations, attitudes, your particular field of knowledge, at different levels of the organization, at different governmental levels, and economic sectors. The only requirement is that you be concrete. Indicate a direction and, if you can, a rate of change (high, moderate, low).

Review the list of changes you have identified and select one that you think is especially important. On the left edge of a third sheet of paper, head a column with this change. Next, place the column beside your list of objectives. Go down the list of objectives, stopping at each one and asking, "How will this change affect the department's chances of achieving this objective?" Mark a plus (+) in the column if you feel the change is helping the department, or a minus (−) if you feel it is hindering or at least not helping. No zeros (0). If you are not sure because you need more information, write a question mark (?) as a reminder to find this information.

When you have compared the change with all your objectives, scan the column. If you see primarily positive signs, your position is good relative to this particular trend. However, if you see primarily negative signs, your position is weak. A number of question marks means that you need further investigation to clear up uncertainties.

At this juncture, you should resist the temptation to "fix" a given item right away. Being pragmatic, most of us want to think immediately about alternative positions or tactics to change a minus to a plus. Later, after you have taken the above step with each change on your list and with other important position references, there will be time to make a balanced judgment about what may need to be changed, what negative can be changed to a positive, and how this can be accomplished.

Prior to reaching a balanced judgment about appropriate tactics to change your position, you need to consider other important position references. One of these references is departmental capability. The department will achieve its objectives only through the contributions of its faculty, staff, and students in addition to the use of its physical and financial resources.

For the fourth part of this exercise, you will need to create another list. This list will be an inventory of your department's capabilities. With this list it is important to be systematic about where you place items because later this list will help in analyzing your position within the institution.

For this reason, please use the following categories as nearly as possible: instruction, research, public service, academic support, student services, institutional support, and operation of plant. These are your assets. Illustrations of what should be included within a given category are given below. Do not worry too much about precision at this point. Remember, you are not going public with this. Items that need further clarification can be cleared up later with appropriate members of your administration.

- *Instruction:* general academic instruction, occupational and vocational instruction, special session instruction, community education, preparatory and adult basic education.
- *Research:* institutes and research centers, individual or project research.
- *Public Service:* conferences and institutes, cooperative extension, public lectures, television, and testing services.
- *Academic Support:* libraries, museums and galleries, audiovisual services, ancillary support, computing support, course and curriculum development.
- *Student Services:* administration, social and cultural activities, counseling and career guidance, financial aid administration, and health services.
- *Institutional Support:* administrative activity, fundraising, public relations, alumni programs, logistical services, purchasing, security, and community relations.
- *Operation of Plant:* maintenance, custodial services, utilities, and repairs.

This will be your longest list yet. From the categories, select the one resource you feel is most important today. Label a column on a separate sheet of paper with the name of this resource and repeat the process used in comparing change with objectives. Given the status of this resource today, ask, "Is the capability of this resource helping the department achieve this objective (+) or not (−)?" Later, repeat this step with each item on your list. The distribution of (+) and (−) will provide you with clues for achieving a stronger position.

There is one very important capability not included in the list above but it must be included here: the capability of generating net revenue. To get a rough idea of your position relative to this reference point, subtract total expenditures attributed to your department from total revenue generated by your department. Estimate the latter by adding together income from research and other grants and tuition revenue. Calculate tuition revenue by multiplying student credit hours generated by your department with tuition per credit hour. An estimate of the tuition per credit hour is obtained by dividing the total tuition charged (exclude room and board) by the average student credit-hour load.

If you arrive at a negative result (deficit) your department is vulnerable. This is not meant as a judgment on your department's quality or value to the institution. It is just a statement of financial position. Often a negative position is associated with a number of low enrollment courses suggesting that a revision of the department's educational objectives may be in order. Whether this is the case or not, try to be honest about your financial position. Remember, this is for your eyes only, and a successful plan for departmental survival must be based on financial viability.

Now it is time to move outside your department to check your position relative to external influences that impact on the department's success. Take another sheet of paper and head columns with the following labels:

- *Chief Academic Officer.* Ask yourself "What objectives the CAO has for the institution and how they affect my department's ability to achieve its objectives" (+) or (−). The dean is more likely to take a favorable position on your next budget request if you can show him/her how your objectives will help accomplish his/hers. In short, look for overlaps between the goals of the dean and your department.
- *Departments of* ——. Identify other academic departments that serve you or that you serve and ask, "What objectives do these other departments have and how do they affect my department's ability to achieve its objectives?" (+) or (−). "Where do our goals overlap?"
- *Departments of* ——. Identify academic departments in other institutions to which you compare yourself, or with which you compete, and ask, "What objectives and capabilities do these departments in other institutions have and how do they affect my department's ability to achieve its objectives?" (+) or (−).

At a later time you may find it useful to inventory other departments in much the same way you looked at your own capabilities. You might discover a special niche that gives you an edge when presenting your next budget to the dean or a grant proposal to a foundation.

Where do you get information about other departments? Within the institution one would hope you could go right to the department chair concerned. If this is not possible, then you must rely on secondary sources such as the catalog, budget documents, the dean's office, the institutional research office, news items, Peterson's Guides for graduate departments, and personal observation.

Information about departments in other institutions will be harder to acquire but some of the same published sources are available. Articles and notes in the professional literature may also supply clues about a department's capability and priorities.

Work through each of these position references in relation to your department objectives. When you are finished, you will have a visible and more objective grasp of the department's strong and weak positions and where to start as you develop an Action Plan to improve your situation.

24

CLARIFYING PRIORITIES THROUGH PAIRED CHOICES

ELWOOD B. EHRLE

All organizations have priorities. In many cases, however, the system of priorities guiding action is largely invisible. Various members of the organizational group will likely have somewhat different views of the priority structure, but few will have much grasp of the composite ordering of priorities in the group. The clarification of priorities, individual and group, may well make the difference between a department that is merely getting by and one that is on the way to a higher quality of life. The clarification of priorities through paired choices can be accomplished in a few hours and can positively influence the behavior and direction of the department for a long time to come.

The paired choices method of clarifying priorities is based on two assumptions: (1) every item of importance must be compared with every other item of importance before its relative priority can be determined and (2) every individual should have an equal opportunity to determine the priority structure of the group.

Many aspects of academic life are of high priority to faculty, students, and administrators. Not infrequently, department chairs, deans and academic vice presidents or provosts are plagued by the belief that everything is a high priority. The question, Is the library important? will get a clear and enthusiastic yes from almost all sides. The real question, How important is the library in comparison to other items (*e.g.,* the improvement of faculty salaries?) is rarely asked. Rather than assuming the library is important and so is everything else, effective leadership and management require one to say *how* important, as compared with all the other important items. In real settings, it is the relative priorities that count.

Many groups determine relative priorities, however vague, through the pronouncements of their most vocal members. In academic department meetings, one often sees the consequences of effective powers of persuasion exercised by one department member or another. If the people speaking most vigorously agree, the rest of the group will probably go along. If they disagree, sides will be taken based on personal relationships, both positive and negative, perceptions of how much influence each contestant has, subtle and perhaps subconscious calculation of how much favor can be gained, or by what is being placed at risk by opposing or joining a vigorous colleague. Quite often the syndrome of, "I'll go along with Harry on this one because I'll need him later on another one," comes into play. Although these discussions culminate in a vote, it may not be clear that the vote represents either a sorting out of the conflicting issues involved or the will of the group. The process may be superficially democratic but the outcome may not indicate that each person's values, opinions, and priorities contributed effectively to the results. This paper describes a systematic way of dealing with these difficulties.

The clarification of relative priorities through paired choices is best conducted in six relatively simple steps. These are:

1. A polar search for descriptors of the organization.
2. A distillation from these descriptors of the items to be put into a priority structure.
3. Making paired choices.
4. Assigning satisfaction indices to each item.
5. Plotting the results of making paired choices and assigning satisfaction indices against one another.
6. Interpreting the results in a manner useful to the department.

THE POLAR SEARCH

A polar search is best undertaken by using a facilitator to elicit for the group as many responses as possible to the questions "What's right about our department (or college, university, and so on)?" and "What's wrong about our department?" The facilitator should attempt to exhaust the first before starting the second. The search should be entirely non-judgmental and no one should be belittled because his/her idea seems strange or somehow wrong. The facilitator should not only refrain from judgmental comments, but should also sharply limit any such remarks that arise from the group. The facilitator will probably have little difficulty filling several sheets of newsprint with the items produced in the polar search and should not be surprised when some items turn up on both lists. The lists should be taped up where they can be easily seen. An effective polar search can usually be conducted in an hour or two.

THE DISTILLATION PROCESS

The best way to distill the priorities is to encourage the group to talk about the results of the polar search. This discussion will usually yield less than twenty items that seem to be of importance to the group. The distillation process often takes the form of combining related items into more generic categories. A lot of "noise" usually drops out.

Once a group has determined the list of items to be put into a relative priority order, each item is randomly assigned a number. The order makes no difference in how they will be treated in the paired choices process, nor on what the resultant ordering of priorities will be.

THE PAIRED CHOICES

The best way to conduct the paired choices process is to lay out all the choices on paper and have the facilitator rapidly read the choices aloud as each member circles his/her choice in each pair presented. A typical paired choice form is presented in Figure 1.

The facilitator must read at a brisk pace so that individuals are not tempted to go back and change a response. Whenever this occurs, people lose their place and the process breaks down. As the facilitator proceeds with each line, it is helpful to ask him/her to shorten the description of the items in order to maintain the pace. If, for instance, the first four items of fifteen being compared are: (1) increased support for the library, (2) improvement of faculty salaries, (3) better equipment budgets, (4) more graduate assistants, the facilitator might read the list as follows: "The first choice on the first line is between numbers one and two. Number one is increased support for the library and number two is improvement of faculty salaries; the next choice is between number one, library and, number three, better equipment budgets; number one is library, number four is more graduate assistants," and so on until the first line is finished. The facilitator then begins the second line, giving the complete description of the choice between numbers two and three and subsequently shortens the descriptions of both as he/she moves across the line. A limit of twenty items is imposed by the tolerance of the group and the stamina of the facilitator.

A PAIRED-CHOICES FORM FOR SEVEN ITEMS

		Total		Sat. Index
$\frac{1}{2}\frac{1}{3}\frac{1}{4}\frac{1}{5}\frac{1}{6}\frac{1}{7}$	1.	_____		_____
$\frac{2}{3}\frac{2}{4}\frac{2}{5}\frac{2}{6}\frac{2}{7}$	2.	_____		_____
$\frac{3}{4}\frac{3}{5}\frac{3}{6}\frac{3}{7}$	3.	_____		_____
$\frac{4}{5}\frac{4}{6}\frac{4}{7}$	4.	_____		_____
$\frac{5}{6}\frac{5}{7}$	5.	_____		_____
$\frac{6}{7}$	6.	_____		_____
	7.	_____		_____

FIGURE 1. A paired-choices form useful in placing seven items in priority order.

When all the choices have been made, each participant marks the total number of times each item was selected in the column on the right. Care must be taken to count the items in the vertical columns as well as those in the horizontal rows. In Figure 1, for instance, item number five occurs in a vertical column all the way from the top line to the line of fives. If participants are not reminded to count both the vertical and horizontal, some will leave out the vertical and the results will be skewed.

THE SATISFACTION INDICES

Each participant then marks an approximate measure of his/her satisfaction on a scale of one (low) to ten (high), in accordance with his perception of how well the department is doing on each item. Once again, the facilitator should read through the items quickly, asking participants to indicate their satisfaction indices as the items are being read. With this completed, the facilitator should collect all papers for processing with a hand calculator.

PLOTTING THE RESULTS

If the facilitator has a helper, it is fairly easy to calculate the group averages for the number of times each item was selected and for its average satisfaction index. If one reads the scores as the other operates the calculator, it all goes rather quickly. The calculation from a group of fifty people working with fifteen items can be completed in just over an hour. The averages are then plotted on a x-y grid, with the priorities arranged along the vertical axis and the satisfaction indices arranged along the horizontal axis. This will divide the items into four quadrants as indicated in Figure 2.

INTERPRETATION OF THE RESULTS

Each of the four quadrants has a particular meaning. The first quadrant (High Priority, High Satisfaction) is called the "Basic Definers Box." This

	High Priority	
Quadrant IV		*Quadrant I*
High-Priority		*High Priority*
Low Satisfaction		*High Satisfaction*
		High Satisfaction
Quadrant III		*Quadrant II*
Low Priority		*Low Priority*
Low Satisfaction		*High Satisfaction*

FIGURE 2. The four quadrants that result from plotting priority order against the satisfaction indices.

quadrant will collect those items most important to the participants and about which they feel quite good. These are the things that tell you what kind of an organization you really have.

The second quadrant (Low Priority, High Satisfaction) is called the "Ho-Hum Box." This quadrant will collect those items that are not very important to the participants but about which they nonetheless feel good. The group does not really care whether or not these items are successful. It is sometimes called the "Instant Hero's Box," since a chairperson or any other member of the department can mount a major initiative on any one of these items without encountering resistance. It is a relatively nonproductive set of items, however, since increased success here is likely to be greeted with relative indifference. "Oh well, that's Charlie's thing. Hurray for him. No thank you. I really don't want to get involved in it."

The third quadrant (Low Priority, Low Satisfaction) is called the "Squeaking Wheel Box." This quadrant will collect those things that people like to discuss at great length but about which they really expect nothing to be done. It is sometimes called the "Let's make a committee" box. These are items on which a committee can work for a year, issue a number of voluminous reports, and still nothing will happen. People do not really care about these items and are quite satisfied if no changes occur in these areas.

The fourth quadrant (High Priority, Low Satisfaction) is called the "Growth Opportunities Box." This quadrant will collect those things that are quite important to the participants and about which they are unsatisfied. There is energy for change in these items. The higher an item comes in this quadrant and the closer it is to the satisfaction line, the easier it will be to engage people in an effort to move it to the right into the "Basic Definers Box." These are the items that represent the best growth opportunities for the department. They are not predictable at the outset. In fact, there are usually a number of surprises in store, even in a group whose members believe they already know their priorities!

One final observation is necessary about the interpretation of the results. The only fixed aspect of the plotted results is the geometric relationship between the points. The axes can be "skidded around" to wherever you want them. This is equivalent to adjusting one's thinking about how high a priority has to be before it is high in the rank ordering and how satisfied a group must be before an item falls to the right of the satisfaction line. By moving the axis around, one can get various views of the priority-satisfaction mix. It will not change the basic fact that relative to one another, some items are more likely to be amenable to change than others. In preparing these plots, it is usually desirable to present an unadjusted report to the group and ask them how they would like to see the axes moved. After some discussion they are likely to see that it really does not matter. The truth will out anyway!

A RECENT EXAMPLE

The paired-choices process was recently used by the chairman's advisory committee in an academic department. The polar search and distillation phases yielded twenty items of concern. When paired choices were made and satisfaction indices assigned, the frequency of selection and the average satisfaction indices produced the scores indicated in Table 1. When the scores were plotted, they distributed themselves as shown in Table 2 and Figure 3.

In interpreting these results it appears that the advisory committee sees the best growth opportunities for the department in various combinations of the items in the fourth quadrant. The four highest priority items (academic program review, department planning, research emphasis and financing, and improving the stature of the department) are all clearly related and can form the basis for the development of an action plan to enable the department to get from where it finds itself to where it wants to be. The other quadrants contain valuable information that can be useful to the department in determining the amount of energy and commitment available to implement various aspects of an action plan.

TABLE 1. Twenty items produced by the Polar Search and Distillation Phases with the Frequency of Paired-Choice Selection (Priority Score) and Group Average Satisfaction Indices (Satisfaction Score).

	Priority Score	Satisfaction Score
1. Department planning effort	13.0	2.4
2. Control of counterproductive behaviors	10.2	2.2
3. Recruiting—undergraduate and graduate	9.0	3.0
4. Alumni relations	4.8	3.0
5. Finding 2–3 funding angels	8.8	2.6
6. Equipment use, acquisition, service contracts	6.8	4.2
7. Program staffing	16.2	4.4
8. Research emphasis and financing	12.6	3.4
9. Student advising and retention	10.8	5.6
10. Upgrading stature of department	12.4	3.2
11. Industry relations	3.4	4.4
12. Spring-summer programs	10.6	4.0
13. Academic program review	13.4	3.4
14. Workload analysis and variability	8.0	4.8
15. Inter-departmental relations	4.8	5.8
16. Seminar programs and speakers	8.8	5.4
17. Logistical support and positions	13.6	4.4
18. Chair position description and evaluation	8.2	4.6
19. Evaluation of professional growth	10.8	3.6
20. Development of electron microscope facility	3.8	2.6

TABLE 2. The Assortment of Twenty Items of Concern into Four Quadrants through Paired Choices and the Assignment of Satisfaction Indices.

	Priority Score	Satisfaction Score
I. The definers (High Priority, High Satisfaction)		
Program staffing (7)	16.2	4.4
Student advising and retention (9)	10.8	5.6
Spring-summer programs (12)	10.6	4.0
Logistical support and positions (17)	13.6	4.4
II. The Ho-Hum Box (Low Priority, High Satisfaction)		
Equipment use, acquisitions, service contracts (6)	6.8	4.2
Industry Relations (11)	3.4	4.4
Workload analysis and variability (14)	8.0	4.8
Inter-departmental relations (15)	4.8	5.8
Seminar programs and speakers (16)	8.8	5.4
Chair position description and evaluation (18)	8.2	4.6
III. The Squeaking Wheels (Low Priority, Low Satisfaction)		
Recruiting—undergraduate and graduate (3)	9.0	3.0
Alumni relations (4)	4.8	3.0
Finding 2–3 funding angels (5)	8.8	2.6
Development of electron microscope facility (20)	3.8	2.6
IV. Growth Opportunities (High Priority, Low Satisfaction)		
Department planning effort (1)	13.0	2.4
Control of counterproductive behaviors (2)	10.2	2.2
Research emphasis and financing (8)	12.6	3.4
Upgrading stature of department (10)	12.4	3.2
Academic program review (13)	13.4	3.4
Evaluation of professional growth (19)	10.8	3.6

CONCLUSION

The paired choices process described herein has enjoyed a wide variety of application in government agencies, the military, business and industry, and various levels of education. To this writer's knowledge it was first applied to academic situations by George T.L. Land[1] and has been used by the Turtle Bay Institute[2]. It has been used with faculty in departments, chairpersons in a college[3] and college deans in a university. It is currently being used in leadership development activities by the American Council on Education.

The paired choice process has two basic virtues. It is fairly easy to use and it works! It should be more widely used in higher education.

NOTES

1. George T.L. Land, *Grow or Die: The Unifying Principle of Transformation* (New York: Random House, 1973).

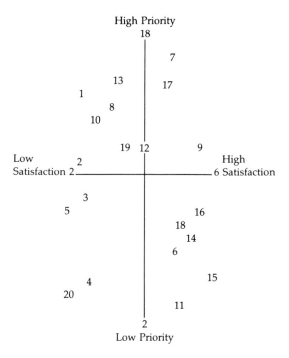

FIGURE 3. The Plotting of Twenty Items of Concern into Four Quadrants through Paired Choices and the Assignment of Satisfaction Indices.

2. George T.L. Land, *Innovation Systems: Workshop and Reference Materials* (New York: Turtle Bay Institute, Inc., 1972).
3. Elwood B. Ehrle, "The Selection and Evaluation of Department Chairmen." *Educational Record* 56 (1 1975): 29–38.

25

THE DEPARTMENT CHAIR AND ENROLLMENT MANAGEMENT: SOME STRATEGIES

ANTOINETTE IADAROLA

For of all sad words of tongue or pen,
the saddest are these: It might have been.

Although Whittier was not referring to enrollment management, his words can be applied with particular aptness to these days of stress and opportunity in higher education. Enrollment management is a term very much in vogue today. And although some may think that it is the sole responsibility of the admissions office or the newly-hired person in marketing, a successful enrollment management system involves every member of the academic community. In a very special way, it involves the department chairperson and faculty, for they have a major responsibility for contacting interested students, developing and updating recruitment literature, encouraging accepted students to enroll, and maintaining contact with students once they are enrolled and are on campus.

Before we examine what department chairpersons can do to achieve sustained, stable enrollments, let us look at the climate of higher learning in order to understand why enrollment management has become a serious concern for most colleges and universities.

A few years ago, Harold Hodgkinson, former director of the National Institute of Education, presented an insightful paper at the Annual Meeting of the National Institute of Independent Colleges and Universities. Hodgkinson described a number of trends that he believed would have important implications for higher education in the next decade.[1] He commented that the fastest growing segment of the nation's population is the 35- to 44-year-old-group, and that by the end of the current decade, 20 percent of the population will be over 65. Colleges and universities must prepare for a declining pool of traditional-age students until 1998, and face an array of other educational providers—business, the military, and government. In addition, women and minorities will enter higher education in increasing numbers.

The implications of these factors are enormous, and they are already affecting administrators and faculty in both the public and independent sectors. Hodgkinson's analysis has been corroborated by recent reports issued by the College Board and the National Center for Education Statistics (NCES). Students today are more likely to be female, over twenty-five years of age, members of minority populations, employed and enrolled part-time. NCES estimated that 225,000 fewer full-time students would enroll in colleges this fall, while the pool of part-time nontraditional students was expected to increase by 157,000. In the words of the College Board, "The nontraditional student is quickly becoming the traditional student."[2]

Given the declining number of traditional-age students, the changing characteristics of students, and the growth of post-secondary offerings by noneducational organizations, rivalry for students has become fierce. In addition, institutions of higher learning are rethinking the content, distribution, and style of academic offerings in order to meet the changing needs of students and the society in which they live. This is all happening at a time when higher education is challenged to be viable, preserve quality, be accountable, and respond effectively to changes that are occurring dramatically and swiftly. And all of these pressures are being confronted within the context of budgetary cuts and increasing competition for endowment funding. Given this situation, it is difficult to imagine an institution that has remained untouched, that will not continue rigorously to question every aspect of its purpose.

Faced with these institutional pressures, it is understandable that colleges and universities are concerned with enrollment management. All are forced to take a closer, more introspective look at programs and activities in order to achieve a competitive edge. And, yet, according to at least one report, ". . . there is little evidence that most campuses have marshalled a concerted, campus-wide enrollment management system."[3]

What can department chairpersons do to contribute to the development of a "campus-wide enrollment management system?" While others have written of the dynamics of enrollment management and the general role of key administrators,[4] this chapter will focus on the department chairperson in enrollment management, for it is he or she who is the primary filter for academic change and the climate within an institution of higher learning. This chapter will not tell you "how to," for, as one writer has suggested, the "how to's" of enrollment management will vary greatly between and among institutions.[5] However, it is meant to provide some grist for further discussion and some suggestions for future directions.

1. USE YOUR POSITION IN THE GOVERNANCE STRUCTURE TO URGE HIGH-LEVEL ADMINISTRATORS TO CLARIFY THE MISSION OF THE INSTITUTION

Today, as in the past, institutions must redefine their educational agenda in terms of the real world. In a searching self-examination, they must see themselves as if for the first time and ask some hard questions. What special role do we play in this network of American higher education? Who is our audience? How are we responding to new types of students, new competitors, and whole new modes of learning? What are the strengths and weaknesses of our faculty, staff, and programs? What comparative advantages do we have over other similar institutions? What services and programs do we provide that students cannot obtain elsewhere better, faster, or cheaper? With our traditions, values, location, human, physical and fiscal resources, what should our college or university aspire to be ten years from now? These questions are basic for institutional health and survival.

Mission statements must be anchored in reality and carefully scrutinized for implementation. If the institution has made a decision to embark on outreach activities for adult students, it needs to ensure consistency between that decision and the implementation of the existing mission statements. For example, the following is a typical mission statement: to comprehend ideas accurately, to define and solve problems by finding and analyzing relationships, to understand the impact of science and technology in our lives, and so on. Now these statements do not need to be changed. But, if no classes are taught in the evening or on weekends, or off-campus, if scholarship aid is made available to full-time students only, and if the learning mode is three lectures per week, then implementation of the mission statement is severely restricted. That is, one component of the mission statement, "to comprehend ideas accurately," has been limited to "to comprehend ideas accurately in 18- to 22-year-old, full-time students from 9:00 a.m. to 3:00 p.m." or "to comprehend ideas accurately through the use of traditional delivery systems." In other words, it is necessary for higher education institutions to reevaluate the ways in which existing mission statements are implemented.

Institutions cannot afford to become isolated and unresponsive to economic and social needs, but they have been cautioned to use restraint in their response, for the marketplace is too transitory a mechanism for determining change. As one observer noted recently: "A university totally serving only the internal claims of those of its members who happen to be its temporary trustees—and that is all faculty and administrators, and students—would cease to serve society; on the other side, one that responds to every current trend and meets only immediately felt educational needs would cease to be a university."[6] Or to put it another way, "the challenge for higher education is to remain sensitive to the short-term needs and concerns of students and other constituencies (such as parents and alumni) without undercutting the institution's evaluation of broader societal needs and its own long-term sense of mission."[7]

The academic department is the dominant educational influence on campuses and the chair can play a key role in defining and implementing the mission at his or her institution.

2. PUT YOUR OWN DEPARTMENT IN ORDER

Working cooperatively with faculty, initiate the same kind of self-examination in your department. The mission statement of a department is its raison d'etre. It serves as the foundation upon which the department justifies its existence within the college or university. How does the mission of the department relate to the mission and goals of the institution? If your department essentially services other departments, is this mission understood and supported by the institution? Has the department geared teaching and learning to new student populations? What changes must be made in curriculum to respond to new social, economic, and job-market realities? What programs should be added? What programs should be dropped? To what extent can existing courses be packaged differently to meet current needs? For example, sociology and related areas might become a major in gerontology. In other words, the department must carry out a kind of "marketing audit." It must come to know itself "warts and all." As one commentator noted: "The department's search for vitality begins with its own assumption of responsibility for its own future."[8]

Department chairpersons and faculty must not wait for a sudden drop in enrollment before asking questions about purpose, programs, and overall effectiveness. It is too late then. One of the most challenging, and yet crucial, of the activities associated with successful enrollment management is faculty agreement on establishing department or division goals. Some chairs develop these goals in isolation and then share them with faculty. And some chairs view the goal-setting process as satisfying the bureaucratic whims of the dean or provost. This is unfortunate, for involvement in the process by the entire department faculty forces everyone to grapple with the issues and to think seriously about long-range program development that will insure vitality.

3. MAKE THE RIGHT CONNECTIONS AND BE SURE TO GET THE DATA

Appoint a faculty member from your department to serve as a liaison to such administrative offices and committees as admissions, marketing, career planning and placement, institutional research, and retention to assure that your department is represented and that you receive the information you need to make informed decisions.

The department must create a comprehensive data base on student recruitment and retention if it is to succeed in enrollment management activities. Academic departments need data that will chart the flow of students in and out of the department over time. For example, how many prospects (inquiries), applicants, and admittees did a department have in a given term? How many have actually enrolled in the department? How many students are majoring in the department's field? How many have graduated? How many are "dropouts?" How many are "persisters?"

Data from students regarding course offerings, teaching, advising, and career planning are also useful. What evidence indicates that students have been adequately prepared for graduate school or employment? How many seniors were admitted to graduate school? How many were employed in positions for which they had been trained? Also helpful is information regarding student characteristics. How many minority students have been recruited, trained, and graduated? From what geographic areas does this department attract students? What is the breakdown of students according to age?

The department can obtain much of this information from the admissions and institutional research offices that collect and store much of this data. However, if this information is not available from these offices, department chairs can assemble such a data base themselves rather inexpensively with the assistance of microcomputers and prepackaged software.[9] Much of this information is unused and this is especially wasteful, given the resources expended in its collection. An important benefit of data acquisition is that it not only increases faculty awareness of its utility in the realm of enrollment effort, but it is also valuable in understanding the current conditions and future trends facing the department. The data also can be valuable in preparing the annual report and in anticipation of program reviews.

Chairs, faculty, admissions personnel, and institutional researchers must be in regular contact regarding the expanded use of such valuable information.

4. DEVELOP ACTION PLANS

Armed with a clear sense of mission and goals, and information concerning employment trends, demographics, changing student characteristics, and student flow, the department can develop action plans for recruitment and retention. Again, it is necessary to have faculty in concurrence in the development of these plans.[10] A chairperson can help unify the department by involving faculty in the process. It may be helpful, too, for the chair to point out the relationships among the statement of mission, the annual report, goals, objectives, tasks, and action plans.

What kind of students does the department wish to attract? Given the competition, the comparative advantage of the institution and the department, the job market demands, and the demographics, can the department attract these students? Will special services be needed to attract and retain these students? Department publications should be carefully examined. Are they updated and accurate? Are they attractive? Are they helpful to current students?

What action plans does the department have for orientation, advising, retention, and career counseling? Departments that assist their students in developing clear academic goals or career objectives, such as employment or graduate study, are satisfying a deeply felt need in students. Department plans can be brief statements of goals and timetables, or they can be more elaborate, indicating strategies for implementation and individuals responsible for carrying out the plan. The chair must decide how much precision and quantification is necessary. The important thing is that these action plans produce results.

5. INVOLVE YOUR FACULTY

Although there is evidence of a growing faculty awareness of enrollment management, studies demonstrate the difficulty of involving faculty in student recruitment and retention activities.[11] And yet, it seems only natural that faculty participate in enrollment management. After all, it is the faculty who are primarily responsible for the creation of curricula, and for the teaching and advising that attract and retain students. Kreutner and Godfrey stress the importance of faculty participation: "Faculty members are the most effective recruiters and it is much more difficult for a student to break ties with a department . . . than it is to leave a university."[12]

Faculty are often asked to be accessible to prospective students when they are on campus. Students want to meet faculty on "get acquainted days," not administrators or staff. Faculty may even be invited to accompany admissions officers on recruiting trips. Today prospective students and their parents are asking sophisticated questions like, "Why should I pay so much money for an academic experience at your college or university?" Or, if it is a private institution, "Why should I pay that *extra* tuition money for an academic experience at your college or university?" Faculty are in the best position to respond to these questions.

Faculty are often willing to convert a prospective student into an enrollee by phoning, writing letters, visiting high schools, participating in college nights, and conducting interviews on and off campus. This past fall Baldwin-Wallace (Cleveland) increased its student body by 100 students over the previous year and it attributed this to faculty involvement in recruitment efforts. Commented one professor: "We are merely extending the mentor relationship between scholar and student beyond the traditional four years . . . We are convinced that faculty involvement in enrolling new students is an appropriate, logical extension of our personalized approach to education."[13]

Chairs can encourage key faculty members to visit "feeder" institutions such as high schools and community colleges and invite instructors in these institutions to campus to put on exhibitions, conduct debates, and produce plays. For example, at the College of Mount St. Joseph (Cincinnati), the Art Department has a display of outstanding works of juniors and seniors selected by the high school teachers. In addition, the faculty give recognition to outstanding art teachers in the high school. These linkages will improve knowledge of respective programs and could lead to the development of agreements between academic departments and two-year institutions. Department chairpersons are in a pivotal position to establish these agreements.

In enrollment management, involving faculty in recruitment activities is a first step, but it is not enough. It behooves department and division chairs to create a core group of faculty, a department retention task force, whose primary responsibilities are retention and attrition issues.

Attrition is expensive. Enrollment declines in a department with high fixed costs have serious financial consequences. The facts are staggering. In four-year institutions, about 50 percent of students do not graduate from the college where they began, and about 30 percent of entering four-year college freshmen finish. The attrition rate at two-year institutions is double the four-year college rate. In other words, the evidence suggests that colleges lose almost as many students as they graduate.[14]

Potential freshmen dropouts can usually be identified by the admissions office. This information can be passed on to a departmental retention task force or a college-wide retention task force. Special services can be provided to these potential dropout students such as remedial programs, career counseling for undeclared majors, and programs enriching the academic and social lives of minority, nontraditional, and commuter students. While it is difficult to control many of the environmental factors contributing to declining enrollments, it is possible for faculty to do something about attrition rates. Therefore, just as recruitment goals are to be included in departmental planning, so, too, should faculty develop retention goals.

6. DEVELOP PARTNERSHIPS WITH INDUSTRY

Lewis Thomas once stated that "the urge to form partnerships, to link up in collaborative arrangements, is perhaps the oldest, strongest, and most fundamental force in nature."[15] The symbiotic relationship between higher education and industry is derived from the important role that education is playing in a knowledge-intensive society. Industry is looking to institutions of higher education for teaching, new windows on research, programs that will help professionals sharpen their skills, and adapt to changing technologies; and, of course, they are looking for a dependable source of employees. While there are hazards and risks in forging alliances, one study concludes that the benefits for higher education and industry far outweigh the potential risks.[16]

Make no mistake: it will not be easy for the department chair to cultivate this new market because it has different requirements and needs than the traditional markets. New initiatives are in order and old patterns and practices may need to be abolished entirely or drastically altered. The department must demonstrate flexibility, creativity, responsiveness, and opportunism. These characteristics are crucial to the design of curricula and delivery formats: an intensive study period organized in modules vs. one hour per day, three days per week for a semester; more active and motivated adult learners in contrast to the more passive and dependent traditional 18- to 22-year-olds; on-site location versus the college classroom; high-quality, experienced faculty with excellent presentation skills versus whoever does not have a full teaching load. If a department is able to demonstrate the above characteristics, it has the capacity to penetrate this new market successfully and retard or reverse declining enrollments. Some steps the chair can take to facilitate this dialogue include:

- Establish advisory committees of area employers on an array of topics (e.g., review of curriculum, development of new programs, review of grant proposals). Although such advisory committees are usually established so that industry can assist higher education, the resulting dialogue will inevitably lead to some areas where the reverse can occur.
- Today, many colleges and universities have launched executive-in-residence programs. Encourage industries to develop faculty-in-residence programs. Such programs are bound to enhance understanding of the needs and interests of both parties, and identify those areas in which the skills of one sector can assist in the solution of problems in the other sector.
- Explore the desirability of delivering degree programs at the industry's facility. On-site instruction is a means of bringing the curriculum and workplace closer together. While on-site instruction may be more convenient for students, it may also encourage them to participate in university offerings on campus.

7. WORK TO STRUCTURE THE REWARD SYSTEM TO INCLUDE FACULTY EFFORTS IN ENROLLMENT MANAGEMENT ACTIVITIES

At most institutions, the teaching role is supplemented by the expectations that faculty will conduct research and provide community service. This tripartite mission is common in public and private institutions. In addition to performing in all three of these areas, faculty today are being called upon to play a role in enrollment management. These pressures are all occurring when tenure is more difficult to achieve, when faculty salaries are inadequate, and when the morale of the professoriat itself is at a low ebb.

If faculty are to play a meaningful role in enrollment management, chairpersons must consider attaching a weighted index for performance in enrollment activities—in addition to the teaching, advising, research, administrative duties, and community contributions criteria involved in the determination of salary increases and in the promotion process. This establishes a more equitable system of distributing workload and allows the faculty to specialize in those areas in which they are the most productive without punishment.

NOTES

1. Harold L. Hodgkinson, "Guess Who's Coming to College: Your Students in 1990." Washington, DC: *National Institute of Independent Colleges and Universities*, 1983.
2. Digest of Education Statistics 1983–84. National Center for Educational Statistics; College Entrance Examination Board. *The Admissions Strategist: Recruiting in the 1980's*. New York: The College Entrance Examination Board, 1985.
3. J. Victor Baldridge, Frank R. Kemerer, and Kenneth C. Green. *The Enrollment Crisis: Factors, Actors, and Impacts*. AAHE-ERIC/Higher Education Research Report No. 3, 1982. Washington, DC: American Association for Higher Education, 1982. 34.
4. Frank R. Kemerer, J. Victor Baldridge, and Kenneth C. Green, *Strategies for Effective Enrollment Management*. Washington, DC: American Association of College and Universities, 1982; Frank R. Kemerer, "The Role of Deans, Department Chairs, and Faculty in Enrollment Management." *The College Board Review* 134 (Winter 1984–85): 5–8, 28.
5. Don Hossler, *Enrollment Management, An Integrated Approach*. New York: College Entrance Examination Board, 1984.
6. *Higher Education & National Affairs*. American Council on Education 34, no. 21 (November 11, 1985): 12.
7. Christopher Lovelock and Michael L. Rothchild, "Uses, Abuses, and Misuses of Marketing in Higher Education." *Marketing in College Admissions: A Broadening of Perspectives*. New York: College Entrance Examination Board, 1980. 46.
8. Dennis L. Johnson, "Quality, Marketing, and the Work Group: The Case for Bottom-up Renewal." *AAHE Bulletin* 36 No. 7 (March 1984). (See especially the "Department Marketing Audit"; also see chapter 23 of this book.)
9. J. Victor Baldridge, Janine Woodward Roberts, and Terri A. Weiner, *The Campus and Microcomputer Revolution: Practical Advice for Nontechnical Decision Makers*. New York: American Council on Education/ Macmillan, 1984. See also Dennis P. Jones, *Data and Information for Executive Decisions in Higher Education*. Boulder, CO: National Center for Higher Education Management Systems, 1982, and William L. Tetlow, ed., *Using Microcomputers for Planning and Management Support*. New Directions for Institutional Research, 44 (December 1984). San Francisco: Jossey-Bass, Inc.

10. Allan Tucker, *Chairing the Academic Department.* New York: American Council on Education/Macmillan, 2nd ed., 1984, chapter 13.

11. Kemerer, Baldridge, and Green, *Strategies for Effective Enrollment Management,* chapter 5.

12. Leonard Kreutner and Eric S. Godfrey, "Enrollment Management: A New Vehicle for Institutional Renewal." *College Board Review* 118 (Winter 1980–81): 6.

13. Baldwin-Wallace College. *Pursuit.* 17, no. 1 (Fall 1985): 1.

14. Kemerer, Baldridge, and Green, *Strategies for Effective Enrollment Management,* chapter 5.

15. Lewis Thomas, "On the Uncertainty of Science." *Harvard Magazine* (September/October 1980): 21.

16. Jana B. Matthew and Rolf Norgaard, *Managing the Partnership Between Higher Education and Industry.* Boulder, CO: National Center for Higher Education Management Systems, 1984.

26

DEVELOPING SUCCESSFUL COMMUNITY-BASED PROGRAMS: A PRESCRIPTION FOR SUCCESS

P. ANTHONY ZEISS

In its first four years, Pueblo Community College's Myers Center for Small Business developed a 550-name client list, helped to start fifty-seven new businesses, helped seventy-one existing businesses to survive, and helped to create 294 full-time and eighty-seven part-time jobs for its community. The annual economic impact of this program-based activity slightly exceeds fourteen million dollars. The Assistance Center, a part of the College's Business Management degree program, has become a national model for small business assistance activities and has been visited by representatives from numerous American states and from thirty-two foreign nations.

In its first two years of operation, Pueblo Community College's comprehensive Career Assessment Center became a nonsubsidized, self-sufficient auxiliary enterprise by providing evaluations to approximately 4,500 persons. The services provided by the Assessment Center have been a major factor in attracting new business and industries representing 4,500 new jobs to Pueblo, Colorado. The Career Assessment Center has become a significant service agent to new industries, existing industries, the local school districts, and to a variety of special needs populations.

These "overnight" success stories, representing the optimum in public-private partnerships, did not happen by accident. Each of these programs was carefully planned according to a clearly identified community need, and each institution became fully committed to meet those needs. Highly successful community-based programs offered by local schools, community colleges, and four-year institutions across the country could be described in similar fashion, but few, if any, occurred by happenstance. Most exceptional community-based programs follow a basic "prescription for success." The following seven-point prescription for developing and implementing community-based programs and services is what Pueblo Community College used to develop the two model programs just described:

1. Know your school and community.
2. Identify a clear need.

3. Develop the concept.
4. Identify funding sources.
5. Sell to the public.
6. Implement with enthusiasm.
7. Evaluate and publicize events.

Far too often, the department chairperson becomes frustrated, un-enthusiastic, and defeated in the development of new programs and services. Most of us are discouraged for one or all of the following reasons: "no one will help"; "the administration won't support it"; or, "I'm doing all this extra work and I'm not getting paid for it." By following the basic "prescription for success," the first two will be eliminated. If the latter excuse sounds familiar, it is an even bet that no successful community-based program will be developed until a strong personal commitment is made, regardless of the prescription followed. In the long run, however, dollars and promotions generally follow enthusiasm, hard work, and initiative. This "prescription for success" can help you to develop an exemplary community-based program, and personal satisfaction and professional rewards will ultimately follow.

1. KNOW YOUR SCHOOL AND COMMUNITY

Before you can hope to develop any successful community-based program, you must know your school and your community. What kind of mission does your school have? What is the vision of the President? What does your school do best? Is your school a proactive vendor of services or is it a re-active social entity? Where does the school get its financing? You must be able to answer these basic questions before considering an exciting new project or program.

Further, you must know your community well, if you expect the new program or service to be successful. If the business community and the leadership of the community does not support your new program, it will be doomed to failure. Are you familiar with the community's major needs? What is the current funding base for the community? What civic, political, or social organizations would want to support your new program? Do you know the directors or presidents of these organizations? What are the political or social sensitivities to your new program? What effect will your past or present political or social behavior have on the promotion of your new program or service? All of these and similar questions must be answered before you even begin to consider the development of a new community-based program.

2. IDENTIFY A CLEAR NEED

Without a concise, easily identified need, no community-based program or service can survive. Your program must be need-driven and cannot simply be the result of a personal desire. The need must also fit within the school's mission and capability. A simple but useful question you can expect to field from administrators, funding sources, and community supporters is; What good is it? Finally, you must be especially honest with yourself to determine if you are willing to provide the extra work and energy to see the project through to the end.

3. DEVELOP THE CONCEPT

One of the best methods for developing the concept of a new program is to begin with a concept paper, which can then be reviewed by knowledgeable friends and colleagues. A brief technical paper, complete with the appropriate research, should also be prepared to focus attention on the essentials and to communicate the program idea to the administration. A technical paper indicates that you are committed to the project and that it has been thought out in a reasonable and specific fashion.

All concept papers should (1) identify the need; (2) list the objectives of the program that will satisfy the need; and (3) describe the benefits of the program. The technical paper should (1) restate the need, objectives, and benefits, and (2) provide the technical data necessary for the program to be evaluated. This brief technical paper should describe the programs to be developed clearly enough so that an interested colleague could continue the project in your absence. It is always wise to seek widespread input and to include informal critiques from peers, superiors, and interested community representatives.

4. IDENTIFY FUNDING SOURCES

The quickest way to extinguish a good program idea forever is not to identify how it will be funded. It is surprising how many times an energetic department chairperson or instructor forgets to examine this essential facet of any new community-based program. Proposing the new program without identifying the funding sources presents a problem to the administration rather than the intended opportunity.

A simple method for identifying funding sources is to ask yourself who needs the services, what agencies or organizations should be interested in the program, and how it can pay for itself. Should the project be funded privately or publicly, or both? A brief visit with a grants writer is usually useful, and involving your friends and colleagues should also provide some good ideas. In any case, it is essential that you provide funding alternatives to the decision-makers. This is also a good time to develop the first year's budget for the new program.

5. SELLING TO THE PUBLIC

It is a simple truth that the acceptance of a new idea or program is directly related to the amount of "ownership" people feel toward it. The more people you can get excited about your new program, the more likely it will be successful. You will have these publics to convince that your new program or service is worthy of their support:

- Internal public: colleagues, superiors, top administration.
- External public: civic, governmental and social organizations; community leadership.
- Recipients: those who will be receiving direct services and benefits.

With each of these publics you should make a list of the people best able to help with development and implementation. You should then visit them personally, to seek their support. Of course, your administration should support the project before you begin developing serious external support. In addition, be prepared to show each person how your new program can affect him/her in a positive manner, and be able to demonstrate that support of this new program is in his/her best interest. Be prepared to share the glory in the project and be sure that you have top-level support from your administration. Such support will help to smooth rough edges later on, and it will identify you as an aggressive professional who demonstrates initiative, hard work, and insight.

You must also identify the potential political and social sensitivities of all the publics. For instance, if you invite the local chamber of commerce to participate in the project, should you also invite the Latino chamber of commerce? If you invite the local job training partnership entity to participate, should you also invite the local job services agency? Ask advice often, send thank-you notes to those who have been helpful, and deliver on all commitments. Above all, keep your top administrators informed of your progress and keep your project developing with the recipient's needs in mind. A small advisory group that includes representatives from all these publics can be especially beneficial with this task.

Reaching the potential recipients of your new program's services must be addressed in a professional manner. You will have to develop a sound marketing plan. This marketing plan must (1) present your program in an easily understood fashion, (2) demonstrate your program's uniqueness, and (3) identify how to reach your program's target markets. Of course, your school's media or information specialist should be closely involved with the process. Help this person to see your project as his/her project. If this can be accomplished, most of your marketing worries will be over. Be sure to speak about your new program to those civic, government, and social groups that should have a special interest in the services.

6. IMPLEMENT WITH ENTHUSIASM

Enthusiasm is contagious. Use it to your full advantage. Be enthusiastic about the project with the maintenance people who will have to help. Be enthusiastic about the project with your peers, with the secretary, with the administrators, and with the appropriate people in your community. Show the news media how excited you are about the project, and always emphasize the benefits for the recipients. Most importantly, share the glory, especially in public settings. After a short while, you will find that others have become the cheerleaders for the project and you can concentrate more on being the coach.

7. EVALUATE AND PUBLICIZE RESULTS

No program or service is ever complete without a valid evaluation and a dissemination of the results. The evaluation process will help to measure your success in achieving the project's objectives and in meeting the community need. The evaluative data will also be useful in fine-tuning the program for the future. Local publication of the results will allow you to re-emphasize the importance of the program to the community and to gain even greater social and financial support from your publics. Be sure your school receives plenty of praise for supporting the project and do not forget to submit the annual report to an appropriate educational journal and to the National Education Resource Information Center.

This prescription for success is by no means a foolproof method for success for all community-based programs or services. However, it has served the author and Pueblo Community College very well in recent years, and the basic developmental processes it involves make good practical sense. In any event, your chances for success will be improved in the development and implementation of any community-based program if this prescription is followed.

INDEX